HOLLIS HATFIELD WEISHAR
JAMES A. DURHAM
editors

Law Practice Management Section
American Bar Association

Commitment to Quality: The Law Practice Management Section is committed to quality in our publications. Our authors are experienced practitioners in their fields. Prior to publication, the contents of all our books are rigorously reviewed by experts to ensure the highest quality product and presentation. Because we are committed to serving our readers' needs, we welcome your feedback on how we can improve future editions of this book. We invite you to fill out and return the comment card at the back of this book.

Cover design by Laura Jacobson for Seven Rays, Inc.

Printed in the United States of America.

Library of Congress Catalog Card Number 99-76093
ISBN 1-57073-740-1

03 02 01 00 99 5 4 3 2 1

CONTENTS

ACKNOWLEDGMENTS

This book has many authors. While we developed the original concept, served as authors, facilitators, managers, and editors for this project, this book would not have been possible without the hard work and dedication of the following individuals who devoted their time, talent, and energy to make this project a success: Stephen Barrett, Burkey Belser, Stephen Brewer, William J. Flannery Jr., David Graves, Lawrence M. Kohn, Robert N. Kohn, Susan Raridon Lambreth, Kelley Kiernan Largey, Roberta Montafia, Murray Singerman, Gregory H. Siskind, and Peter D. Zeughauser. We would like to thank all of these individuals who contributed to this project.

We would also like to thank the many marketing professionals who, through their books, tapes, lectures, and shared experiences, have contributed immeasurably to the advances and the body of knowledge in the legal marketing industry. Particularly, we would like to thank the people at the ABA's Law Practice Management Section for having the vision to recognize the importance of this fast-growing area, and for their commitment to making this project a success. If ever there were an example of excellent teamwork, it is in the development and creation of this terrific book.

Hollis H. Weishar
James A. Durham

INTRODUCTION

James A. Durham

The practice of law has not really changed all that much in the past decade, but the *economics of the business of law* have changed dramatically. It is no longer sufficient to rely exclusively on excellent technical skills to succeed as a lawyer. Law firms that have a large number of lawyers making large amounts of money by contributing nothing more than billable hours are going to be struggling in this competitive legal marketplace. Everyone is being asked to contribute to the firm's success by developing new business, offering value-added services, and ensuring client retention. No one in the legal profession is immune from the market pressures that are driving lawyers to have a much greater focus on marketing and client development.

With so much emphasis on marketing and business development, Hollis Weishar, the American Bar Association's Law Practice Management Section, and I believed it was imperative to make an extraordinary effort to pull together the best thinking on these subjects as we move into the new millennium. This book represents that effort.

Even the best creative thinking, however, does not displace the important, long-standing, and timeless marketing concept of "learning what clients want and delivering it." But because lawyers are a profession of people principally impressed by logic and data, we assembled the information in this book to allow legal practitioners to explore in more depth the specific tasks and skills needed to succeed in a competitive marketplace. There is great value, for example, in knowing not only that you need to use technology more effectively in your practice, but also the specific ways in which technology might be better used to deliver value and efficiency to clients. Similarly, it does no good to know that you need client feedback if you never learned the best ways to solicit and respond to it. Similarly, the impact, quality, and value of ideas can be greatly enhanced if you know what to expect and what is possible. This book is intended to provide the valuable insights, and more.

The list of things you will learn from reading this book is nearly as long as the book itself; it is packed with practical ideas, outlines, strategies, and even some so-called "big-picture concepts." All this wit and wisdom is presented in the relevant context of practicing lawyers and busy law firm managers—it is not just "textbook" information.

Although we have made every effort to offer a comprehensive guidebook to marketing in the new millennium, I am compelled to remind you of Dr. Wayne Dyer's observation in *You Will See It When You Believe It:* "you cannot *taste* water simply by reading the word 'water'. . . . You cannot *see* a sunrise simply by saying the word 'sunrise'. . . . In order to *taste* water and *see* the sunrise, you must touch the former to your lips and gaze upon the sun at the crack of dawn." Obviously, no amount of talking or reading about marketing will draw clients to your practice—you must *do* something to experience marketing.

Law firm marketing has been described, appropriately, I think, as "a contact sport." It involves getting face-to-face with clients and prospects, asking questions, and listening to the answers. You can, however, listen and respond better if you have read about what is going on in the industry and studied the best practices. Though being helpful to people—personally or professionally—may, in a nutshell, be what business development is all about, certainly it helps if you are aware of some creative ways to help them. This book will help you do that.

Marketing versus Business Development

I always start a business development training program by making a clear distinction between those things that I perceive to be "marketing tools"—brochures, advertising, public relations, articles, and speeches, and those things that "create clients"—conducting face-to-face meetings, networking effectively, developing super-satisfied clients, cultivating referral sources, giving referrals, and creating client-specific products and service strategies.

Because every lawyer has his or her own definition of "marketing" and "business development," it is helpful to have a common understanding of the concepts. In this book, however, the terms "marketing" and "business development" will be used interchangeably. Whether we call it marketing or business development, it is helpful to define the specific goals of these activities. I believe the overriding goal of marketing and business development activities is to generate satisfying, profitable work and to increase revenue for the law firm. There are a number of ways to meet this goal:

- *Keep* all the *existing work* that clients are currently giving you.
- Turn "*first-time*" client matters into *future work* (get a case, make it a relationship).
- *Ensure* that clients who use the services of a *specific practice area* are giving you *as much of their work as possible* in that area.

- *Expand* beyond *practice areas.* Turn litigation-only, business-only, employment-only, and other single-practice-area clients into "firm clients" who work with lawyers in other parts of the firm.
- Ensure that your *clients* are *referring* their business colleagues to you *without qualification* or *reservation.*
- *Increase* and *maximize* the *profit margin and realization* from all the work you are doing.
- *Attract new clients* to all areas of the firm.

The best way to accomplish all the above is *to provide extraordinary value in all of your relationships.* You can do this by taking the following actions:

1. Communicate clearly and consistently with your clients:
   - Discuss in advance the scope, cost, and strategy of all work, and keep the client informed of all developments, including actual fees versus budget.
   - Manage the client's work cost effectively: that means recognizing the difference between "bet-the-farm," important, and routine ("commodity") work, and approaching each accordingly.
   - Seek feedback so you know the client's level of satisfaction with your work and service; respond to the expressed concerns.
2. Get to know your client and prospects so well that you can identify creative ways to help them achieve their business goals and can go to them with ideas (for example, preventative law, product development, training, case disposition, strategic introductions).
3. Develop risk-sharing arrangements and cooperative relationships with clients by learning what "partnering" really means, and offering some "win-win" arrangements to clients.
4. Make sure *everyone in your organization* understands how important it is to give extraordinary client service, and train them to deliver that level of service.
5. Use your network of contacts and relationships as an asset; put people together, give referrals, do favors for people, and be available as a resource.

You Will See Myriad Examples of Management's Role in Marketing

There is an extraordinary connection between a firm's marketing success and the support and direction marketing gets from management. If your firm rewards only billable hours and the one person whose initials appear next to a new client's name, then much of what you read here will fall on deaf ears. Similarly, if your firm does not measure nonbillable time, if the lawyers in your firm are not willing to contribute 2,500, 2,600, or maybe even 2,700 hours a year to their professional lives, if the lawyers do not invest time "off-the-clock" to enhance existing client relationships, or if there are other firm policies that are anathema to a marketing culture, then you will not benefit a great deal from the specific ideas and concepts set forth here.

In a recent workshop at the National Conference of the Legal Marketing Association, we attempted to define a perfect marketing culture for a law firm. The list we compiled included the following elements:

- The firm has a client service orientation.
- People work in teams, demonstrating a sense of "Firm."
- Client satisfaction is a factor in compensation.
- Management is supportive of—and delegates—appropriate responsibility, authority, and resources to a marketing director and practice group leaders.
- Everyone in the firm is expected to contribute to business development efforts.
- There is a waiting list of lateral partners who want to come to the firm with big "books of business."
- Staff persons see themselves, and everyone else sees them, as integral parts of the client service team.
- Every lawyer knows what is important to the firm's success.
- The path to individual success in the firm is crystal clear.
- Everyone is incentivized to act in accordance with the firm's culture.
- There is regular and continual communication with clients.
- The workplace is diverse and enlightened—there is respect for alternative lifestyles and a family-friendly environment.
- There is excellent internal communication.
- The firm's culture embraces technology; it uses integrated databases, the Internet, an intranet, teleconferencing, and more.
- There is uniformity of presentation—graphically and stylistically.
- Management lawyers are trained in all areas of effective leadership.
- The firm has an industry focus—the lawyers understand industries, as well as individual client needs.
- There is a common vision of "who we are."
- Clients belong to the firm, not to individual lawyers.
- The firm has a strong "brand identity."
- The firm monitors and then aspires to the "best practices" of the most successful firms and other organizations.
- The firm contributes to the community; it is a good corporate citizen.
- The firm embraces change and is flexible.
- Everyone trusts one another.

The link between marketing and management is obvious. If you believe this list describes where your law firm needs to be, then you should use this book as a resource and guide to help you determine the steps you need to take to move from where you are today to where you want to be tomorrow.

Although many of the best legal marketing people in the country have contributed their best thinking to this book, what you learn here is only part of the story. We can all learn the rest of the story by listening to clients. Clients are often quite good at developing business strategies, and they certainly know what they want from their lawyers. If you read this book and then listen to the marketplace, you will know exactly what to do—whether you do it is up to you. Don't wait for the next milestone in our civilization (does the date 2001 have particular significance? 2010?), or the next shock wave in our profession (like the day accounting firms are set free to compete fully with law firms). Our law schools did not teach us business development or client service skills, and most firms have not done it very well. To keep up with the dynamic changes in the legal industry, we must become students of the business of law. This book offers a terrific, advanced course of study.

Jim Durham

SECTION I

Developing Your Approach

CHAPTER 1

Overcoming Objections and Obstacles: Persuading Your Pessimistic Partners

Susan Raridon Lambreth

Ten years ago, law firms needed to be convinced of the importance of marketing themselves. Today, most lawyers realize they have to market their services, but they are still unsure about *how* to do so most effectively. Because many lawyers have had limited success with their marketing efforts, they are frustrated with—or skeptical about—the whole process.

Part of the frustration or skepticism, even cynicism, results from the many obstacles lawyers and law firms can face in developing and implementing marketing programs. Many of these obstacles can be removed, or at least minimized, however, by following these steps:

1. Identify the apparent barriers or obstacles to marketing—both real obstacles and excuses.
2. Understand why and how the real obstacles inhibit marketing and why the excuses exist.
3. Take steps to overcome the obstacles.

Identification of Obstacles to Marketing

There are both external and internal obstacles to marketing. The external obstacles include competitors, ethics, client reaction, and community attitudes. Though these obstacles are out of our control and cannot be addressed directly, they are usually less problematic than the internal obstacles. Internal obstacles are actually more troublesome, and include a firm culture or mindset that does not support marketing, compensation systems that are not linked to marketing efforts, insufficient practice management, lack of accountability, and inadequate training or budgets. However, internal barriers can be overcome by employing specific strategies.

Internal obstacles generally fall into one of two categories: those that affect the marketing of the firm as a whole (institutional obstacles) and those that hinder the implementation of marketing tactics by individual lawyers (individual obstacles).

Institutional Obstacles

Firmwide obstacles include the following:

1. *Firm Culture or Historical Mind-Set.* The majority of lawyers grew up in law firms that either disavowed marketing as unprofessional or discouraged it as unnecessary: "Don't worry about bringing in business, we've got plenty." "Just get the work done and keep the clients happy." Even though these same firms are now encouraging or even requiring marketing, years of discouragement are not overcome with a simple mandate. Change requires firmwide education, correct (and not mixed) messages from firm management, and the right incentives for team marketing and cross-selling.
2. *Complacency.* Some lawyers still think they can avoid the need to market. However, the next few years will continue to "shake out" firms that are mismanaged or that market poorly. Look for more dissolutions of firms that fail to develop a marketing direction and follow through on it. Complacency can be addressed by the messages sent by firm leadership, changes in incentives, and education.
3. *Compensation Systems.* Systems that are primarily production oriented ("eat what you kill" or "billable hour as king" types) discourage lawyers from cross-selling, delegating, or working as teams in developing business, or even ensuring client service. Systems that reward origination, but not teamwork and cross-selling, are also divisive and hinder effective team marketing. Similarly, even if a compensation system rewards production, marketing efforts, and results, there must still be a way to ensure accountability, to prevent "worker bees" from being as highly compensated as those who produce revenues and new business. Too many firms give lawyers more incentive to
   - bring in new clients than to expand existing ones,
   - land prospective clients by themselves than to work with others as a team,
   - keep contacts with clients and prospects to themselves than to share them freely with others or make them part of the firm's contact database, or
   - attract new pieces of marginally profitable work for which they get credit, than to work with teams to land more profitable matters for which they will share credit.

Compensation systems must at least reward some business development and practice management activities, not just results.

4. *Lack of Internal Communication.* Midsize and larger firms, particularly, miss some terrific opportunities because they do not communicate well with each other. The lawyers do not know much about each other's practice strengths, selling points, clients, or success stories. Most firms fail to cross-sell well, to do effective team marketing, or to integrate laterals or other offices, because internal communication is lacking. Typically, it is lacking for two reasons: the firm's compensation system does not encourage internal communication, much less require it, and the firm's value system does not monitor, measure, or reward cross-selling or the expansion of existing clients.
5. *Lack of Practice Management.* Today's frequent purchasers of legal services have become sophisticated consumers, demanding efficient, cost-effective service. However, our data shows that without good practice group management, service does not meet client expectations of excellence. Good practice management means more than paying lip service to associate training and annual evaluations. It includes devoting substantial attention and resources to workload allocation, case management, delegation, supervision, effective training, mentoring, peer review, and more. As a result, practice group management—including workload monitoring, lawyer development programs, business planning, and quality control—has become a higher priority in many firms. Marketing without practice management dilutes the marketing message and disappoints clients.
6. *Lack of Accountability.* Poor follow-through is probably the most prevalent problem hindering law firm marketing. Lawyers make the mistake of going through "fits and starts" or bursts of marketing activity after firm meetings or annual retreats. Instead, well-thought-out, ongoing, regular follow-through is necessary for business development success. And, this follow-through will not happen without individual and firm accountability. Accountability means measuring, monitoring, and rewarding marketing, which in turn requires establishing tracking systems, communicating regularly about efforts and results, and providing strong compensation incentives.

Individual Obstacles

Obstacles to individual lawyer marketing are also significant. They include the following:

1. *Lack of Time.* This is the most frequent excuse lawyers give for not marketing. It often masks more deep-seated reasons, such as compensation

disincentives, lack of accountability, or problems with time management.

2. *Discomfort.* Even though marketing is now "accepted" in many firms, there are lawyers in every firm who are not comfortable with the idea. Some mistakenly equate it with advertising, which they find offensive. Others accept public relations and image campaigns, but don't want to meet personally with clients and prospects "one-on-one." They may want the firm to spend countless dollars on image building, but they are unwilling to do their parts. Many lawyers believe that only good schmoozers or natural salespeople are effective marketers, and because they do not have these skills, they should be relieved of any obligation to bring in business.
3. *Fear.* Closely related to discomfort is outright fear—fear of failure or rejection. Lawyers mention fear as an obstacle in almost every sales training program.
4. *Lack of Understanding.* Many unnecessary battles are fought in law firms because lawyers simply do not understand basic marketing concepts and tools. Some who view marketing as little more than advertising or slick salesmanship fight every proposed marketing initiative. Lawyers who recognize that outstanding client service and excellent personal relationships are the keys to marketing cannot understand why all lawyers do not embrace it.

External Obstacles

Potential external obstacles include strong competition, ethical restraints, fear of client reaction, and community culture or attitudes.

1. *Competition.* Aggressive efforts by competitors can sometimes dilute the effectiveness of marketing efforts. However, competition often raises client awareness of all marketing. Also, a competitor's efforts can shake the complacency of some lawyers and motivate them to market more. If you feel your competitors are "beating" you by being more aggressive, there are several strategies you can use to respond. Because it is unlikely your competition is doing all these things, you can achieve a marketing advantage by
   - improving internal cross-selling efforts by implementing "key client" plans that lead you to understand everything about a client and to suggest creative ways to meet the client's needs,
   - ensuring a large number of your partners are trained in the latest relational selling techniques (many firms who believe they are "marketing aggressively" are actually doing the wrong things), and
   - targeting niche markets or specialties, rather than trying to be "all things to all people."

2. *Ethical Restraints.* The ethics rules were not designed to protect sophisticated business executives from the persuasive wiles of lawyers. They were designed to protect injured persons or unsophisticated laypersons. To my knowledge, there has not been one example of a law firm disciplined for "business-to-business" marketing. Most lawyers who raise ethical limitations as an obstacle to marketing are actually using it as an excuse to avoid marketing. Nevertheless, ethical rules do govern a variety of lawyer marketing activities, and they must be understood and respected.
3. *Client Reaction.* Many clients, particularly businesses, react positively to appropriate law firm marketing. A CEO in a client interview told us many years ago, "Lawyers are so arrogant they think they don't have to sell like the rest of us. Every successful businessperson sells something, whether it's products, services, or ideas." Clients expect law firms to tell them about their areas of expertise, and they rarely react negatively to substantive business-to-business marketing. Individual (nonbusiness) clients respond favorably as long as the marketing is not intrusive, is understandable, and is not condescending.
4. *Community Culture or Attitudes.* Most communities not only accept law firm marketing (other than tacky billboards or television ads), they expect it. Law firm contributions to charitable organizations have grown rapidly, despite data showing that this is often not a good use of a firm's marketing budget. Research data suggests that as long as law firm marketing is tasteful and professionally executed, community reaction is not an issue.

Understanding Why Obstacles Exist

Before exploring ways to overcome obstacles, we must understand why they exist. The major reasons for law firm marketing obstacles include insecurity, rapid change, and lack of solid business management.

Insecurity

There is tremendous insecurity in the legal profession due to increased competition and the rapid change that has characterized the industry in recent years. This is causing many lawyers to go into a "bunker mentality" or to "stick their heads in the sand" because they are overwhelmed by the prospect of even more change ahead. Psychologists tell us that "you can teach an old dog new tricks." It is next to impossible, however, to teach "scared dogs" new tricks. The legal profession is full of "scared dogs." Insecurity leads to the following reactions (that is, obstacles):

- lack of follow-through
- discomfort and "fear of marketing"

- lack of understanding
- perceived lack of time
- complacency

Rapid Change

Although rapid change can be a reason for insecurity, the rate of change has resulted in firms in which management and leadership structures do not yet support marketing efforts. This is reflected in obstacles such as

- historical mind-set
- out-of-date compensation systems and accountability
- lack of internal communication
- insufficient practice management

Lack of Solid Business Management

Despite all the talk about management committees, increased use of legal administrators, and growing use of management consultants, many law firms are only beginning to implement what the business world considers basic management principles and structures. This results in many obstacles, such as

- lack of strong practice group management and leadership
- insufficient firm management support for marketing
- lack of management, marketing, and technology training
- insufficient compensation incentives and accountability

Overcoming the Obstacles

Although there are no "magic bullets" to eliminate marketing obstacles, there are some sound ways to attack the problems. It should be noted, however, that the solutions are hard to apply in many law firms, because they require a willingness to change, a time commitment, and a proactive approach (in what is typically a reactive environment). Some suggested solutions follow.

Correct the Incentives

One of the most important ways to overcome obstacles is to ensure that the firm's incentive system supports the right behavior. If you tell your lawyers to cross-sell, but the compensation system discourages them from doing so, your efforts will lead to frustration, not success. In fact, in firms in which the compensation system does not provide accountability for marketing, less than 25 percent of the partners typically make sufficient efforts to market.

Incentives can be monetary or nonmonetary, but the best systems use both. Monetary incentives reward not only new client origination, but also marketing efforts (within clearly defined guidelines), such as cross-selling initiatives and team marketing. Many firms now use partner "models" or personal business plans to provide accountability and to measure performance.

In addition, firms should set realistic expectations for individual and group marketing efforts, and for the results to be achieved. Frustration arises when unrealistic goals and expectations give lawyers a sense that they are not experiencing success. Research shows a typical partner should spend three to four hundred hours per year on marketing and should understand that it takes four to six years of efforts before significant results will be seen. Many lawyers get so discouraged before they reach this point that they quit doing much marketing. Actually, many lawyers spend enough time, but because their efforts are unfocused, the time does not pay off and frustration levels rise.

Marketing Education

It is important to create a common understanding of marketing within a firm to build acceptance and enthusiasm for it. This can be accomplished through programs and presentations—by either outside experts or knowledgeable people within the firm—at firm retreats, firm meetings, seminars, and practice group meetings, and by circulating articles or other marketing information.

All of a firm's education efforts should emphasize that legal marketing depends on personal contacts and relationship building. The education should also provide guidance on the most effective tools for advancing personal relationships and managing one's network. Many firms are still using marketing approaches that have lost effectiveness.

Lawyers need to learn that each of them can play a valuable role in business development. Many times lawyers' discomfort with marketing stems from their misconception that only certain models of behavior work, and that effective rainmakers have a unique style of their own. In fact, there are many routes to take. Each lawyer can take a different approach to building relationships and developing contacts—one that suits his or her talents and interests. Often, when lawyers see comfortable roles for themselves in the process, they are more willing to participate in the effort.

Finally, marketing education should include specific skills training. Because the most effective law firm marketing is personal contact, lawyers must feel comfortable with—and be effective at—making contacts and building relationships with existing and prospective clients. They need to be good at personal "selling." Many of them may also need presentation skills training to help them in responding to "beauty contests."

Internal Communication

Because most firms miss their best marketing opportunities through a failure of internal systems, internal communications should get some serious attention.

Simply stated, lawyers do not know enough about each other's strengths, success stories, networking contacts, prospecting efforts, and the like. I have yet to see a law firm that spends too much time or money on internal communication. On the contrary, some of the most effective marketing programs consist principally of internally focused efforts (cross-selling plans and seminars, internal newsletters, and lawyer skills databases, for example).

Though many law firms now have internal marketing newsletters, others resist because "our lawyers won't read it" or "it's only a brag sheet." An internal marketing newsletter (or electronic bulletin board for more technologically sophisticated firms) is one of the easiest, least expensive, and most effective steps to improve marketing. And, they work in firms from 15 to 1,000 or more lawyers, can be produced without the aid of outside consultants, and, in smaller firms, even without an in-house marketing professional.

With or without an internal newsletter, lawyers need to communicate marketing success stories to each other on a regular basis. These success stories should include information about new clients attracted through team marketing, positive feedback after a competitive bidding contest, business acquired or contacts made through a speech, and significant outcomes ("wins") for clients, such as deals completed, cases won, or partnering structures achieved, just to name a few.

Another important element of internal communication is making sure that marketing activities have a high profile and a perceived high priority within the firm. Marketing should be an agenda item for most partner, firm, practice area, and staff meetings. Individual lawyers should report their successes at regular meetings. Send the message to the entire firm that marketing is important. The managing partner should be visible in his or her support of marketing, as should the practice group managers.

Practice Management

Strong practice group managers who have been trained in their roles and who have accountability can help overcome obstacles by implementing training and development programs for the associates and partners in their groups, by encouraging individual and practice group plans, by using quality control systems, by applying new technologies, and by creating model documents and other initiatives that bring the lawyers and clients close through improved communication and service.

Early Success Experiences

Many lawyers are skeptical about marketing; past marketing "failures" or fits and starts have fueled cynicism about the subject. Although education and internal communication are extremely important, firms must find ways to measure and then point to marketing successes—large and small. You should begin your marketing program by identifying projects that, if implemented, are almost guaranteed successes (such as face-to-face meetings with clients, small industry-focused seminars, or targeted-industry speeches with direct audience follow-up). Identify two or more lawyers and staff persons with the best track record of follow-through and get them involved in one of these projects. After each project is completed successfully, communicate the success widely and regularly throughout the firm. Success breeds success. When lawyers see their colleagues succeeding, some will be encouraged to get on the bandwagon.

Client Input

Another way to overcome some of the obstacles to business development is through client input. It can be gathered through a formal client assessment survey by having clients speak at retreats, or as a result of personal visits by your managing partner. When clients tell lawyers what they want and expect, it is a powerful motivator—and most of what clients request, from legal updates to creative fee structures, is the stuff we call marketing.

The following chart is a summary of specific marketing obstacles and some suggested ways to overcome them. As you can see, there is a lot of overlap—you cannot view a particular obstacle in a vacuum, and there are various strategies to address each obstacle. Adapt these and other ideas you will find throughout this book to your firm's culture; do not let the apparent obstacles to marketing be real obstacles—the marketplace demands change.

Ways to Overcome Marketing Obstacles

Obstacle	**Ways to Overcome**
Historical mind-set	Incentives/accountability, education, internal communication
Complacency	Incentives/accountability, education, early successes
Compensation system/ accountability	Incentives/accountability
Lack of internal communication	Education, firm meetings to focus on marketing, internal newsletters
Poor practice management	Incentives/accountability, strong firm and practice area leadership and management
Lack of follow-through	Accountability, internal communication, early successes, monitoring by administrator or in-house marketing professional, training
Lack of time	Incentives/accountability, education, realistic expectations, finding right role for each lawyer
Discomfort	Education, training, realistic expectations, right role for each lawyer
Fear	Education, training, realistic expectations, right role for each lawyer
Lack of understanding	Education, training, realistic expectations, right role for each lawyer, and internal communication

CHAPTER 2

Strategic Marketing Planning

Hollis Hatfield Weishar

If you are a managing partner, marketing partner, or marketing director of a law firm, then sooner or later you will be faced with the task of developing a written, strategic marketing plan for your firm or a key specialty area of practice. There are three questions that you must ask when creating your plan:

1. Where are we now?
2. Where do we want to be in three to five years?
3. How are we going to get there?

Before we explore these questions, let's review some key concepts . . .

What Is Strategic Planning?

You need a clear understanding of who you really are, what you're capable of, what business you're in, what value you create for your clients, and how you differentiate yourselves in winning and keeping your clients. The key is to create the means to make the most of whatever the business environment presents. The task is to use *strategic thinking* and create a strategic plan to create success.

Some Thoughts on Why Law Firms Lose Their Way

Many law firms appear to be no more than a collection of individuals practicing under one roof. Sometimes it may seem that midsized or large firms have fifty different businesses going on at once. Often these businesses don't enhance one another, and can even be in competition for a firm's marketing budget and resources. Remember, if a law firm is at war with itself, it can never be very effective on the battlefield of business! This is an important concept to accept and explore when you are entering the strategic planning process.

Leadership Is Important

In the process of developing a plan, answers come through a careful process of creative thinking and logical reasoning that must be unique to each firm. The process of strategic planning or goal setting has fundamental features that makes it relevant to almost *any* challenge facing *any* law firm, but leadership is necessary to achieve success. Someone needs to work hard to craft the vision and define the direction. Someone has to put the right people in the right places and build a "marketing team." Someone has to build consensus about the plan and communicate it widely and frequently, and at least one individual needs to face difficult issues and make tough decisions.

In Planning Your Strategy, Set Clear Rules of the Game

Sure, you could probably assemble a dozen of your best and brightest lawyers around a conference room table in your office and work for a day to develop a strategic plan. Every law firm is full of highly intelligent people who love to offer their opinions and expertise regarding marketing. But maybe it is smarter to do some external research (in addition to your internal conference table sessions with your best and brightest) to identify some driving patterns, including economic considerations, demographics, client feelings and preferences, and the ways in which information technology and globalization are changing the way we do business.

Designing a Strategy: How Not *to Do It*

Many law firms have planning systems that are bottom heavy. They spend a great deal of time and effort getting all the practice group, departmental, and individual tactical plans written, but little or no time thinking about the basic strategy or direction of the business. To correct this strategy, law firms must try to set some firmwide goals. These can include tactics that involve the entire firm, such as starting a client interview program, or beginning a marketing training program for lawyers or support staff, or sending out regular press releases. These are examples of marketing tactics that benefit the whole firm. Firms must then go beyond simply planning, and begin doing. Many firms create grandiose strategic plans, supported by elaborately detailed budgets, resource estimates, tactical plans, and timetables, most of which ultimately have little connection to the success of the business.

Designing a Strategy: How to *Do It*

Think about the future. Where does your firm want to be in three years? In five years? Focus on "*futuring,*" instead of just *planning.* "Futuring" should be used to help law firms form pictures of where they are going. Ask the tough questions: Is our labor practice becoming obsolete? Should we still be focusing on serving labor unions, or should we train our people to focus on the growing area of employment law, such as sexual harassment in the workplace and age discrimination? Although developing a plan is necessary, it should be focused on the future "picture" and how to achieve that picture. Law firms should not get caught up in the *process* of planning, but should be able to move beyond process.

The Six Levels of Strategic Planning Success

1. *A Vision.* Who is ABC law firm and who do we want to become?
2. *A Mission Statement.* It is helpful to create a written statement of how the firm must do business, how it defines clients, what value it creates for clients, how to keep clients' business, and how the firm can work with clients to get critical feedback regarding their desires and the firm's performance. Many firms come up with documents to serve as their strategy statements, philosophy statements, values statements, or company policies, but too often even the most basic document of this kind never gets far beyond the management committee. Your mission statement should go beyond "wordsmithing" to form an *image of the firm.* Someone who is reading the statement should be able to ascertain the qualities that make your firm unique relative to other firms. Your statement should be short, memorable, and catchy so that people can remember it!
3. *External Information about the Market.* You need some indication about what is going on in the *external* world—with your competitors and throughout the economy—concerning technological, political, and social changes within your defined geographic market.
4. *Internal Information about Your Strengths, Weaknesses, Opportunities, and Threats.* Work with your lawyers to obtain their perspectives about your firm and your practice. Ask questions including these: Who are we? What are we good at? Are we a team? What are we committed to? What are our best opportunities?
5. *Goals for Growth.* These can include both qualitative goals, such as, "We want to become the Number One healthcare firm in Kansas City," or quantitative goals, such as revenue/growth targets, market-share targets, or cost-reduction targets. These goals should be as specific as possible, and be supported with detailed tactical plans.
6. *Implementation and Measurement.* Don't keep your plan a secret! Set realistic targets, provide training to individuals who are responsible for implementation, keep the strategic marketing plan as simple as possible, and try to make it measurable. And remember, success is never final, and neither is the strategy.

Purpose of a Strategic Marketing Plan

A variety of factors in today's business environment make practice development and marketing efforts vital for any law firm—not only as a means of expansion, but also to prevent loss of the firm's existing client base.

Survival

Any professional practice is caught in a never-ending process of losing clients for perfectly valid and acceptable reasons—companies expand, merge, relocate, and close. To stay at the same level of fee income, at the very least, you must replace these "natural" losses, whatever their causes, and continue to provide quality, "world-class" service.

Competition

The marketplace is becoming more competitive. Accounting firms are now strong competition for law firms. Clients are becoming more sophisticated and have higher expectations. Law firms are reporting 15 percent more marketing hours than ever before. All this makes for a highly competitive marketplace. To compete effectively, law firms must develop and market unique selling features, which are not available elsewhere, and also must substantiate billing rates by emphasizing the "value-added" services the firm can provide.

Change

Your law firm has been very successful. You made it through the 1990s, which was the decade of the client. Now, a change in philosophy has occurred in the marketplace. Clients expect more. Your practice needs to continue to become more consultative. You are expected to help clients *avoid* legal problems. Many types of legal work have become a commodity in the marketplace.

The Big Picture

By taking a "big-picture" view of marketing and by placing the client at the center of that picture, you come to realize that marketing is a means of survival. Don't ever forget that your strategic marketing plan should have the client as the center of your efforts. This can include existing and potential clients.

Fulfillment

The purpose of strategic planning and developing an ongoing marketing program is to improve the flow of quality clients into the firm and increase client satisfaction with the firm's services. However, marketing should also fulfill the needs of professionals and staff persons to work at a firm they feel is a successful and productive member of the community and the profession. Marketing is not advertising or cold calling but a continuing sophisticated combination of ascertaining the ongoing legal and business needs of target groups, and organizing people and services to meet those needs in a first-class manner at an appropriate profit.

The Future

An equally important aspect of marketing is determining the services clients will want in the future, which the firm may not currently provide. Your strategic marketing plan needs to identify the hot markets for work in the next five to ten years, and move in the direction of capitalizing on these opportunities. At the same time, your firm should also be aware of any practice areas that may be on the wane.

Clear Direction and Control

A good strategic marketing plan can provide control and direction, as you maintain and increase the growth of the firm. Your plan should detail growth objectives and the strategies and actions required in achieving those objectives. The implementation of the actions will result in a stronger, healthier, and more fulfilling practice.

Now That We Know What to Do, Where Do We Begin?

Step 1: Situation Analysis/Meetings with Key Individuals

You will need to call a meeting with key individuals, including the managing partner, management committee, director of marketing, and other lawyers who are interested in the process and important to the law firm's marketing program. You will also need to review the firm's current marketing literature and determine how members of the firm are using it.

Step 2: Vision Session/Retreat/S.W.O.T. Analysis

It can be helpful to this process to have either a half-day retreat or a ninety-minute "vision" session over lunch in the office. In larger law firms, it is necessary to do a series of "vision" sessions. The purpose of the retreat or vision session is to get information from the group and build consensus.

Typically, a S.W.O.T. (Strengths, Weaknesses, Opportunities, and Threats) analysis is performed during either the retreat or vision session. This session must be facilitated by an individual who can use a variety of exercises to help the group focus on (1) the perceived position of the law firm in the marketplace and in the minds of the clients, (2) desired growth patterns and potential for the law firm, and (3) opportunities to cultivate new clients.

PLANNING A MARKETING RETREAT OR "VISION SESSION"

- First, Identify Your Goals
  - Encourage open discussion.
  - Solicit ideas from the *entire* group.
  - Build consensus.
  - Encourage out-of-the-box thinking.
  - Ask the hard questions.
  - Formulate conclusions for each session.
  - Keep the discussion focused.
  - Cut off discussion when necessary.
  - Make sure you have fun.
  - Provide a written plan for follow-up.
- Then, Look Back for a Brief Historical Overview
  - Why are we here? How has the legal environment changed over the last ten years?
  - What types of changes have *we* experienced in the last ten years, in terms of practice areas, clients, and personnel?
  - What have been the primary forces generating this change? What have been our marketing "actions" and firm "reactions"?
  - What has given us the ability to adapt successfully? Have we experienced some cultural success with marketing?
  - What are the key strengths and weaknesses of our firm?
  - How is our firm different from our competitors?
  - Why do clients use our firm?
    - performance/quality of work
    - personal relationships
    - competence/experience
    - special skill
    - knowledge of client industry/business
    - written and verbal communication skills
    - professional image/reputation
    - location
    - cost/fees/price
    - financial terms and conditions
    - dependability/reliability
    - persistence
    - availability
    - bottom-line results
  - How has our financial growth been impacted?
- Now . . . Look Forward
  - What are the primary forces that will change our firm or areas of practice in the next ten years?
    - physical issues

        - clients
        - competitors
        - economic issues
        - technological changes
        - social issues
        - political issues
        - legal issues
    - Where do we want to be in three to five years?
    - What are our major opportunities and threats?
- Developing a Unified Approach
    - Summarize three to five key points relating to your discussion.
    - List your desired client types.
    - Discuss how you can develop new programs, including key-client focus, creative partnering, risk-sharing arrangements, legal budgeting for clients, and advanced case management.
    - Identify ten priorities to accomplish over the next six months.
    - Plan how to communicate the goals and key priorities.
- Finally
    - Create a written, strategic marketing plan.
    - Identify your goals (for example, grow Intellectual Property [IP] practice by 10 percent).
    - List the tactics planned to achieve goals (for example, develop new brochure for IP practice, establish client teams for key IP clients, sell service to firm clients who do not presently use IP).
    - Set priorities.
    - Budget appropriately.
    - Develop a detailed marketing calendar.
    - Implement, monitor, and revise.
    - Measure your success every three months.

Step 3: Client Feedback/Client Analysis

Client interviews can be performed during the strategic planning process, if desired. Generally, it is helpful to interview up to ten clients to evaluate their views of the law firm. It is best to conduct personal visits with your clients, but mailed surveys work well, too. In addition, performing an analysis of the law firm's existing client base is essential. Through a client analysis, the law firm should identify which clients provide 80 percent of revenues in any single area of practice. From this list of clients, the firm can identify industry strengths, geographic strengths, and practice area strengths, and can also explore which clients are profitable. Client profiles could be developed for each partner's top five clients, profiling billing trends over the past three years, areas of law presently being provided to the clients, pertinent information about the clients' businesses, and other law firms that the clients use on a regular basis. These client profiles can then be reviewed, and opportunities to expand the client relationships can be included in the marketing plan.

Step 4: Market Research/Market Analysis

Information about the marketplace is essential to any law firm, and this information is easily available. Several companies execute market research studies, and can provide valuable data about the marketplace, which can be helpful to the process. Every law firm also needs to have an active prospect list of up to a dozen companies that the law firm would like to secure as clients. Research of these companies can be performed (by the firm's librarian, if available) and a one-page marketing plan can be developed for each prospective client. This makes it easier to track marketing success or failure.

How Do We Apply the Knowledge We Have Gained?

At this point in the process, your firm or practice group will have a clear view of where they are. Moving forward, you should ask, "What are the opportunities for the law firm?"

Step 5: Crafting the Mission Statement/Positioning

The mission statement communicates the goals of the law firm in a simple statement. It will be communicated internally within the law firm, as well as externally to the world. The mission statement should go beyond "wordsmithing" to form an *image* of the law firm. It should be the "headline" about your business, and is important because it defines you and sharpens your focus. A clear mission statement enables you to clarify your purpose to anyone you engage—from your banker to prospective clients. It differentiates you from the pack, which is an important aspect of your ability to compete. Your mission statement should clearly describe (1) the nature of your practice or service, and (2) the markets you want to serve.

SAMPLE MISSION STATEMENTS

"Our firm's mission is to assist our clients in achieving their legal, business, and financial goals. We provide creative solutions that are cost-effective and consistently exceed client expectations. The firm's commitment to excellence is reflected in our long-term relationships with our clients, in the professional development of our people, and in our reputation in the community."

"We strive to be a preeminent, New York business law firm that delivers consistently high-quality, responsive, and cost-effective legal service. We will work to build lasting client relationships based on honest dialogue and the timely exchange of information. We will always treat others with dignity and respect. We will share with our community a portion of the leadership, skill, and other resources we enjoy, and will fulfill our ethical and professional responsibilities to the legal system, our clients, and the public."

Your mission statement is one method by which you can position your firm, or differentiate it from other firms in the marketplace. Positioning the law firm to the external world is very important. Law firms can own any number of market positions—positions based on geographic location, industry expertise, price, and so on. Many law firms base positions on their business sense, service, value to the client, spirit of innovation, or an individual lawyer's reputation. To position your firm effectively, and differentiate it from all other law firms, you should explore service offerings, professional and employee attitudes, marketing communications (every piece of paper published by the firm—letters, forms, advertisements, and brochures—reflects the firm's market position), as well as the community involvement efforts of the firm's lawyers.

Step 6: Planning on Many Levels—Firm Strategic Marketing Plan, Practice Group Plans, Niche Area Plans, and Individual Lawyer Plans

FIRM STRATEGIC MARKETING PLAN

The final step in the strategic marketing planning process is the development of a written marketing or strategic plan (or plans) for the law firm. The written plan should be concise (no one will read 300 pages) and address client relations, firm-specific activities, plans to develop marketing support materials, any planned advertising, and a public-relations program, as well as a comprehensive "action items" list, implementation schedule, and marketing budget. The plan will contain defined goals and targets, as well as key-result areas, which should be achievable and measurable. (See the sample at the end of the chapter.)

PRACTICE AREA OR NICHE AREA STRATEGIC MARKETING PLAN

You may also find it helpful and meaningful to develop a strategic marketing plan for specific practice groups, niche areas of practice, or even individual clients. Use your firm strategic marketing plan as a model for these (so you have consistency in format), and remember that these plans should be goal-oriented and concise.

INDIVIDUAL MARKETING PLANS

Each lawyer in the firm should complete an individual marketing plan. This is valuable for three reasons: (1) It helps the individual articulate goals, organize efforts, and set priorities. (2) It helps you identify clients or prospects that more than one individual is marketing, so you can establish client or prospect "teams" to facilitate the marketing and development of clients. (3) It will provide you with a way to assign marketing budgets to individuals. Individual plans can also be evaluated for opportunities to cross-sell new services to existing clients. (See the sample form at the end of this chapter for ideas regarding what to include in individual marketing plans.)

Overview of the Strategic Marketing Plan

A comprehensive marketing plan is inclusive, beginning with the marketing goals of the firm, continuing with an implementation schedule, and ending with a marketing background section and budget. Most marketing plans contain three major components:

1. Marketing Goals, Priorities and Action Plan: Specific marketing goals should be developed from information gathered and analyzed during meetings with lawyers, the management committee, or marketing committee. The overall goals should cover no more than a three-year period. Specific priorities should be clearly identified for each year, and immediate priorities can be listed in boldface type. (Or placed in a separate marketing summary for the given year.) An action plan should follow each goal and provide a step-by-step strategy to achieve it.
2. Marketing Background: The marketing background section includes your vision and mission statements for the organization, as well as a list of present areas of expertise, and the market segments and potential niche strategies for the firm.
3. Budget: This is simply a detailing of the costs associated with implementing the tactics contained in the plan.

Remember that the objective of any strategic marketing plan is to establish order, control marketing activities and expenditures, and provide direction for the management and growth of the firm.

Specific Elements of the Strategic Marketing Plan

Market Position

You should identify the market position that your firm occupies at present. This could include information about the size of the firm, its location, the strength of its position in its current market, the types of clients it serves, and the services provided those clients. You may also want to include information about any law firm networks or alliances with which you are affiliated.

The Six Market Segments

Every law firm should direct its marketing activities in six market segments, which should be reflected in the strategic marketing plan. These market segments are the sources of new clients for the firm.

MEMBERS OF THE FIRM

This group includes all professional and support staff, as well as lawyers. The lawyers need to make everyone in the firm aware of all capabilities and expertise, and get everyone in the firm involved in client relations and business development, to the greatest extent possible.

EXISTING CLIENTS

Existing clients should be your best referral source. If you provide prompt, quality service and value, you will obtain referrals. Cross-selling is part of this. You need to make a concerted effort to educate your clients about your services. Research has shown that clients typically are not aware of the range of services available from their law firms. Lawyers must thoroughly analyze the needs, expectations, and desires of clients, and model their service offerings accordingly.

SPECIFIC LOCAL CLIENTS

This group includes clients that the firm does not presently represent, but with whom the firm would like to do business. A list of prospects for both the short term and long term should be included in the individual marketing plan of each lawyer, and the firm should have at least a dozen firmwide prospects.

GENERAL INTERNATIONAL/NATIONAL/REGIONAL CLIENTS

Your firm wants to represent those included in this group because they currently do business in your state or region or may do so in the future. Your firm could offer practice areas in which the firm has built—or could build—sophisticated expertise that is not easily replicated, or practice areas in which the firm's lawyers have the ability to do nationally high-quality work, but at far less expense than other firms.

IN-HOUSE COUNSEL

Members of a client's in-house counsel staff frequently make decisions about which firms to retain for legal services. Your firm should (1) develop a database of those businesses in your market area that have in-house legal departments and the need to use outside firms, and then (2) develop a program to make those businesses aware of the firm's capabilities in specific areas that may interest them.

OTHER REFERRAL SOURCES

Last, but not least, general referrals may turn out to be the most important part of the firm's marketing efforts. A major push should take place to maximize specific referral sources and build relationships with key individuals who can send your firm business. Individual members of the firm should make a concentrated effort in this area. This includes building strong relationships with accountants and other lawyers, through trade associations and similar organizations. Individuals in your firm need to do significant courting of these individuals, particularly on the local level, to make sure they know your firm wants new work, has a desire to develop new clients, and has a dedication to client service. Your firm should make these referral sources aware of your full range of capabilities.

Niche Strategy

To build a successful niche strategy, it helps to isolate a specific number of practice areas that are likely to grow and develop needs during the next five years. This could include service niches (such as estate planning, litigation, healthcare, or intellectual property), or geographic niches (defined by city, state, region, or country), or specialty-market niches (such as closely held businesses, physicians, construction companies, or corporations). Individual lawyers can consider these broad niches in their marketing plans. By focusing marketing efforts on a select number of niche areas, each lawyer can create a successful and *manageable* marketing program. If your lawyers try to be all things to all people, they will fail. Your firm should build a reputation for having experts in selected areas, and then strongly market the services in those areas.

Overall Strategies for Success

Strategies are courses of action necessary to achieve firm goals, capitalize on firm strengths, and overcome firm weaknesses. Every strategic marketing plan needs them. Strategies include

- People
- Product (service)
- Place
- Promotion
- Price

PEOPLE

In a service business, people are the most important asset. Clients judge services by the professionalism and technical competence of the firm's people. Because a law firm does not necessarily have a "product," and the services that a firm provides are intangible, clients, prospective clients, and contacts will search for clues by which to judge the firm. Among those clues is the image projected by people. The professional dress and conduct of staff persons, and the manner in which the phone is answered and clients are greeted, are extremely important. Therefore, your firm should continue to stress professionalism, attentiveness, and concern at all levels of the organization, at all times. Your firm should also stress the importance of working as a team. THIS

IS A PRIORITY! Implementing your strategic marketing plan should be the responsibility of ALL members of your firm, from the managing partner to the receptionist and mailroom workers.

As a part of your marketing plan, you should establish a philosophy that encourages the continued professional growth and development of all personnel—maximizing their potential and thereby maximizing client service.

SERVICE

Expanding the range of services that the firm can provide clients, and focusing on specific services that clients desire, are necessary steps to addressing clients' needs fully. Through a survey of selected clients and regular client contact, your firm can better understand the additional services clients may desire. All lawyers should strive to serve these evolving needs by developing current personnel, hiring necessary expertise, or establishing relationships with qualified individuals to whom they will refer clients to ensure needs are met.

PLACE

Your firm should clearly articulate the location of your marketplace. Some lawyers may have a practice that is national in scope, while others may focus their energies on the local marketplace.

PROMOTION

Your marketing objectives are probably focused on client satisfaction, retention, and development, and your marketing efforts should not lose sight of that. Marketing should be divided between maintaining existing clients and adding new ones. Generally, as a rule of thumb, you should spend about 75 percent of your "marketing time" on taking care of and expanding existing client relationships. The other 25 percent should be devoted to establishing new relationships and business development.

Your firm should support individual participation in community and professional groups, as deemed appropriate. Lawyers should be encouraged to develop individual marketing plans, which serve as outlines for individual participation in the firm's marketing program. Activities such as writing articles, speaking, participating in seminars, and community involvement will be detailed within these plans.

PRICE

In comparing your firm's fees with those of other firms, on both a local and national basis, your firm should strive to maintain a "value-added" philosophy, to offer clients more for their money, and to create positive feelings in clients (especially when they are paying your bills). Pricing is an important component to consider when developing any marketing plan. You may want to get some feedback from your clients regarding their comfort level with your fees.

Individual Marketing Plans

Key questions for any individual marketing plan:

- How many hours per week, on average, are you willing to devote to business development and client retention activities?
- Are there areas of practice in which you specialize? If so, what areas?
- Are there other areas in which you would like to become more specialized?
- List three clients or prospects who might benefit from your existing, or new, area(s) of expertise.
- How will you present this specialization to these clients or prospects?
- List the five most valuable clients with whom you work.
- Based on this list of clients, identify how you can improve your relationships in the following areas (list specific names of clients below each activity):
  - Improve communication (for example, take the client to lunch or dinner, visit the client's place of business, send the client advisories)
  - Learn more about the client's business or industry, and present business ideas to the client
  - Conduct a client satisfaction interview, and look for ways to cross-sell new services
  - List other ways in which you could improve your level of service to the client
- If you were to target three potential clients this year (to whom you could sell firm services other than your own), who would they be?
- List one step you will take to move each of these prospects closer to "client status."
- List your three most valuable sources of referrals.
- To whom do you make the most referrals?
- List one or two new people to whom you can refer business.
- List one way you will thank or acknowledge each in the next thirty days.
- In which organizations are you active? (include professional/business/civic).
- Write one goal for increased leadership or contribution this year.
- In which other organizations would you like to become active this year?
- If you were required to write an article on two topics this year, what would they be?
- On which topic will you try to speak or write this year?
- If you were to follow up on three clients that you or the firm lost, who would they be?
- Describe other business development/marketing activities not mentioned that are important or interest you.

- Based on the above questions and answers, what will be your *primary* marketing goal for 1999?

Weekly Marketing Plan Checklist

It can be helpful to your program to provide individuals with *gentle reminders* that they should be marketing. Offer them a laminated card, or something they can post in their offices. It reminds them to market—every week! An example follows.

√ ***Check those items accomplished every week:***

80% OF YOUR TIME SHOULD BE SPENT ON "RELATIONSHIP BUILDING"

☐ Contact your **existing clients** at least weekly.
☐ Make a list of and call or visit your **referral sources** on a regular basis.
☐ Make a list of at least **three targets** and contact your target clients at least every two weeks—remember it can take seven contacts before they remember you.
☐ Have your library or a member of your support staff do some **research** about your target clients and think of ways you could help them solve their problems or capture opportunities.
☐ Make your **friends/family/social contacts** aware of the capabilities of your firm.
☐ Work to build relationships and communicate with **other partners/professionals** in your firm.
☐ Create a list of **other professionals outside your firm** who might be referral sources.
☐ Have someone else do a **client interview** with one of your clients.
☐ Send your clients, contacts, and referral sources an **article** of interest to them.
☐ Take someone to **breakfast, lunch, dinner.**
☐ Invite someone to a **sporting or cultural event,** or to **play golf or tennis.**
☐ Send out your card, **a firm profile,** or information on a specific practice area or area of expertise.
☐ Invite selected contacts to a **seminar.**
☐ Send **personal notes** of congratulations for accomplishments.
☐ **Join organizations** that are meaningful to your clients and contacts.
☐ Update your **mailing list.**
☐ Send **holiday cards** every year.
☐ Send **thank-you notes** for referrals.

- ☐ Become *actively* involved in the **community.**
- ☐ Involve your **secretary/support staff** in your marketing efforts.
- ☐ **Track your results** and remove unproductive prospects/referral sources/clients.
- ☐ Think about ways you can expand services to clients; **cross-sell** other firm professionals.
- ☐ Develop a **client service team** and prepare a marketing plan for an individual client.
- ☐ Offer to help clients with **project/case management** and **budgeting.**

20% OF YOUR TIME SHOULD BE SPENT ON "REPUTATION BUILDING"

- ☐ Identify three newsworthy matters about which you can **write** an article or client alert.
- ☐ **Read** a variety of industry publications to learn what issues are important to your clients/contacts.
- ☐ **Join** an association that supports your practice specialty.
- ☐ Obtain the **mailing list** for group(s) in which you participate.
- ☐ **Send** at least one article, letter, or client update per month to those individuals on your mailing list.
- ☐ Update your **résumé and bio** to include recent achievements.
- ☐ **Speak** when you can on your area of expertise.
- ☐ Send a **letter to editors** who might be interested in publishing articles prepared by you; include a list of topics for them to consider, and then stay in touch and get to know them.
- ☐ Get more involved in **industry groups** related to your area of expertise.
- ☐ Make sure a **press release** is issued for your accomplishments.
- ☐ Make sure your accomplishments are **communicated internally** to your firm.
- ☐ Contribute to your **Web site**; announce areas of interest/important accomplishments or developments.
- ☐ Make sure you are aware of **conferences/seminars/trade shows** to attend within your area of expertise; offer to speak or moderate a program.
- ☐ Respond to **RFPs** if this is appropriate for your area of practice.
- ☐ Watch for **upcoming events in the community** that will provide you with an opportunity to meet people.
- ☐ Work on preparing a **"twenty-second infomercial"** about your firm and your practice.
- ☐ Attend a **networking event** and *really* network.
- ☐ Make a list of ways that your **practice is different** from your competitors' practices.

Sample Strategic Marketing Plan

(In your own strategic marketing plan, you may want to include a section on marketing background, such as a summary of your client interview program, market research data, economic reports, or any other materials you used in developing the plan.)

Marketing Goals, Priorities, and Action Plan

The goals and objectives will be revised on an ongoing basis, as needed, and are an important part of the long-range planning effort of the firm. These marketing goals reflect specific activities that presently are viewed as offering the best opportunity and highest payoff for the firm. The goals presented here are for a two- to three-year period. In an effort to identify a manageable level of activity, and to establish priorities for the next year, all items listed in **bold-face type** throughout the plan will be executed in [year].

This marketing plan was created for ABC Law Firm as a formal outline of planned marketing activity for the next two to three years. The marketing plan, as a whole, details a very comprehensive approach to marketing. Considering personnel, time, and monetary constraints, it is necessary to prioritize activities to ensure successful completion of this plan.

Overall Objectives for ABC Law Firm

GOALS FOR GROWTH

- 5%–7% net increase in chargeable hours per year ($_____ x 6% = $_____ additional revenue)
- Increase in chargeable hours for all personnel per year as follows: one-half from new business and one-half from existing clients ($_____ new and $_____ existing)

MARKETING GOALS

1. Maintain client satisfaction, develop central client database, and develop new business from existing client base
2. Cultivate active referral sources and develop a program to maximize referral opportunities
3. Target market-specific niches and develop a specific prospect list of clients from whom the firm will generate new business
4. Position the firm to expand and strengthen awareness of ABC Law Firm in our market
5. Build a marketing culture and improve marketing firmwide

Goal #1: Maintain Client Satisfaction and Develop New Business from Existing Client Base

ABC Law Firm will strive to retain the firm's existing client base and to continue building on the satisfaction of those clients by providing superior client service. This also includes generating new business from those clients through cross-selling of new services. The firm will strive in [year] to improve communication with existing clients and referral sources.

The firm will focus on expanding relationships with existing clients in an effort to (1) further develop the "value-added" concept, (2) strengthen key client relationships and cultivate our primary source of new business, (3) expand our services to existing clients, (4) better understand how clients view us, and (5) specifically promote selected niche areas.

EXISTING CLIENTS

Existing clients continue to be our most valuable new-business source. We must constantly recognize the importance of providing quality service to them. This includes proper use of the telephone and voice mail. Clients should be given options when calling the office, and voice mail should be used appropriately. Quality service—a much broader concept than quality in the technical sense—entails providing our services to clients on a timely basis at a reasonable cost. Quality service means assisting clients in improving their profitability and operations through value-added legal services. We need to be *proactive* with our clients and help them plan their legal strategies. The specific programs relating to existing clients follow.

CLIENT CONTACT PROGRAM

- We will emphasize ongoing involvement at both partner and associate levels in this program. Reporting of these efforts should be a requirement.
- An initial minimum goal of the client contact program will be one client meeting of a practice development nature per week, with a further goal of meeting with each client every six months.
- "Welcome to Our Firm" letters from the engagement partner will be sent to new clients.
- Targeted seminars will be held for selected clients, prospects, and referral sources.
- A client satisfaction/needs survey will be developed and conducted.
- A checklist will be developed and used as a reminder about additional services to provide existing clients.
- Exit interviews will be conducted, as an analysis of lost clients. A memorandum should be prepared and forwarded to the marketing committee whenever a client is lost.

STRATEGIES TO ACHIEVE GOAL #1 IN [YEAR]

Maintain Client Satisfaction and Develop New Business from Existing Client Base

ACTION STEP	RESPON-SIBILITY	PRIORITY	DATE
EXISTING CLIENTS			
Mail "Welcome to our Firm" letter for all new clients, which will be sent to them from the firm.	________	________	________
Conduct yearly client satisfaction survey:			
Develop survey and obtain principal approval	________	________	________
Send survey out to clients/perform personal interview	________	________	________
Tabulate results and report	________	________	________
Implement key principal visibility program, which would involve having each principal meet with existing clients to ask: "How are we doing? What can we do better? How can we improve our service to you? It will be important to report results (that is, a memo to the marketing committee), which can be summarized and reported on an ongoing basis.	________	________	________
Send birthday greetings to clients on an annual basis.	________	________	________
Conduct exit interviews for all outgoing clients.	________	________	________
Develop a strategy to deal with transition issues resulting from retirement of partners.	________	________	________
Update our client listing to include the following information: bank name and key bank contact, law firm and principal lawyer, and SIC codes.	________	________	________
Institute program whereby professional staff will write letters (samples available on system) to selected in-house counsel and other referral sources, thanking them for their assistance during the engagement. These letters			

will go to agreed-upon individuals at least once a year. The engagement partner will approve these letters.	________	________	________
Consider conducting a seminar for our clients and potential clients before [date].	________	________	________
Conduct in-house seminars once or twice a year in the office to address specific topics of interest to clients.	________	________	________
Design a more complete "client service opportunities" or "client needs analysis" checklist in an effort to further develop and cross-sell the practice. Tie this into a client education program.	________	________	________
Use the "Guide for Clients" on a regular basis for all new clients.	________	________	________

Goal #2: Cultivate Active Referral Sources and Develop a Program to Maximize Referral Opportunities

By using a well-established network of referral sources, the firm can generate new business. Individuals have to ask for the business!

For all referral sources, specific programs include

- Interfacing with our counterparts (partners and associates, middle management).
- Encouraging referral sources to view us as a resource.
- Inviting referral sources to conduct training sessions for our staff on what they do.
- Joining their trade association (if possible).
- Making targeted technical presentations to their trade associations or to their companies.
- Referring business to key referral sources on a selected basis and making sure they know who referred it.

ACCOUNTANTS/CPAS/OTHER LAW FIRMS

We must expand our network of professional service firms to focus on relationship building with the following:

- Targeted law firms, including those that specialize in specific practice areas that we do not provide.
- Specific CPAs who want to conduct seminars for our firm.

BANKS

Commercial bankers continue to be one of our major referral sources, and we will keep targeting and networking with them. It is critical that our professionals interact with their counterparts at these banks. Our lawyers must make it a point to know the loan officers assigned to their clients and should begin developing relationships with them (one bank at a time).

- Targeted banks include _____, _____, _____, and _____.
- We will hold at least one bank reception in the fall of each year.

STRATEGIES TO ACHIEVE GOAL #2 IN [YEAR]

Cultivate Active Referral Sources and Develop a Program to Maximize Referral Opportunities

ACTION STEP	RESPON-SIBILITY	PRIORITY	DATE
REFERRAL SOURCES			
Update database of referral sources.	________	________	________
Develop a specific plan regarding how to market referral sources, including accountants, other lawyers, brokers, and insurance consultants.	________	________	________
Identify and create a list of specific referral sources.	________	________	________
Organize receptions to be held in our office for the following banks:			
________________________________	________	________	________
________________________________	________	________	________
________________________________	________	________	________
Host cocktail receptions for the following CPA firms:			
________________________________	________	________	________
________________________________	________	________	________
________________________________	________	________	________
Host a dinner or reception with one or more stockbroker firms:			
________________________________	________	________	________

Host a dinner or reception with one insurance agent: ________________ ______ ______ ______

Identify banks or groups of commercial lenders for a seminar, and conduct one seminar before the end of the year. ______ ______ ______

Ensure that significant emphasis is placed on the cultivation of referral sources, particularly bankers and other lawyers, but also existing clients, in all individual marketing plans. ______ ______ ______

Develop a referral card system to track referrals. ______ ______ ______

Goal #3: Target Market-Specific Niches and Specific Prospective Clients to Generate New Business

The firm needs to take a more proactive approach to business development. If the right process is followed within key niche areas, the firm will secure new clients. The firm must bring in a constant flow of new clients to survive. Specific prospect lists will be gathered and contacts will be made. Brochures or flyers describing niche services will be developed. Specific mailings will be done to target niches and prospect lists. The firm has a particular interest in increasing market share of small- to medium-sized emerging companies, which typically have $5–$50 million in revenue and in-house legal staffs.

SPECIFIC PROSPECTIVE CLIENTS

[Include a list of at least twelve.]

NICHE MARKETING PROGRAM

Specific marketing plans will be developed for specialized services (niches), and partners and associates will be encouraged to increase their credibility and name recognition to develop a "famous person" concept within niche areas. The "famous person" is the one potential clients consider the expert in any given area of practice. As part of this effort, the firm will expand and continue to develop skills, materials, and other resources needed to broaden our service offerings in consultative areas.

The following areas will be explored and evaluated:

[List areas]

STRATEGIES TO ACHIEVE GOAL #3 IN [YEAR]

Target Market-Specific Niches and Specific Prospective Clients to Generate New Business

ACTION STEP	RESPON-SIBILITY	PRIORITY	DATE
TARGET AND NICHE MARKETING			
Obtain a written action plan from niche leaders for marketing business niche services through [date].	______	______	______
Meet with all lawyers and legal assistants to develop written individual marketing plans and finalize them.	______	______	______
Expand the mailing list for newsletters and consider developing specific newsletters or "legal briefs" for various industries.	______	______	______
The firm will develop a top-ten desired-client list within each selected niche area, and research will be performed to develop a marketing plan for each. Ten prospective clients will be targeted, then individuals will gather information on these clients (their bankers and lawyers, for example). An attempt will be made to secure a meeting or, at a minimum, to get them on our mailing list for newsletter mailings.	______	______	______
Use the newsletters to "sell a theme," such as estate planning or healthcare.	______	______	______
Implement a system to track proposals (proposal control sheet), to monitor the status of proposals, and to determine the win/loss ratio and the principal reasons for success or failure.	______	______	______
Review the existing proposal letter format and narrative, evaluate it, and consider revisions as necessary.	______	______	______
Create "model" proposals for specific services/client types.	______	______	______
Target dental schools and other healthcare providers as a prospective client group.	______	______	______
Identify all reports and procedures required in tracking marketing.	______	______	______

Develop specialty-area marketing brochures or collateral materials, develop a direct-mail list, and execute the direct-mail program.	________	________	________
Implement an eighteen-month follow-up program for new business development.	________	________	________

Goal #4: Position the Firm to Expand and Strengthen Awareness of ABC Law Firm in Our Market

ABC Law Firm needs to clearly identify a position in the marketplace that differentiates the firm from all other legal service providers and highlights the firm's unique capabilities and diversity. Using a consistent "look" or corporate identity will be an important part of this process. The firm will continue to strengthen the market's overall awareness of who it is and what it does.

ABC Law Firm will be positioned as experienced, knowledgeable, and professional, and as providing close personal attention and quality service—particularly as business advisor—to closely held business owners and privately held companies. The firm's mailing list of clients, contacts, and community leaders is a key part of this effort. The firm will explore improved processes to ensure the mailing list is updated and expanded on a regular basis.

COMMUNITY INVOLVEMENT

- *Active* participation in business, charitable, and civic associations, with emphasis on enthusiastic and regular participation, will be strongly encouraged.
- Every member of the professional staff will be encouraged to participate in at least one organization, which could be a business, charitable, recreational, or religious organization.

PUBLIC RELATIONS

- We will issue press releases for significant accomplishments.
- We will work with the press for potential feature-story coverage and article-writing opportunities.

NAME RECOGNITION

- The firm will design and develop an "institutional" firm advertisement for publications and program book usage on an as-needed basis.
- We will identify various trade shows in which the firm will participate during the coming year.
- The firm will keep its Web site up-to-date.

COLLATERAL MATERIALS

- The firm will develop product brochures for the selected niche areas.

- More individuals in the firm will use the firm brochure.
- The firm will continue quarterly publication of its newsletter.
- The firm will consider promotional items for client/staff use, such as coffee mugs or T-shirts.

SEMINARS/SPEAKING ENGAGEMENTS

- The firm will hold at least three seminars per year and will follow each one with a specific contact program.

STRATEGIES TO ACHIEVE GOAL #4 IN [YEAR]

Position the Firm to Expand and Strengthen Awareness of ABC Law Firm in Our Market.

ACTION STEP	RESPON-SIBILITY	PRIORITY	DATE
AWARENESS OF FIRM IN MARKET			
Issue regular press releases, for items such as promotions, major appointments, speeches or presentations, and firm anniversaries. Information for press releases is to be generated by the marketing committee.	______	______	______
Design and develop industry niche brochures for selected niches.	______	______	______
Give a supply of the firm brochures to each partner and encourage the partners to use them on a more regular basis.	______	______	______
Determine and formalize a process that will ensure the quarterly update of the firm's mailing list. Expand the mailing list for the newsletter to include closely held companies not presently serviced by the firm.	______	______	______
Develop more-formalized presentation materials to be used in proposal presentations (such as PowerPoint, or preprinted flip charts with graphics).	______	______	______
Through contacts at appropriate business and industry media, arrange for articles to be written by the firm or quote certain principals as appropriate. A "media guide" could be prepared and sent to key editors, listing resources in the firm.	______	______	______

Identify publications in which the firm will advertise in the coming year, and develop ads that can be used in a variety of situations.	______	______	______
Identify various industry trade groups that the firm, as well as specific individuals, should join. Encourage attendance at meetings, and hold seminars sponsored by these groups.	______	______	______
Identify three individuals with the firm who, as part of their individual marketing plans, will write articles for local business or trade publications on selected niche areas of practice.	______	______	______
______________________________		______	______
______________________________	______	______	______
______________________________	______	______	______
Each individual identified above will write at least one article before [date].	______	______	______

Goal #5: Internal Marketing—Build A Marketing Culture and Improve Marketing Firmwide

There is a desire to improve marketing on all levels at ABC Law Firm. A marketing culture needs to be initiated, and each firm member needs to be involved as an active participant in client relations and business development. Training and ongoing exposure to marketing concepts is key.

Active, focused, and enthusiastic participation in practice development is considered to be a positive characteristic of those individuals who will advance within our firm. Practice development always will represent much more than selling—or even marketing—the firm. It also will encompass the concept of providing quality service to our clients.

ABC Law Firm will encourage staff persons to participate in the firm's marketing, in whatever manner is most comfortable for them. We will emphasize that marketing is everyone's responsibility. We will determine specific roles for each individual in fulfillment of the firm's marketing program.

INDIVIDUAL MARKETING PLANS

- The firm will assign [name] to act as a facilitator in the development of individual marketing plans.
- An "Individual Marketing Plan" will be completed by every member of the legal staff and will become part of the ongoing counseling process.

MARKETING TRAINING PROGRAM

- Training will be provided regarding the variety of services the firm provides.
- Presentations on the basics of client relations will be held for partners and associates.
- Client-relations training will be conducted for all members of the support staff.

ANNUAL FIRM MEETINGS

- Annual meetings will be held to discuss marketing success and set marketing goals for the upcoming year.
- Marketing incentives will be offered and communicated.
- Short presentations on significant new clients will take place quarterly.
- Short presentations on new products or services will take place regularly.
- A monthly new-client list will be distributed via the weekly bulletin.
- Members of the staff will serve on the marketing committee.

STRATEGIES TO ACHIEVE GOAL #5 IN [YEAR]

Internal Marketing—Build a Marketing Culture and Improve Marketing Firmwide.

ACTION STEP	RESPON-SIBILITY	PRIORITY	DATE
INTERNAL MARKETING			
Organize and locate all marketing materials in one section of the office and issue a memorandum to all personnel notifying them of such.	________	________	________
Develop a plan for training the firm's professionals on marketing-related matters. Such training would begin in the first year of an individual's career and would continue each year. Training programs would include but not be limited to the following: how to develop a marketing plan, developing a personal marketing style, listening skills, oral and written communication, developing a strong referral network, practice expansion skills, and so on.	________	________	________
Include a section in weekly online bulletins, currently being developed, that is devoted to marketing-related activities. The marketing section is to include cross-selling activities, wins on potential clients, seminars, articles, community service, networking opportunities, and similar items.	________	________	________

Use e-mail to notify all personnel of prospective client activity to take advantage of contacts within firm, which may be helpful in securing clients.	______	______	______
Hold biweekly meetings of the marketing committee. The meetings will begin at 8:30 a.m. and will last approximately one hour.	______	______	______
Expand the marketing committee to include professional and support staff representatives.	______	______	______
Upon approval of the marketing plan by partners or the management committee, hold a meeting with all personnel to review the marketing plan.	______	______	______
Encourage staff persons to write newsletter articles.	______	______	______
Encourage staff persons to write for the Web site. A monthly tax column or legal tip will be included on the Web site.	______	______	______
Institute quarterly "brown bag" luncheon meetings to discuss marketing topics. All lawyers and support staff will be invited to the meeting, attendance will be optional, and the discussion will be informal, relating to any area of marketing or practice development: new clients, proposals outstanding, or marketing ideas, for example.	______	______	______
Issue a monthly marketing calendar to all personnel, which will indicate all action items targeted for that month as well as any other marketing activities occurring in the month.	______	______	______

Typical Marketing Budget

Your firm should plan to spend between 1 percent and 5 percent of gross revenues on marketing and client development. Because law is a relationship business, one-third of this lump sum should be devoted to individual lawyers, to pay for their relationship-building activities. The following list includes typical categories of a law firm marketing budget. The salaries of marketing personnel generally are not included in the marketing budget. In planning your marketing budget, it is helpful to identify the lump sum that you plan to invest in marketing, and then assign money to each category, based on your priorities. That way, if you run out of money midyear, you will have financed the most important aspects of your marketing program early.

Breakdown of expenses	**Budget this year**	**Last year's expense**
Business entertainment	________	________
Computer/library/publications	________	________
Marketing consultant/outside services	________	________
Professional dues for trade and professional	________	________
organizations	________	________
Seminars and special events	________	________
CLE (relating to marketing)	________	________
Holiday cards and gifts/postage	________	________
Newsletter printing/postage	________	________
Brochures and other marketing materials	________	________
Staff incentive program	________	________
Referral gifts or receptions	________	________
Advertising	________	________
Print	________	________
Community books	________	________
Specialty advertising/promotional items	________	________
Postage	________	________
Charitable contributions	________	________
Client survey printing/postage	________	________
Professional and support staff training	________	________

A Strategic Planning Success—Built on the "Voice of the Client"

Situation

A law firm with two offices and 125 lawyers came to a marketing consultant, seeking assistance with strategic planning on a firmwide basis. Although the firm had been successful, the lawyers felt that as a group they needed to identify a "shared" vision for the future of the firm. Key questions included these:

- Where are we going in the next five years?
- What is our mission?
- Do we want to grow or remain the same size?
- Should we maintain two offices or consolidate?
- What makes us unique compared with other firms?
- How do we effectively position ourselves?
- What are our strengths?
- Where does our future lie?
- Are we a group of individuals practicing together or a firm?

These are questions that law firms routinely face. So, how does a firm facing these questions respond? Can a large law firm develop a meaningful direction and strategic plan for the *entire* firm?

Solution

The consultant worked with the firm to form a strategic marketing committee. The goal of the committee would be to work in concert with the consultant to develop a more cohesive direction and more clearly defined objectives for growth.

Achieving consensus by committee is no easy task. In the initial meeting, it was made clear that although there was no doubt this committee could sit around a conference room table and come up with a strategic plan for the firm, this was not the desired outcome of the process. The consultant suggested that this firm base its marketing plan on something meaningful and concrete—the "*voice of the client.*"

FOUR VARIABLES USED IN DEVELOPING THE PLAN

1. Personal interviews with twenty-five of the firm's clients
2. A market research study of the top two hundred purchasers of legal services in the firm's market
3. A "macro" economic analysis of the regional trends
4. An internal analysis of key lawyers in the firm

Through this research, the firm could identify and consider what its clients wanted and expected, the market demands for legal services, and the general economic trends that could impact its business. Overall, a strategic plan was developed that summarized the major goals of the firm for the next three years based upon these variables. The firm is reporting a great deal of success in implementing the plan.

Remember, success is never final and neither is the strategy. Try it—it works!

SECTION 2

Getting Organized

CHAPTER 3

Marketing Intelligence for Intelligent Marketing: Using Research to Get and Keep Clients

Stephen Brewer

Competing for Clients in the New Legal Marketplace

Before the 1990s, the legal profession was a *seller's market.* In a seller's market, demand exceeds supply and sellers dictate the terms of the relationship, including naming their own prices. In a seller's market, marketing consists primarily of opening the doors in the morning and letting the business roll in.

In the 1990s, however, due to an oversupply of lawyers and a trend among clients of taking more work in-house, law firms found themselves—for the first time and for the foreseeable future—in a *buyer's market.* In a buyer's market, supply exceeds demand, buyers dictate the terms of the relationship (including the prices paid for the products or services involved), and firms and their services are seen as commodities. In a buyer's market, marketing becomes a necessity for keeping the doors open.

In the current buyer's market, lawyers and law firms are increasingly "on trial," to use a legal analogy. At issue in this trial are the following:

- The value of the firm's services
- The relevance of the firm's services
- The manner in which these services are delivered
- The firm's ability to understand and meet its clients' changing needs

In this trial, the judge and jury, which come from both external and internal sources, are the firm's clients and prospects (external) and its lawyers and staff (internal). Verdicts are rendered on a daily basis—hire the firm or fire it, stay with the firm or leave it. The penalties associated with these verdicts are harsh: law firms go out of business, downsize, and merge; lawyers experience growing disaffection with the profession; long-term clients feel less loyalty to firms, and even defect; CPAs and other professionals perform an increasing amount of legal-related services; and law firms frequently endure "Requests for Proposals" (RFPs) and competitive presentations to get new business.

Here, as with any trial, the key to success is having superior factual information.

- Superior factual information is the basis for superior strategy.
- Superior strategy is the basis for superior tactics.
- And superior strategy and tactics are the bases for winning.

In litigation, the information-gathering process is called discovery. In marketing, it's called marketing research—or, in a broader sense, marketing intelligence. In both cases, the party with the better information wins. In other words, information is a *competitive advantage* in marketing, just as it is in litigation.

How does your firm measure up in today's highly competitive legal marketplace? Do you have the factual information needed to present a compelling argument to clients, prospects, and others who will determine your firm's ongoing success and profitability? Do you know *what* information to get and then *how to use it* to develop an effective strategy?

The Role of Research

The critical issue for your law firm is getting and keeping profitable clients. Without a sufficient number of profitable client relationships, no law firm can survive. Because the best relationships—either personal or business—are based on each party having in-depth knowledge of the other, marketing intelligence and the information systems it creates are crucial. However, only a handful of law firms throughout the country have made a commitment to develop an ongoing marketing information capability that is the fundamental ingredient in building superior relationships.

In a buyer's market, profitable client relationships become increasingly harder to get and keep. As competition increases, so does the need for marketing intelligence as a means to find a competitive advantage and build strong, enduring client relationships. *Marketing research is the most effective means of gathering the factual information you need to develop successful strategies for creating, maintaining, and expanding your relationships with existing and prospective clients.*

Without accurate and timely information, your firm can waste much time and money on marketing efforts. Just think about the number of confusing or pointless advertisements you've seen done by law firms—ads that are driven by lawyers' preconceived notions of what's important, but that do little to address clients' and prospects' real concerns or needs.

The need for in-depth, accurate information explains why so much time, money, and effort in a litigation matter is spent in discovery. Discovery is simply a formalized information-gathering process designed to reveal facts used to make strategic and tactical decisions. Likewise, *marketing research* is a systematic process of gathering and analyzing data from and about your firm's various constituencies, to give your firm adequate, factual information that can be used to build successful marketing strategies and business development programs.

Who are the various constituencies that your firm needs to understand and ultimately satisfy? They include

- Existing clients
- Prospective clients
- Existing and prospective referral sources
- Relevant members of the judiciary
- Perhaps most important of all, lawyers and staff within your firm

Data versus Information

"Data" and "information" should be distinguished, as the two terms are often confused. Data are facts, figures, observations, and experiences that have not been organized or analyzed in a systematic way. Using the litigation analogy, data are the documents, deposition transcripts, and interrogatory answers that are gathered during the discovery process. Information, on the other hand, consists of facts that have been winnowed from the data, analyzed in a systematic way, and used to draw conclusions about a specific issue, topic, or situation. In litigation, this would be the equivalent of the specific facts extracted from discovery to develop a trial strategy or to support or refute one or more specific assertions.

Likewise, marketing research information consists of relevant facts that have been accumulated, organized, and analyzed to help solve a marketing problem or to develop and exploit a marketing opportunity.

How Information Helps Build Relationships

Obtaining reliable marketing information is the essential first step in planning and executing any effective marketing program. Why? Because before you can communicate with somebody or persuade someone to take desired action, *you must first learn about that person's wants, needs, perceptions, and motivations.* Before you can meet someone's needs, you must first understand those needs.

Understanding wants, needs, perceptions, and motivations allows you to create relationships with prospects and maintain and expand relationships with existing clients. *Creating relationships with prospects is the key to expanding your firm's client base, and maintaining and expanding relationships with existing clients is the key to maximizing your firm's profits.*

The information gathered through various research methods—such as client surveys, market surveys, one-on-one interviews, or even internal firm surveys—is the marketing "discovery" process that can help your firm

- Win a greater number of competitive new-business presentations
- Convince prospects to hire your firm without a competitive presentation
- Identify dissatisfied clients and save them before they defect
- Identify other law firms your clients use, for which services and why
- Identify new business opportunities with existing clients
- Identify developing market needs so your firm can position itself to meet them
- Determine who your competition really is, versus who your lawyers think it is

Unfortunately, in today's buyer's market, *high-quality legal work is not enough.* Clients and prospects expect skillful and competent legal representation. The key differentiators in today's market are

1. the actual or perceived value a lawyer or firm delivers, and
2. the ability of the lawyer or lawyers involved to understand the client's business or industry.

Those who understand this reality will flourish, and those who do not will stagnate or perish.

Research also can help improve the profitability of your firm. Superior profitability in any business is directly tied to stable, ongoing relationships. The longer a law firm or any other business can retain its clients or customers—and maintain or increase their spending levels—the more exponentially profitable these relationships become. Client satisfaction surveys and face-to-face client interviews can help firms identify and fix client problems before they become client defections. Moreover, these research activities can help your firm find profitable new ways to serve existing clients.

Likewise, the less turnover the firm has, the more profitable it will be. Internal surveys can help you keep your pulse on lawyer and staff morale, spot emerging problems, and find new ways to better manage the firm.

One of the keys to creating loyalty and cementing relationships—internally and externally—is to create an ongoing dialogue among the parties involved. Surveys and face-to-face interviews are cost-effective ways to maintain a consistent dialogue with key constituencies inside and outside the firm.

CREATING A DIALOGUE THROUGH RESEARCH

The key to any ongoing relationship—a marriage, a friendship, or a business relationship—is a mutual exchange of *value.* (There's an old saying that the best relationships are "60/40" relationships—each party thinks he or she is getting 60 percent of the value and the other party is getting 40 percent.) Developing an ongoing dialogue is the only way individuals or businesses can consistently create, maintain, and expand relationships. Marketing research should be thought of as a formalized dialogue process involving clients, prospects, referral sources, and even the law firm's own lawyers and staff persons.

Although the primary objective of this formalized dialogue process is to generate factual information that will aid in making better marketing decisions, an equally important objective is to communicate to your clients and prospects that your firm is interested in becoming their business partner. A dialogue lets your clients know your firm is interested in learning about business issues they face, market trends that affect their profitability, problems they might have with your firm's procedures or systems, or any one of a myriad of other concerns.

Moreover, the dialogue process stimulates clients to think more about the benefits your firm offers, which may result in those clients using more of your services. Cross-selling is also an inevitable by-product of this dialogue process. By learning more about your clients and their businesses, you will identify opportunities to provide them with additional legal services. An informal poll of marketing directors throughout the country showed that firms conducting regular face-to-face satisfaction interviews with their clients could expect to generate significant new engagements with these clients 70 to 90 percent of the time.

What types of research should your firm undertake to learn about clients and prospects and to initiate a marketing dialogue? Before this question can be answered, your firm needs to address twelve fundamental marketing questions, which will allow the firm to focus its research efforts to glean the most accurate and meaningful information and focus its marketing strategies and priorities to yield significant new business opportunities.

Twelve Basic Marketing Questions

The most common marketing problem that law firms face is a lack of commitment to a consistent marketing effort. The second most common problem is a lack of focus in marketing efforts. Achieving a clear marketing focus typically helps generate a more consistent marketing effort.

Your firm's marketing focus can be improved if the lawyers understand that marketing is based on principles, just like the practice of law. If your firm's management understands these principles—and in particular, will concentrate the firm's research efforts on the following fundamental marketing issues—your firm will enjoy a much more focused and successful marketing effort.

QUESTION 1: WHAT BUSINESS IS YOUR LAW FIRM IN?

This is a critical question, because the way in which managers define their business determines how they run it. For example, years ago, professional sports teams viewed themselves as being in the "sports business." Today they understand that they are also, particularly from the fans' perspective, in the entertainment and licensing businesses. By redefining their business—*from the buyer's standpoint*—professional sports teams have generated billions of dollars in additional revenues.

This is a critical concept for any professional service firm to understand, because there is often a huge gulf between what professional service firms think they are selling and what their clients are really buying. In the marketing game, only the buyer's perspective matters.

QUESTION 2: ARE YOU MEETING OR EXCEEDING CLIENT EXPECTATIONS?

Studies cited in several *Harvard Business Review* articles show that clients who say they are "somewhat satisfied" with their law firms are six to eight times more likely to defect than clients who say they are "very satisfied." Market surveys conducted among larger client organizations in a number of U.S. cities since 1991 show that, on average, 25 to 30 percent of most law firms' clients are less than "very satisfied." *This indicates that, on average, the needs or expectations of every third or fourth client in most law firms are not being fully met.*

Marketing research can measure the specific numbers for your firm, as well as identify which clients are dissatisfied, the extent of their dissatisfaction, and the source or sources of their dissatisfaction. Because client retention is the number-one priority, an annual, quantifiable client satisfaction survey should be standard operating procedure for your law firm.

QUESTION 3: WHO ARE YOUR COMPETITORS?

Law firms, like all other businesses, have both direct and indirect competitors. For most law firms, direct competitors are usually easy to identify geographically by practice area. However, as with litigation, one of the cardinal rules of marketing planning is not to speculate. It takes research to shed light on these direct competitors—who they *really* are, what they *really* are doing, and how they *really* are doing it.

Research can also help identify indirect competitors and track the inroads they are making with your clients and prospects. Today, the legal profession—including your firm—has a growing list of indirect competitors. These include accounting firms, which are taking big chunks of market share away from the legal profession. In-house departments are also indirect competitors. They are doing a larger share of the less-complex legal work, directing more work to non-law firm suppliers, increasingly auditing law firm performance, and hiring nonlawyers to do work in-house. Other indirect competitors include human resources consulting firms, environmental consulting firms, management consulting firms, and other providers of nonlegal professional services.

QUESTION 4: WHAT TARGET GROUP OR GROUPS OF CLIENTS DOES YOUR FIRM WANT TO SERVE?

No law firm can be all things to all clients. In today's competitive legal market, the decision about which groups of clients to serve—or not serve—is one of the most critical and fundamental business decisions any law firm or lawyer must make. Determining your target group of clients or customers is called "market segmentation." The idea is to focus on segments of the market that your firm can serve most profitably. The most common forms of segmentation are based on business type (as defined by Standard Industrial Classification codes), geography, business size (Fortune 100 or Fortune 500, for example), legal needs, or some combination of these.

Marketing research is the quickest and most cost-efficient way to determine which segment or segments of the client universe that your firm, its practice groups, or its individual lawyers can serve most profitably. Marketing research can also be used to qualify specific client organizations within the chosen segments, to determine which organizations are the most promising prospects, and to learn the identity of the decision makers.

QUESTION 5: WHAT IS YOUR BASIC COMPETITIVE STRATEGY?

Marketers of any product or service can choose from four basic competitive strategies:

- Pursue a *broad market,* competing on the basis of *low price.*
- Pursue a *broad market,* competing on the basis of *value-added differentiating factors* other than price.
- Pursue a *narrow or "niche" market,* competing on the basis of *low price.*
- Pursue a *narrow or "niche" market,* competing on the basis of *value-added differentiating factors* other than price.

Choosing a competitive strategy is a valuable way to become more focused at the firm level, at the practice group level, and at the individual lawyer level, even though the competitive strategies may be different at each level. In other words, the firm's basic competitive strategy could be broad/differentiated. At the same time, a practice group within the firm could choose a narrow/differentiated strategy. An individual lawyer in this same practice group could have a personal broad/low price competitive strategy within the niche chosen by the practice group. (The individual lawyer's basic competitive strategy would be to serve as many clients as possible within the niche and attract them on the basis of being the low-cost provider.) One competitive strategy is not necessarily better or more profitable than another. The important thing is to dominate the chosen quadrant—that is what determines profitability.

QUESTION 6: WHAT POSITION DOES YOUR FIRM WANT TO OWN?

Your marketing position is "who you are" or "what you stand for" in the minds of your clients and prospects. This perception is measured in terms of the attributes they consider important in a law firm. Firms have defined areas of expertise in areas such as products liability defense, international law, and high technology, as well as a host of other specialized fields. Unfortunately, the position most law firms own in the minds of their clients and prospects is "just another law firm." What position, if any, does your firm own? The only way to find out is to conduct marketing research among your clients and prospects. This will help you determine

- Positions that are meaningful to clients and prospects
- Available positions (that is, those not owned by another law firm)
- Credible position(s) for your firm

Whatever your firm's positioning strategy, it should be stated in a six- to eight-word phrase that promises value to the firm's clients and prospects and presents a clear mission statement for everyone inside the firm.

QUESTION 7: HOW CAN YOUR FIRM BE MEANINGFULLY DIFFERENTIATED FROM ITS COMPETITORS?

Differentiation strategies are the specific ways in which your firm adds value to its services or to its relationships with clients. These differentiation strategies can be unique services, levels of expertise, service policies, or other enhancements to the basic relationship, which are meaningful to clients and prospects and offer them clear benefits for doing business with you rather than your competitors.

Marketing research is an excellent tool for determining the ways your law firm can effectively differentiate itself from direct or indirect competitors, as well as for determining the relative appeal various differentiation strategies might have for clients and prospects.

QUESTION 8: TO WHAT EXTENT ARE CLIENTS AND PROSPECTS AWARE OF THE SERVICES YOUR FIRM OFFERS?

Clients or prospects can't buy services from your firm if they don't know all the services offered. Market studies in a number of cities, as well as proprietary client surveys conducted by many law firms, show that *clients and prospects typically have little or no awareness of the services their law firms offer beyond those the client currently uses or has used in the past.*

Marketing research can help you determine the awareness and perceptions of your firm's services and expertise in the eyes of its clients and prospects. This can help your firm develop more-targeted and cost-effective strategies and programs for client retention, cross-selling to existing clients, and new-client acquisition.

QUESTION 9: HOW EFFECTIVE ARE YOUR FIRM'S MARKETING COMMUNICATIONS EFFORTS?

Many law firms spend money on advertising and other communications without determining the benefits or results these activities produce for the firm. Marketing research can be used to determine the effectiveness of your firm's advertising, public relations, seminar programs, and other marketing communications activities. This information can help your firm refine these activities to make them more effective, and can also be used by the firm's managers to channel marketing communications dollars into the most effective activities.

QUESTION 10: HOW DO LAWYERS AND STAFF PERSONS FEEL ABOUT YOUR FIRM?

Ultimately, *your firm's external relationships will be only as good as its internal relationships.* How people inside the firm—lawyers and staff persons alike—feel about the firm and each other is a critical factor in determining the firm's success. Most law firms never bother to investigate this central aspect of their business. Moreover, lawyers and staff persons are often a source of good ideas on how to improve the performance and profitability of the firm, yet these ideas rarely come to the surface because they are almost never solicited. Marketing research is an excellent tool for "taking the temperature" within the firm, as well as for tapping into the operational and marketing insights of lawyers and staff persons.

QUESTION 11: WHAT ARE YOUR FIRM'S MEASURES OF SUCCESS?

Most firms measure success in financial terms—revenues per lawyer, profits per partner, and so on. However, because your firm is in the relationship business—internally and externally—the real marketing question is this: How closely does the firm monitor and track the quantifiable aspects of its internal and external relationships? For instance:

- Does the firm track the *profitability of each client* in addition to the revenues from each client?
- Does the firm track, on a progressive basis, year to year, the variances in the billings of each of its major clients?
- Does the firm have a centralized database with current information on the key contact persons for each client?
- Does the firm have clients annually evaluate the performance of the lawyers and staff persons who service their accounts?
- Does the firm conduct annual satisfaction surveys with its clients, lawyers, and staff persons?
- Does the firm track the turnover among its partners, associates, paralegals, and support staff? When people leave the firm—and equally important, when they join the firm—does management know why?
- Does the firm have a system in place for tracking and analyzing internal and external complaints?
- Does the firm's management know which external individuals and/or organizations refer business to the firm on a regular basis, and why?
- Does the firm track the amount of time clients have to wait in the firm's lobby before they are received by the person they came to see?

Because a firm's business objective is to maintain and expand profitable relationships, these and other measures of the firm's performance are critical pieces of marketing information. The research should be done in a consistent and timely fashion, so the firm always has current information available to identify trends, opportunities, or problems, both internally and externally.

For example, for a three-month period, one firm tracked the amount of time clients waited in the firm's lobby until they were received by the individuals they came to see. The results were eye opening. The "wait times" ranged from 15 minutes to 45 minutes and averaged 25 minutes. If you were a client, how would you feel about cooling your heels for an average of 25 minutes every time you came to visit your law firm? After this information was shared with the firm's lawyers, the lobby "wait time" for clients dropped to five minutes.

QUESTION 12: DOES YOUR FIRM ACTIVELY TRACK MARKET SHARE AND "CLIENT SHARE"?

Your firm, or individual departments within your firm, may have billing increases or decreases in any given year. Although this is certainly important to the partners from an income and compensation standpoint, it is not relevant from a marketing standpoint. *Market share and client share are the only ways to keep score from a marketing standpoint. Only your firm's performance relative to the market as a whole, and relative to each client's total spending on inside and outside legal services (versus simply spending with outside law firms), will tell you where you stand.* For example, if the market is going up faster than your firm's revenue increases, then your firm is losing market share. If the market is declining faster than your firm's revenues are declining, then you are gaining market share. If your firm's percentage of a client's total spending for *inside and outside legal services* is increasing, your client share is increasing.

Market share is one of the key measures of the overall strategic health of your firm—that is, the firm's ability to relate consistently and profitably to the needs of clients relative to competing firms in the marketplace. Your firm's strategic health will ultimately determine its financial health.

Market share is often difficult to gauge. The key is to establish some relative (but not necessarily exact) yardstick by which to measure your firm against its direct competitors. This might be as simple as periodically dividing the number of lawyers in your firm into the total number of lawyers in the local firms with which your firm competes most directly, and tracking the resulting percentages. It may mean tracking the number of certain types of lawsuits that are filed in a particular jurisdiction and determining what percentage of those suits are filed by your firm and by other firms.

Client share is a key measure of the ability of your firm, its lawyers, and its practice groups to provide *superior value* to individual clients. As such, client share is a predictor of client retention and profitability. Client share is determined by having periodic, in-depth discussions and performance reviews with clients to assess the usage of your firm relative to other internal and external legal resources they might have.

However your firm does it, it is important to establish some method for tracking market share for the firm and, to the extent possible, client share for the firm's practice groups and individual lawyers. Market share and client share are the only ways to keep meaningful score, from a marketing standpoint.

Marketing Research Steps

Organization and focus are the critical ingredients in a successful marketing effort. A productive and informative first step in this process is to address the twelve issues discussed above. The information and insights gleaned from this exercise will raise questions that only research can answer. These questions may include the following:

- Who are our real competitors, both direct and indirect?
- How are we perceived by legal decision makers in our key geographic or vertical markets, relative to our competitors?
- How are particular practice areas of our firm perceived by current and prospective clients?
- What key factors do clients use when evaluating or selecting a law firm? How are we perceived in connection with these factors?
- Are legal services decision makers satisfied or dissatisfied with their current firms, including ours? Why?
- What do clients want in terms of day-to-day interaction with their law firms, including items such as billing procedures, return phone calls, and regular feedback, for example?
- What problems, needs, or attitudes exist inside the firm that may be causing client acquisition or retention problems?

Answering these and many other questions are essential to creating successful business development and client relationship programs.

To make the most of any research project, it must be organized properly. Though there are many different types of research—such as mail surveys, telephone surveys, executive interviews, and focus groups—they all require the same basic organizational steps, which are

1. Define the problem, opportunity, or issue that the research will address.
2. Establish specific objectives for the research project.
3. Determine the information needed to meet these objectives—that is, what you want to know when all is said and done.
4. Identify and prioritize possible sources of data that can lead to needed information.
5. Select the research technique(s) that will be used to collect the desired data.

6. Determine the identity of the respondents and the sample size (that is, the number of respondents), or other sources of data you will use.
7. Design the questionnaire or discussion guideline or other data collection instrument or technique.
8. Prepare a brief written research proposal that includes the objectives of the project, its value to your organization's marketing effort, and a budget.
9. Gather the desired data.
10. Process and analyze the data.
11. Prepare a written report detailing the useable marketing information derived from the research data.
12. Prepare and prioritize written recommendations for putting the resulting marketing research information to work.
13. Assign responsibility and accountability for follow-through.
14. Set deadlines for specific activities and follow-up.
15. Determine additional marketing information needs.

Research can be sorted into several categories. The two that will most affect you are *primary research* and *secondary research.*

Primary Research

Primary research is research that a law firm or other organization undertakes for a particular purpose. There are generally three methods for generating primary data: experimentation, observation, and surveys or other interviewing techniques. The last method—surveys or other interviewing techniques—is the most frequently used method in business-to-business marketing research. It typically consists of mail or telephone surveys, the Internet, focus groups, or one-on-one interviews.

Once the research objectives have been established, primary research can be divided into these basic steps:

- Research design: the methodology or techniques that will be used
- Sample design: the group of people, or universe, from whom the primary data will be obtained, as well as the specific qualifications that these people must meet
- Questionnaire design: the questions that will be asked and how the questionnaire will be structured to generate the desired data from the research effort
- Data collection: the method or methods actually used to collect the desired data from the universe of potential respondents
- Analysis: study of the resulting data to provide useable marketing research information
- Use: drawing upon the marketing research information as a basis for developing and implementing marketing and business development programs

Within the realm of primary research, there are two general categories: *qualitative research* and *quantitative research.* The primary distinction between the two is that quantitative research is, to a greater or lesser degree depending on the number of people interviewed, statistically projectable and quantifiable. Qualitative research, on the other hand, generally is not. Instead, its role is to help researchers understand the wants, needs, perceptions, feelings, and beliefs that influence behavior or perceptions among people in the market segment(s) being studied.

QUALITATIVE RESEARCH

The most frequently used methods of qualitative data collection in business-to-business marketing research are

- Focus groups
- One-on-one, discussion-type interviews that can be conducted either in person or by telephone

A focus group is a group of six to twelve people who meet the screening criteria of the sample design. These people typically meet in a conference room for a couple hours with a professional focus group moderator. If the focus group participants are geographically scattered, a meeting can be conducted via a long-distance conference call or in conjunction with a trade show, association meeting, or conference that the desired participants attend. Following a prepared guideline, the moderator leads the group through a discussion of the issues being explored in the research. The moderator's purpose is to generate as much qualitative information as possible about the marketing issues being explored.

Business-to-business focus group facilities are typically constructed with hidden viewing rooms adjacent to the conference rooms. Representatives of your law firm can sit in a viewing room during a focus group session to hear and observe the proceedings firsthand. Focus groups are always revealing and generally yield significant marketing insights. As one lawyer commented after observing a focus group consisting of eight of his firm's clients, "I was forced to listen for a change—the viewing room made it physically impossible to interrupt."

Allowing sellers to obtain candid, personal feedback from buyers or prospects, which many sellers fail to do in the normal course of business, has tremendous value. Another benefit of focus groups is that the proceedings can be videotaped and audiotaped from the hidden viewing room. These tapes can be edited and used as part of firm training materials, presentation materials for competitive new-business presentations, and even sales materials.

Like focus groups, individual face-to-face interviews should be approached with a preplanned guideline, to keep the discussion as relevant as possible. In many cases the interviewees will consent to having the interviews audiotaped or videotaped.

QUANTITATIVE RESEARCH

As mentioned earlier, quantitative research is statistically projectable, unlike qualitative research. For example, client focus groups might reveal a general dissatisfaction with your firm's billing format, while a follow-up quantitative telephone survey showing that 78 percent of 200 client/respondents are dissatisfied gives a more precise measure of the level of dissatisfaction. Quantitative research could also measure the specific areas of dissatisfaction with your billing system (confusing billing statements or objectionable charges, for example).

The two most popular methods of quantitative data collection in business-to-business marketing research are mail surveys and telephone surveys. Mail surveys typically involve written questionnaires. Recently, due to advances in technology, these surveys are increasingly taking the form of mailed diskettes that are programmed with the survey questionnaire. Respondents simply insert the diskettes into their computers, follow the guidelines provided, and then mail the diskettes back to the organizations conducting the research. This approach typically yields significantly higher response rates than written questionnaires, especially when the research is being conducted in businesses or industries with high degrees of computer literacy. Also, some firms use the Internet to administer e-mail surveys or Web-page questionnaires and have experienced a great deal of success with both.

Telephone interviews in business-to-business situations are typically conducted by trained executive interviewers using computer-aided telephone interviewing (CATI) equipment. The interviewer sits at a computer that has been programmed with the questionnaire. The computer prompts the interviewer regarding which questions to ask and the order in which to ask them. The computer also does calculations based on the response to each question and literally adapts the interview to the individual respondent's knowledge base. In other words, during a client satisfaction survey, each respondent would be asked to rate your firm only on the specific performance factors that had emerged as the most important to that individual respondent.

Telephone interviewing is generally considered more effective for business-to-business marketing research than written surveys. There are two reasons. First, respondents must deal with telephone calls immediately, whereas they can, and often do, put aside and forget written questionnaires. Moreover, the people who take the time to respond to written questionnaires are typically those who have stronger-than-average positive or negative emotional involvement in the subject. This could bias resulting data, either positively or negatively. Telephone interviews tend to yield a truer cross section of the universe of prospective respondents.

HOW QUALITATIVE AND QUANTITATIVE RESEARCH WORK TOGETHER

The problem with a strictly quantitative approach to research is that the researcher is forced to make assumptions about the wants, needs, feelings, perceptions, and priorities of the potential survey participants. Because there is often a significant gap between the perceptions and priorities of sellers and buyers in any business or profession, these assumptions can seriously compromise the research results. Consequently, focus groups or other types of qualitative data collection are typically used at the project's outset to identify the issues that need to be addressed in the quantitative research. This approach helps provide a factual understanding of how prospective respondents view the world, so the researcher's assumptions are minimized or eliminated. The quantitative research yields data that show how the issues identified or verified in the qualitative research play out in statistically measurable terms across the universe of prospective respondents.

Thus, the strength of qualitative research is that it provides factual insights into the perceptions or behavior of potential respondents from whom the sample is to be taken; its weakness is that the impressions gained from several focus groups or one-on-one personal interviews are not statistically accurate and may not reflect the realities of the marketplace. The strength of quantitative research is that it yields a statistically measurable and projectable picture of the views held among the universe of respondents; however, its weakness is that the assumptions made in developing the quantitative questionnaire may be erroneous, compromising both the research results and the marketing decisions that are based on the results.

QUESTIONNAIRE DESIGN

Quantitative research always involves some form of questionnaire, which ensures that each question is asked in a consistent way. The questionnaire is presented directly to the respondent as a written document or computer diskette, or indirectly as a telephone or face-to-face interview.

As mentioned earlier, marketing research is analogous to the discovery process in a litigation matter. The design of the research questionnaire is just as important to the outcome of the research project as the questions asked in interrogatories and depositions are to the success of the discovery process. In each case, the quality of the data obtained depends on

1. which questions you ask, and
2. how you ask them.

The questions you ask in the questionnaire depend on the research problem and the method of data collection selected for the research project. How you ask the questions is a function of the types of questions you ask, as well as their wording. Research questions must be worded as clearly and concisely as possible so that they will elicit straightforward, unbiased answers.

This is why questionnaire design is the most critical factor in the success of any research project, as well as the most difficult step in the project.

For example, a question in a client satisfaction survey that asks whether the firm "charges reasonable fees for services" will yield different information value than a question that asks whether the firm "provides superior value compared with other firms you use." A client could perceive that the firm charges reasonable fees for services, but not that the firm has particularly good value relative to other firms the client uses. Which perception is more valuable for a law firm in today's competitive legal market?

As with interrogatories and depositions, marketing research questions should be as precise and specific as possible to yield accurate information. One of the most frequent mistakes made in questionnaire design involves questions that include more than one variable; for example, "Are the firm's phones answered *promptly* and *courteously*?" This question will yield imprecise information because the respondent could react to either or both variables; the question should be asked as two separate questions or presented with two separate rating factors.

Keep in mind that there are no set rules for questionnaire design—it is an art rather than a science. However, a simple procedure that can help ensure effective questionnaire design is to write the *information objectives* of the project in bullet form before you begin developing the questionnaire. Then divide the written objectives into "need to know" and "nice to know" categories. The result is a clear road map for the questionnaire's content.

Also keep in mind that different types of questions will yield different types of information. There are six types of questions that are typically used when constructing a primary research questionnaire:

1. yes/no questions (*Do you frequently try new law firms?*)
2. multiple-choice questions (*Which of the following law firms do you use?*)
3. preference questions (*Which of these law firms do you most prefer?*)
4. rating questions (*On a scale from 1 to 9, with 9 being "liked very much" and 1 being "didn't like at all," indicate your feeling about the law firm by circling the number that corresponds to your feeling.*)
5. ranking questions (*Rank in order from 1 to 5—with 1 being the best and 5 being the worst—your opinion of the following law firms.*)
6. open-ended questions (*Why do you choose to use that particular law firm?*)

Questionnaire design is a critical aspect of the research process. If you ask the wrong questions or fail to address key issues, the results will be inaccurate or misleading, which means your expensive and time-consuming marketing efforts will be based on the wrong assumptions.

THE DUAL BENEFIT OF PERSONAL INTERVIEWS

Conducting personal interviews is typically a very expensive method of quantitative data collection, because a survey involving a statistically meaningful number of personal interviews (usually fifty or more) takes a significant amount of time and interviewer training. However, as a qualitative data-gathering tool, personal interviews with law firm clients have a dual benefit that can more than offset the cost.

First, because this information comes directly from the source, you gain important, firsthand information about your clients' wants, needs, expectations, and feelings about your firm, its people, and its performance. Some firms are nervous about being exposed to this level of candor, because they may encounter problems or criticism. However, the alternative is to lose the chance to identify and solve problems before clients become so dissatisfied that they fire your firm. Problems or criticisms raised by clients should be welcomed—you can't correct a problem or situation if you don't know it exists. Keep in mind that no matter how difficult the conversation, most clients appreciate a lawyer's or firm's willingness to take the time to have a discussion. Typically, client relationships with lawyers and firms are strengthened by this process, and rarely weakened by it. If necessary, discomfort can be minimized by having a trusted consultant or third party conduct the interviews.

Second, this type of interview offers the potential of gaining additional business from the client being interviewed. In a very informal "straw poll" of law firm marketing directors across the country whose firms regularly conduct client interviews, the respondents estimated that 70 to 90 percent of these interviews led directly to significant additional engagements for the firm. This is because the interview process created a dialogue, which is the key to a healthy, mutually satisfying firm-client relationship. Clients frequently suggest problems or needs the lawyer might never imagine. During the course of the dialogue, the lawyer can explain the types of expertise the firm offers and easily explore other ways the firm can help the client.

Secondary Research

Secondary research is research involving data and information already compiled by other sources for other reasons. The information may have been gathered by—or is available through—state and local governments, libraries, trade associations (including the ABA), trade publications, marketing research firms, other law firms, universities, the Internet, or any number of other resources. As compared with primary research, secondary research can typically be gathered more quickly and less expensively. Drawbacks of information gathered through secondary research include the following:

- It may not address the issue at hand.
- It may not have been gathered or analyzed in a reliable fashion by the organization or individual that originally compiled it.
- The respondents or data sources may not be entirely relevant.

Secondary marketing research data can be found both inside the firm (internal data) and outside the firm (external data).

INTERNAL SECONDARY DATA

Internal secondary data is all the data originating and collected within the firm during the normal course of business. This could include billing records, out-of-pocket expenditures on behalf of clients, payables, receivables, realization, receivables aging, new business origination credits, client billing records, results of cross-selling efforts, or analysis of the firm's current client base by Standard Industrial Classification code or services used. Sales and cost data are two of the most fundamental and important internal data in any business. In law firms, interestingly enough, they are generally not as closely tracked and monitored as they are in most client businesses. In fact, the matter codes in most law firms are far too general to enable the firms to extract meaningful sales information, even when the lawyers take the time to enter them when opening a file.

It is difficult to make marketing planning decisions or business development decisions without an accurate picture of sales trends and services the firm currently sells. *Part of every law firm's internal data program should be the collection of accurate sales data based on a specific matter code for every conceivable matter that any lawyer in the firm might perform.* Also, law firms that do not adequately use cost accounting against the revenue derived from each client and from each matter handled for each client don't really understand which clients or matters are profitable. *Cost accounting by client and by matter is a critical facet of any firm's internal data collection process, because profits are the lifeblood of any business or professional service organization.*

EXTERNAL SECONDARY DATA

One of the most frequent complaints clients have about their lawyers, as well as about lawyers soliciting their business, is that the lawyers haven't taken the time to learn about the client's business or industry. External secondary data is an excellent source of background information for lawyers preparing to conduct one-on-one client satisfaction audits, make competitive new-business presentations, or visit prospective clients.

There is a tremendous amount of external secondary data available on a wide range of industries and specific companies within these industries. Sources for external secondary data include the following:

- LEXIS/NEXIS
- Counsel Connect
- Dunn & Bradstreet
- *The Thomas Register of American Manufacturers*
- Governmental agencies
- Business, trade, and professional associations
- Business-oriented media
- Trade journals
- Universities and foundations

- Corporate annual reports and/or Securities and Exchange Commission filings
- Commercial data services
- Securities brokers
- Other professional services organizations, such as accounting firms and investment banking firms
- Brochures and Web sites of competing law firms
- Brochures and Web sites of your firm's clients and prospects

There are also organizations and publications that offer a variety of previously published research on a variety of industries, markets, or topics. These include the following:

- *The Off-The-Shelf Catalog* (Northport, New York)
- *FINDEX: The Directory of Market Research, Reports, Studies, and Surveys* (Bethesda, Maryland)
- *The Marketsearch International Directory of Published Market Research*
- *The Directory of Industry Data Sources* (Cambridge, Massachusetts)
- *The Guide to American Directories* (Coral Gables, Florida)

The U.S. Department of Commerce classifies all industries and businesses by means of a numeric coding system called the Standard Industrial Classification (SIC). The SIC system is organized as follows:

- "Major Groups," which are expressed as two-digit numbers
- "Industry Groups," which are designated by the two-digit Major Group number plus an additional digit to identify the Industry Group
- "Industry Number," which is designated by the three-digit Industry Group number plus an additional digit to identify the Industry Number

SIC codes can be valuable to law firms internally as well as externally. Specifically, a firm could conduct an analysis by client and SIC code to identify the source of revenues and profits, and to monitor and track changes in its client base. In fact, forward-thinking firms are now making SIC code identification a mandatory part of their client intake procedures.

Ways to Put Research to Work

Marketing research is the foundation upon which your firm's marketing efforts should be built. Listed below are just some of the ways law firms use marketing research today:

- To perform marketplace surveys
- To perform internal surveys
- To perform client satisfaction surveys
- To develop new products and services

- To conduct seminar follow-up
- To measure effectiveness of advertising and communications
- To profile clients
- To profile prospects
- To select branch office locations
- To conduct due diligence in law firm mergers
- To qualify targeted prospects
- To perform end-of-matter reviews with clients
- To administer "issues" surveys by region or industry, with results sent to clients and prospects as a goodwill/lead generation tool

Where should your firm start? A guide follows.

Step One: Make a Commitment to Research

The time and expense invested in acquiring research information is wasted if your firm doesn't do one simple thing: make a commitment to marketing research on a consistent, ongoing basis. *The success of a firm's research or marketing program is determined largely by the degree of commitment the firm's management and partners are willing to make.*

For many firms, commitment to research and marketing is sporadic and inversely proportional to revenues. When revenues are up, interest is down. When revenues are down, interest goes up. Firms clamor for market research information when business is down and they want to learn what their clients and prospects are thinking, but when business improves, they assume they know. For market research—and by extension a marketing program—to work, a law firm must *make a consistent commitment that is not a function of high or low revenues.*

Market research provides the maximum amount of information when it is done systematically over a sustained period of time. This not only provides current information about your clients, prospects, and perceptions of your firm, it also provides a historical perspective that shows measurable trends.

Step Two: Determine What Your Firm Needs

There are unlimited ways to use research to create the foundation for your marketing program. As with any other business decision, the criteria to be considered are economic. The economic question for any research is this: Will the value of the information be greater than the cost? You must employ certain fundamental forms of research that are essential to even the most basic marketing program. Remember, without factual, timely information on your clients, your prospects, and the marketplace where your firm does business, your marketing program will be inefficient at best, and disastrous at worst.

What follows are recommendations for a two-part research program. Phase One includes the most essential research components, in which every law firm should invest. Phase Two describes a more sophisticated research program that is designed to enhance a firm's integrated marketing/information system.

RECOMMENDED RESEARCH PROGRAM: PHASE ONE

Phase One includes three essential market research surveys that give your firm the information it needs to create, expand, and maintain relationships with its lawyers and staff persons, clients, and prospects. All three surveys create dialogues with their respective target groups. Indicated in parentheses is the frequency recommended for each component. Keep in mind that all three surveys establish benchmarks that will help your firm measure the success of its marketing efforts, both internally and externally.

Internal Survey (annually): The goal of this survey of lawyers and staff persons within your firm is to identify problems or opportunities with clients or each other, and reveal good ideas. In addition, your firm's "culture" will be enhanced because people at all levels will have a chance to provide input and feedback about the firm, how it does business, and its clients. This is an excellent means for opening or stimulating lines of communication and developing a shared sense of purpose among lawyers and staff persons. The survey also serves as a benchmarking tool because of how precisely it can measure positive or negative morale in your firm. The survey can be distributed as a written questionnaire or on computer diskette. Respondents typically have the option of remaining anonymous.

Client Survey (annually): This is a systemic (and preferably ongoing) research program that surveys each of your firm's clients annually. The purpose is to take the pulse of your clients—to learn what the firm is doing right and ways in which it can improve the delivery of services to clients. It is also an excellent way of creating a dialogue with clients that often leads to additional business. Beginning this process with focus groups helps eliminate or minimize the chance of making any wrong assumptions in designing the quantitative questionnaire. The questionnaire can be a written or telephone survey, though a telephone survey is typically more productive. It can also be done via diskette, e-mail, or the Web, in combination with a telephone interview, which is highly effective.

Market Survey (every three years): This can be either a proprietary or franchised survey of your firm's marketplace. Typically, executive interviewers survey legal decision makers (chief legal counsel or CEOs, for example) at major companies and not-for-profits in your area. This survey focuses on the wants, needs, perceptions, and hiring factors that are important to these key legal decision makers in your firm's marketplace. Your firm will get quantifiable information on how it is perceived in the marketplace—that is, the relative strengths and weaknesses of various practice groups compared with those of your competitors. Frequently, the survey includes verbatim comments from respondents.

This survey is an excellent planning tool for your marketing department. It provides factual information on market opportunities, identifies barriers to your firm's marketing efforts, and serves as a benchmark to measure—every three years—the success of those efforts. It also allows you to compare the market's perceptions of your firm with those of your clients and prospects.

RECOMMENDED RESEARCH PROGRAM: PHASE TWO

Phase Two is for those law firms willing to make a consistent, long-term commitment to collecting as much marketing information as possible, creating an integrated marketing program based on this information, and establishing practical systems for using this information on a day-to-day basis. Phase Two incorporates—on a consistent, ongoing basis—the research recommended in Phase One, and also includes the following components.

Client Base Analysis: This in-depth analysis of your clients entails grouping them first by revenues, then by profitability—both in terms of gross profit dollars and profit margins. Gross profits and profit margins are important because buyers' markets are characterized by downward pressure on prices and profits. The focus should be on examining the profit margins for each client in general and, more specifically, the profit margins for each type of work being done for each client.

Revenue and Profitability Analysis by SIC Code: Each client is first identified by SIC code to determine the types of industries and businesses represented in the firm's client base, and then clients are sorted by revenue and profitability. This analysis shows your firm where it is commanding premiums for its work—in other words, which clients are the most profitable and what types of work you are doing for them. It also reveals the businesses or industries that are willing to pay these premiums, which is important information to consider in your firm's business development efforts.

As part of this process, you divide your clients into four categories: A, B, C, and D, with A being the most profitable. Most firms find that 80 percent of their clients are in the C and D categories and generate about 20 percent of their profits, while 20 percent fall into the A and B categories yet generate 80 percent of the profits. The goal is to use this information in your business development efforts to reduce the percentage of C and D clients and increase the number of A and B clients.

Face-to-Face Client Interviews: These interviews should be conducted with only key clients (those in the A and B categories mentioned above). These interviews are very time and resource intensive, because they require extensive preparation (usually including secondary research about the client's business and industry). However, they are an excellent opportunity to discover significant new engagements for the firm. One guaranteed benefit is that these interviews help build a very strong relationship between the client and your firm.

Survey of Your Firm's Current Referral Sources: This survey is typically done by mail or telephone, with telephone being the more effective approach. The purpose is to gauge the respondents' perceptions of various factors, such as your firm's expertise in various practice areas, the value of the firm's services, and the practice areas to which the respondents refer business. It also helps to educate the respondents about various services the firm offers.

Finally

The key to managing extensive amounts of marketing information productively is to create a system for integrating it, updating it, and applying it to the firm's marketing efforts, day-to-day operations, and, ultimately its culture. Only by doing this can the information be a readily accessible, valuable resource for lawyers and marketing personnel. This requires a commitment of technology and resources; however, it gives the firm a significant competitive advantage in understanding its clients and expanding its business with them, as well as determining where to focus its new business efforts.

When your firm engages in marketing research, it will acquire a wealth of information that can make a dramatic difference in its ability to create, expand, and maintain its relationships with existing and prospective clients. It can also be used to improve your firm's internal relationships, which in turn will have a positive impact on your client relationships. But most important, it will provide your firm a unique competitive advantage: the ability to initiate and maintain a dialogue with clients and prospects based on an intimate, accurate understanding of their wants, needs, and expectations.

CHAPTER 4

Developing Your Visual Image

Burkey Belser

For hundreds of years, lawyers have adopted uniformity in their dress and in the materials they produce for courts. It's no wonder they have difficulty understanding the value of appearing unique. And yet, in today's swiftly changing and highly competitive marketplace, unique is exactly what they now, suddenly, are being asked to be. In this chapter, you will learn

- the *real* goal of marketing communications
- how people find and choose lawyers, and what they want to learn from you
- how often those people want to hear from you
- what works, and why and how it works

The *Real* Goal of Marketing Communications

Advertising, brochures, and Web sites do not sell professional services. The right person with the right service in front of the right audience at the right time sells legal services. Well-done marketing communications, however, do serve two important functions: They *condition* the sale before you meet your prospect, and they *reinforce* the sale after you succeed. This happens by establishing a corporate personality—a visible persona that *is* the law firm in the minds of its various publics.

Law (like engineering and science) concerns itself with substance and scorns preoccupation with form. However, if only substance were important, magazines would publish only typewritten articles, and in-house counsel would choose the unattractive and unlikable lawyer as easily as the attractive and likable lawyer. Buyers—even lawyers who buy legal services—are not immune to the *substance* of form. Design gives form substance. And, whether we like it or not, people base their buying decisions on that truth. In this chapter, you will learn how to bring it under your control. Form does not rule over substance; neither does substance rule over form. Use them both!

How People Find and Choose Their Lawyers

All buyers (whether sophisticated or not, and whether they're buying candy bars or cars or legal services) go through distinct stages in the buying process. You need to address them all.

Finding Lawyers

The "finding" or "information-gathering" phase begins before people decide to hire outside counsel. Most buyers start by calling people they trust. Our research shows they are equally likely to ask someone inside their company for referrals (42 percent begin this way) as they are to ask someone in an outside firm (41 percent). Only 21 percent of sophisticated legal buyers resort to legal directories. With them, *Martindale-Hubbell* is by far the most popular (88 percent). To find the "right" lawyer, buyers also attend seminars, read ads, search the Web, and look for articles authored by individual lawyers—in firm-sponsored newsletters or independent media.

The list of candidates usually narrows down to no more than three or four, though the shortlist may double if the matter is of "bet-your-company" status. However, once the shortlist is created, all candidates are functionally equal; that is, one candidate may have more-appropriate experience, but the other may be more likable. One may have international offices, but another may have fewer potential conflicts. The finding or information-gathering process is predominately intellectual, but once all the variables are weighed and valued, the process becomes predominately emotional.

Research shows the most important factors in the finding process are (1) expertise (prior experience with the same type of matter with positive results); (2) cost (not the lowest hourly rate, but the best value when all factors considered); (3) individual lawyer's reputation; and (4) innovation (fresh way of treating a routine matter, or an innovative approach to a complex one). Other factors that buyers consider, which may be more or less important, include knowledge of the buyer's industry and company, chemistry, firm reputation, billing practices, and client orientation. Some of these factors can be learned through brochures, newsletters, or other communications, while others require in-person meetings.

Choosing Lawyers

Typically, people make decisions only because they run out of time—the matter is urgent, supplies ran out, or the car is waiting. At this point, because the choices are roughly equal, the buyer must make a predominately emotional decision. *This important fact of buyer behavior is at the heart of all advertising and other marketing communication tools.* You must make the buyer feel good about the decision he or she is about to make and feel good afterward. (You'll learn how to achieve that in the section entitled, "What Works, and Why and How It Works.")

Two factors dominate the process of finding and choosing a law firm: Expertise in the pertinent area of law is usually the top criterion, and cost/value considerations rank second, becoming relatively more important in the selection stage. However, as the list of possible firms narrows, personal chemistry and law firm reputation move up the ladder of importance. In our research, the reputation of the firm became the most important factor for some (19 percent). That's not surprising, because those who regularly buy legal services often must justify their choices upstream to management. A strong firm reputation makes that chore decidedly easier.

Other important factors include individual lawyer reputation, knowledge of the buyer's industry, firm location, billing practices, responsiveness, and prior experience with the firm. Notice that the factors are slightly different—and in a slightly different order—than in the finding stage. Some are surprised to learn that responsiveness is so far down the list. But responsiveness is, in marketing jargon, a "post-purchase evaluation"—something that cannot be measured until the service relationship begins. (Studies show that prospective buyers consider lawyers responsive if they deliver brochures or other materials within forty-eight hours. To prove you are responsive, start *being* responsive right away.) Prior experience with the firm is also near the bottom of the list. That should terrify every lawyer—and with good reason. On average, companies with revenues between $100 million and $1 billion use fifteen firms, and those with revenues in excess of $1 billion use sixty-six firms! (So the best defense is a good offense: Keep in touch with clients through regular communications, preferably phone calls and letters, or newsletters and other communications.)

Buyer's Remorse

Anticipating the buyer's emotions immediately after the sale is as important as understanding the emotions immediately before the sale. "Buyer's remorse"—that sinking feeling in the pit of your stomach—is the fear that you've made the wrong decision. Everyone goes through this stage, just as certainly as everyone goes through confusion in the finding and choosing stages. You can address this issue through reassurance programs. For example, after buying a car, did you ever receive a communication shortly afterwards, with some reassuring message such as, "Hope you're liking your new Jeep Grand Cherokee. Come in after three months and get a free oil change." This message really says, "You were smart to buy from us." Sellers of legal services can benefit from programs like this as well. The reassurance can be simple, such as a letter or useful gift (perhaps a booklet with the direct-dial numbers for all the lawyers in the firm).

Why is all this detail about buying patterns important to the law firm marketer? Imagine your brochure to be a hammer and your ads a power sprayer. Imagine your newsletter to be a drill and your announcements, saws. Each tool has a defined use and does poorly at the job designed for another. Understanding buyers' minds and habits will allow you to understand and use your tools efficiently and precisely. For example, if you understand all the strategic uses of a firm brochure, you will recognize that many different brochures are possible—as many as there are types of hammers! Other businesses have known this for years and are sophisticated users of marketing tools. Lawyers, for the most part, are just learning the vocabulary.

What Works, and Why and How It Works

Let's examine each marketing tool to understand its precise role in the sales process. You need not simply believe this author; test these thoughts against your own experience for confirmation.

The Firm Brochure

The granddaddy of law firm marketing communications is the brochure. Firms spend thousands of dollars each year writing, printing, and distributing firm brochures in hopes of catching the attention of potential clients. But most lawyers have heard in-house counsel admit that the brochures that cross their desks often land in the trash—without anyone taking even a few seconds to glance through them. How did brochures get such a bad reputation?

First, many firms develop bad brochures. And second, good brochures are often used in bad ways. Research shows that 56 percent of in-house counsel request brochures, and two-thirds of corporations with revenues above $500 million ask for brochures. Although lawyers increasingly recognize that brochures are essential, they often still treat them as a necessary evil—something like expanded business cards. For these lawyers, the firm brochure is a wasted opportunity.

What can a firm brochure do? It can tell your story in an organized way, arguing your case from beginning to end. It can speak for you after you leave a meeting, when the decision to hire is made. The best brochures can even act as scripts for sales calls—when you make the same points in both a meeting and the brochure, the brochure serves as a powerful aid to memory. Brochures can institutionalize cross-selling by telling existing clients about your firm's other capabilities. They can correct an outdated image and give the firm a personality—a visible persona in the marketplace. Brochures can also help clients "self-select." Because law firms are often afraid to turn away *any* new client, they do not make the hard decisions necessary to locate the *right* client. A brochure can help do that.

THE FIRST GENERATION OF LAW FIRM BROCHURES

The first generation of firm brochures were hardly more than catalogs of services—A-to-Z lists that began with Antitrust and ended with Zoning. Though these brochures succeeded in defining the scope of services, they utterly failed to *sell* those services. (After all, what can you tell an in-house counsel about antitrust law in one or two paragraphs that he or she is unlikely to know already?) Moreover, a catalog fails to reveal a firm's personality and how the firm defines value in legal services in the marketplace—the primary goal of a firm brochure. As a practical matter, these brochures are obsolete the moment they come off the presses. And finally, they are boring. This beginning effort at the law firm brochure reflects a lack of understanding of its purpose. Your clients want information about *you*. How do you create a really effective sales tool?

BEFORE THE DESIGN PROCESS BEGINS

A firm brochure is a mirror through which lawyers see the firm as a whole, often for the first time. Because brochures should have a long shelf life, the mirror should reflect the future, not the past. Matching present-day reality with a vision of the future is difficult for any business. First you must "know thyself," and then, "know thy dream." And, even if the story of the firm exists in a business and marketing plan, actualizing that plan through a brochure is a challenge. That's when substance becomes form, and form, substance. This is hard work, but delightful when breakthroughs come.

An effective brochure is possible only if you establish a design goal that reflects your positioning strategy. But firms often begin developing brochures without plans. And so, the resulting bad brochure begets the bad reputation brochures enjoy. Ask yourself, "How hard is it to develop a winning case? How much creativity does it require? How careful must I be with the details?" Why should brochures be any different?

IDENTIFY THE KEY MESSAGES

Every firm is unique. The mix of lawyers—their experience, their diversity, their different talents—make a sound that can be tuned into a single note. Lawyers who are uncomfortable with self-promotion can take some solace in the fact that the note will never sound true if it is dishonest. The message that overrides every other must be accurate about the firm's vision of itself, and must be accepted by the partnership and understood by the entire firm. (Therefore, the development process should include giving everyone the opportunity to hear that the firm's management believes the message is genuine.)

Behind a key message are other themes you should develop. For example, your network of offices might make you uniquely positioned to offer international, national, or regional coverage that others can't match. Your deep experience in two or three industries gives clients a head start when you take the case. Your open culture gives clients access to teams of the best talent the firm has to offer. There are dozens of other themes you could explore. There are very few that fit your firm. Those that do become your "voice."

WHAT IS A DESIGN STRATEGY?

There are many organizational schemes for a law firm brochure, and they can be combined with different levels of emphasis. For example, you could organize your brochure around case studies to group practice areas from a business's point of view. You could focus on characteristics of service (such as speed, innovation, or multilingual capabilities). You could focus on geography, laying claim to a region or state or area of the world. This is strategy.

You could illustrate your case studies with photographs or drawings. You could present your service characteristics with solid colors. You could tell the story of your Southeast Asia experience by turning the globe upside down. This is design in service of strategy. Design animates strategy, brings it to life, and, if creatively done, makes people respond. (If you feel fiercely about Coke or Pepsi, then (1) you are human, and (2) you have responded *emotionally* to a brand.)

CLIENT FOCUS

Some of us forget to ask others about themselves, so focused are we on ourselves. Most brochures exhibit similar bad manners. They focus on the firm, not on clients' needs or concerns. Few things are more difficult than turning away from the gravitational pull of your busy workday and toward your clients' concerns. Understanding clients' needs—telling your story from their point of view—wins just as many clients as asking about others wins friends. In fact, consider the marketplace like a holiday party: Those companies that seem to care about their customers or clients seem to be the best liked and most successful.

READERS DON'T READ, THEY SCAN

You should design brochures based on the way readers behave, not on the way you want them to behave. Readers rarely read according to your table of contents. Instead they skip around and read the most accessible material on each page. As readers scan, they constantly make "reading" decisions; then, if they choose to read, they constantly assess whether they should go back to the scanning level. Studies of readers' eye movements confirm this. (If you don't believe this, study your own reading patterns and you'll find a close parallel with the reading patterns of most people.) Therefore, your brochure should be designed for scanning readers. Tell your story in headlines, subheads, pictures or illustrations, and captions. Use bullet points. Keep copy brief. Do anything scanning readers want, because the more time they spend with your materials, the more likely you are to gain their trust and to have preconditioned the sale.

A PURPOSE FOR EVERY PAGE

Be rigorously goal oriented. Define the overall goal for your brochure, and then the key message for every page. These goals are always informational *and* emotional. They may be achieved through headlines, color, images, or any of a dozen other tools in the designer's toolbox. But the designer and the law firm should be clear about the key messages and should carefully study the developing brochure to confirm these goals have been achieved.

Enhancing Memory

Many factors encourage and enhance memory. Not all of them are known. What is known is that memorability increases if we burn multiple pathways into the brain—sound, sight, touch, and smell. Memory must be reinforced if we want material retained in short-term memory to transfer to long-term memory.

THE IMPORTANCE OF A NAME

The first memory to establish is your firm's name. Short names, no more than four or five syllables, stand a better chance of being remembered than longer ones (which are always reduced to shorter monikers anyway: Ford Motor Company becomes Ford, International Business Machines becomes IBM, the Food and Drug Administration becomes the FDA, and so on). Memory has little room for polysyllabic handles, so compression constantly occurs. Because smart marketers recognize this, an entire industry has grown around naming products and services.

Law firms often carry unmemorable "company" names, but, fortunately, the public is there to help reduce Skadden, Arps, Slate, Meagher & Flom to Skadden Arps or, even better, Skadden. A few firms market services under a "street name" (like Jones Day), but retain an official name of the partnership (Jones Day Reavis & Pogue). Other firms, like Proskauer Rose, have taken the plunge and simply shortened their firm names.

A slogan (which marketers call a positioning statement) reinforces memory by attaching an association to a name. An example is "Federal Express: absolutely, positively overnight." The benefit of the company's service is directly linked to the company's name. Law firms trying to stake a clear market position have followed that model, as shown in this example: "Howrey & Simon: In Court Every Day."

THE IMPORTANCE OF VISUAL IDENTITY

Corporate identity has been defined as the "communicated essence" of a corporation. A visual identity attempts to project what makes a firm unique. And it provides a visual pathway for memory.

VISUAL PATHWAYS

The development of marketing tools is solidly rooted in the history of our cultures. In fact, the development of logos—the modern equivalent of heraldry—parallels the rise of capitalism. Throughout time, no one has doubted the power of the image. Before humans could read, they could understand symbols, learning to love them or fear them, hate them or laugh at them. On that foundation, that basic activity of memory, rests the tradition of the corporate logo. Logo has come to mean the graphic associated with a company, product, or service.

WHAT IS A LAW FIRM'S VISUAL IDENTITY?

Of course, the logo is just one visual element in the identity scheme. Though it is the cornerstone of the identity program, only the consistent application of that logo, coupled with a family of colors and selected type styles, gives your clients a memorable vision of the firm. Inconsistent messages are confusing. Consistency, the spirit of effective communication, can't be overdone. Most businesses have too few opportunities in front of clients to waste them with more than one message.

The style of illustration or photography you choose—even the shape of your materials and the paper choices—influence memory and affect the impression your audience retains about your firm. Why? Legal services are intangible, and therefore their quality and reliability cannot be felt or seen or heard. So consumers place inordinate emphasis on every tangible indicia of you and your work—such as your letterhead, your business card, your fax form, and your brochure.

Chemistry is so important in business relationships—and what influences chemistry? Your appearance, posture, tone of voice, conversational style—and your printed materials. This is nothing other than your *personal* visual identity! Extrapolate to the entire firm and you will understand the idea: Visual identity attempts to create a firmwide chemistry.

Consider IBM and Apple Computer, or CBS and NBC. Each has a distinct personality, but they provide look-alike services. Consumers understand what each has to offer because the companies have communicated their unique personalities (their corporate identities) through words, images, and music—all your senses they can reach. A law firm should communicate its visual identity, its image and personality, in all printed materials—from letterheads to labels, brochures to wills. Most firms still fail to communicate their personalities to their publics. Letterheads often come straight from a stationer, treated as office supplies rather than the most important indicator of the firm's presence.

WHAT A VISUAL IDENTITY CAN DO FOR YOUR FIRM

A clear, distinctive identity gives the firm a platform for doing business. A well-managed identity can become the basis for building relationships

- *among law firm partners.* Building consensus is difficult when individuals have no allegiance greater than their individual goals. A clear identity requires shared values and shared goals. Building consensus is made easier by consistent, tangible expression of a firm's culture through an identity program.

- *in newly merged firms.* A clear identity can guide and motivate a firm in transition. And it can also make a firm being acquired appear more valuable.
- *among recruits.* New lawyers want to join a firm they understand. Studies prove that recruiting the best lawyers, and retaining them, are critical factors in profitability. A firm needs to present prospective lawyers with a clear definition of itself. A visual identity, properly developed and implemented, communicates stability, as well as the firm's philosophy, energy, and market position.
- *among clients.* Clients deserve the same succinct definition. A strong firm identity signals for clients a law firm's clear position in the industry and the marketplace, and that the firm knows who its clients are and why it is in business.
- *among employees.* Employees like being left out of the picture even less than they like being underpaid. If they understand the firm's objectives, and where their work fits in, their satisfaction increases. A shared identity helps employees understand these qualities, and it can motivate superior performance and develop emissaries for the marketing effort.
- *with the firm's administrator.* Poorly coordinated identity systems cost firms thousands of dollars each year through waste and inefficiency. Thirty-two percent of all printed materials are thrown away because they become outdated. A well-designed identity system often pays for itself in savings.

CONSISTENCY IS THE GOAL

Very few companies have the opportunity to reinforce their visual identity with the entire American public every day. To achieve that level of awareness, those companies spend hundreds of millions of dollars! To achieve more-limited awareness, a few regional or local companies spend millions of dollars! All these companies understand that each impression has *value;* thus each presents a consistent impression to squeeze the most value from its advertising and promotional dollars.

For law firms, this idea is not always welcome. A large firm may have as many as twenty-five designs for business cards, dozens of letter formats, or eighty fax designs. Many firms that coordinate a consistent look for all their promotional materials exempt their "holy" letterhead and business card, leaving their traditional stationery unchanged. Because a law firm has so few opportunities to make repeat impressions, valuable opportunities are wasted when the letterhead and business card (along with the fax, the most common carrier of those impressions) are not included in the identity program. *Everything* published by the firm (with the exception of court documents) is an opportunity to remind viewers of the firm's consistent market position.

THE QUESTIONABLE VALUE OF FIRM ANNOUNCEMENTS

Firm announcements are a time-honored tradition of law firm marketing. They are, as one legal marketing consultant notes, "a venerable news release. . . . Gentle reminders of the firm's existence." Too gentle, perhaps. The changing tradition of the law is forcing the examination of traditional tools. While the firm announcement is undergoing radical change in its format and design, budget-conscious marketers might ask whether they should be produced at all. The costs of engraving, printing, paper, postage, and handling should cause every "occasional mailing" of the firm to be scrutinized.

WHAT DOESN'T WORK

Rarely do announcements hail a single lawyer. Usually, to save money, the announcement gangs two, three, or more names together on the same card or set of cards. The impression that a single name might have made on a more collegial community in years past has been diminished by today's crowded and competitive marketplace, which demands that large firms recruit dozens of new lawyers every year. Because of their cherished history, announcements will probably continue to be published. In the nearly forgotten world of etiquette, announcements acted on the same set of sensibilities as a cotillion ball. Today, some in-house counsel say they regard stacks of them almost with irritation. Instead of being helpful, they are a nuisance in the daily mail.

WHAT DOES WORK

Continual contact with clients is critical. Announcements do remind the recipient that the firm is still in business. As repeated impressions are key to effective visual identity, announcements can play a part in the process. Morale is also important. Almost as a perk of partnership, announcements signify a formal welcoming into the society of lawyers that is a law firm, though the tradition may be more important for family and friends than for clients. Announcements are improved by adding a small biography of the new partner, which helps clients place the individual somewhere in their hierarchies of need. Improved announcements also employ design, color, and innovative typography consistent with the firm's other identity materials, giving them personality and certainly improving their effectiveness as marketing tools.

If you cherish the tradition, then mail to a select list. Include biographies. Add portraits. If you see this tradition as a "legacy system," then abandon it. Use the legal media to announce new partners. Publish "substantive" news of changes within the firm biannually or annually, giving more information about the strategy behind those hiring decisions and your goals for the future.

MANAGING CHANGE

The change from old to new is legitimately hard. It hurts to see a cherished way of doing things pass away. The introduction of a new visual identity can cause a firestorm of protest. The success—or failure—of the process is in direct proportion to your ability to manage change. The following steps may be helpful.

SURVEY THE FIELD

The dominance of tradition in the legal culture inevitably makes every lawyer's first question, "What are other firms doing?" So the first step in designing a visual identity change is to collect as many examples of law firm identity programs as possible. Not every partner will need them. But the partners who need that reassurance need it badly. Check with the major engravers in the legal field. Ask lawyers in your own firm to collect letterheads that they like from other firms.

SHOW PROCESS

Bitter experience encourages marketing partners and directors to make committees as small as possible. Nevertheless, keeping the design process confined to a small committee will be fatal in the development of a firm identity. Committee members learn quickly and, during the visual identity process, are not even aware of how much they have learned. They may consider solutions that would shock the rest of the firm. Rather than simply roll out the new identity program as a *fait accompli,* show the partners how the process led to your conclusions. Teach the new viewers about typography, placement, letter design, and color so they understand and support your committee's decision.

SEPARATE ISSUES OF CHANGE FROM ISSUES OF TASTE

Objections to a new design often are based on emotional reactions to change, rather than on the design itself. For example, "I prefer black ink" simply may be another way of saying, "I want my old letterhead back." Or, "I prefer the traditional typeface," is most often code for "I like what I had, thank you." Lawyers find "traditional" to be that with which they are familiar. Be sympathetic. Lawyers were raised in the cathedral of logic. Visual "substance" may seem lightweight when compared with legal "substance." So attack with logic and seek to answer real objections, not straw men.

Yes, Your Clients Read Newsletters

The good news: 92 percent of in-house counsel read newsletters. Buyers of legal services like to be kept up-to-date on breaking issues that affect their businesses. The bad news: Some in-house counsel receive as many as two hundred newsletters each month! Nevertheless, newsletters that are not too long (most readers prefer no more than four pages) and that are packed with brief and usable information attract the attention of in-house counsel.

PUT *NEWS* INTO NEWSLETTERS

A newsletter worth reading may leave the client or prospect with just one new idea or one new piece of information. What kinds of ideas or topics are appropriate? Anything that's new and relevant can be "news"—new regulations, new laws, new services that benefit clients, new ways of doing business, strategies for new markets, or new opportunities. News about the firm itself may also interest clients, when it is relevant to their businesses. The addition of an environmental practice, the opening of a foreign office, the overhaul of a computer system that gives the firm new capabilities—these developments can be important to clients. And though firms typically use announcements to introduce new partners and associates, corporations typically use newsletters to introduce new employees, in greater depth than formal announcements allow.

But few of us have time to spare. A considerate editorial strategy would be to make news stories brief. Readers appreciate summaries of new laws and activities that are no more than two paragraphs in length. Send readers to your Web site or offer a phone number for those who want more detail. If you believe the full story needs to be told, offer an executive summary at the beginning to allow readers to answer the question, "Does this story affect me?" Short summaries lead to (1) reduced lawyer resistance to writing articles; (2) better stories (Mark Twain once said, "If I had more time, I would have written a shorter letter."); (3) more interested and appreciative readers (test against your own behavior—which items are *you* most likely to read in your favorite magazines or newsletters?); and (4) the possibility of regular publication.

PERIODICALS SHOULD BE PUBLISHED PERIODICALLY

In the magazine or newsletter publishing business, the worst sin is not publishing on time. Yet law firms frequently announce quarterly newsletters with a grand splash in the first issue, and then get only one more issue out that year or, even worse, never publish again. If regular newsletters are part of your individual practice area marketing plans, then you must deliver on your promise. Otherwise, all your investment is wasted. A publication is a *contract* between the reader and the publisher. So, before you begin, answer the same questions you would before starting any business: What are our goals and strategies? How many resources do we have? Do we have management support? If any answers come up short, do not even start. There are other ways to keep in touch with your clients and prospects that may work better for your firm.

DEVELOP A VOICE

You may not even realize that your favorite publications keep your allegiance and command your affection because they have developed a voice you admire or like. Consider *The New Yorker, Atlantic, Metropolitan Home, Vanity Fair,* or *Forbes.* All magazines that lead their markets do so with a strong editorial voice. Let your voice—your personality—come through. Have opinions and a point of view. You will be read. Editing for clarity, power, and personality is what good publications do best.

THE DESIGNER'S ART MAY OFFER YOUR ONLY CHANCE TO BE READ

"Style," said the well-known illustrator Edward Sorel, "is personality." The goal of a well-designed newsletter is not only the orderly presentation of information. It must also present the editorial personality visually. Newsletters that succumb to the false dichotomy between form and substance fail to reveal a personality, particularly when "substance" holds "form" in contempt.

The departments, feature stories, editorials, contents pages, and publication information in magazines are strategically organized to increase readership. Newsletters can employ the same mix of editorial features to increase interest and develop loyal readers. Readers get comfortable with the organization of your newsletter, just as you do with your local grocery store. Both of you can save time "shopping" if the layout is routine. Badly designed newsletters make all elements equal, then pour the most interesting material on the front page, followed by material of decreasing interest steadily toward the back, which tells readers they need go no further than page one. Publication design requires some skills unlikely to be found in the mailroom or in the template directory of word processing programs. Buy style. If budget is a key concern, have a designer incorporate elements of style into an electronic template that you can interpret each time the newsletter is published. Elements of visual style are headlines, subheads, body text, folios (page numbers), and sidebars. These elements make the visual dictionary an editor can use to present a story.

Requests for Proposals: Becoming a Way of Life

Nearly two-fifths of companies that employ fifteen or more law firms issue Requests for Proposals (RFPs). As buyers of legal services become more sophisticated and pressure on the corporate legal dollar increases, more firms are being asked to submit proposals for legal work. Many firms are improving the structure of their responses, but few take full advantage of the organizational and presentation opportunities a visual image presents. A well-designed proposal can increase the likelihood that yours will stay on top of the heap. To be hired, every professional must do three things: (1) demonstrate understanding, (2) demonstrate professionalism, and (3) reduce uncertainty.

DEMONSTRATE UNDERSTANDING

Responding to a proposal begins by asking questions about (1) the company requesting the service, (2) the matter at hand, and (3) the competition. Demonstrating understanding of the company and its legal concerns is the first step in your presentation. Presenting your qualifications is the second.

DEMONSTRATE PROFESSIONALISM

An effective proposal should address the creative or strategic handling of the case, and its management, with the following organization:

- executive summary
- statement of the challenge
- expertise and experience
- management plan for the case

REDUCE UNCERTAINTY THROUGH PACKAGING

Because RFPs are specifically designed to streamline selection, the process is colder and more distant than in the past. Proposals are a way of prequalifying firms without the investment of time and emotional energy of face-to-face meetings. Therefore, because consumers of professional services fear they will be the victims of your worst work and not the beneficiaries of your best, you need to reduce uncertainty by packing as much personality as you can in your proposal. Packaging can be the single differentiating factor in your firm's presentation and, believe it or not, can make the difference between success and failure in winning the assignment.

FOLLOW THE BIG-SIX MODEL

Create a distinctive cover design and binding. Employ the firm's identity on the cover. Use its logotype and colors. If your firm responds to enough proposals to justify the investment, use metal spiral binding with paper covers instead of plastic strips or plastic coils. This helps an open proposal lay flat, avoids the off-the-shelf plastic look, and prevents thicker proposals from pulling apart with use.

USE TABBED DIVIDERS

Give readers a chance to make their own decisions about what to read first. Some go to the dollar numbers first, others to the biographies, and still others to the executive summary. The numbered tabs that are often used for briefs are inconsistent with a custom presentation. Develop tab dividers that reflect the cover and the firm's identity.

FORMAT THE INTERIOR PAGES

Using sheets preprinted with color and the firm's name vastly improves the presentation of word-processed material. Develop templates and style guides for headlines, body text, footnotes (if you must), sidebars, page numbers, and other details. When possible, use graphs, maps, pie charts, tables, and photographs. The more time your client or prospect spends with your proposal, the more likely you are to win.

Advertising and the Visual Image

All the basic rules of marketing communication previously discussed apply to advertising—plus some. You must establish an objective, develop goals and strategies, and define your target audience. You must understand how the media defines markets and market segments, and compare media attributes, editorial stance, and readership. You must determine the value of media concentration or media mix, and identify your key message. You must decide how to evaluate your success, and how to refine your message, your budget, and your media plan. Advertising is too expensive to be done badly.

MEASURING RETURN ON THE ADVERTISING DOLLAR

Sales records of companies almost never show a correlation between sales and advertising volume. Advertising is only one of many factors influencing sales; determining out how much other factors—such as the firm's reputation, the rainmaking skills of individual lawyers, fee structure, service quality, competitive pressure, and the economy—contribute to a "sale" demands a mathematical model not yet invented. Even results from direct mail, the most "measurable" of all sales tactics, are muddled by contributing factors such as the reputation of the company, the state of the economy, and the effect of supporting advertising on television, radio, and newspapers. If you regard advertising as an expense, as standard accounting procedures do, then calculating the value of advertising is very frustrating indeed. Some advice: Do not even try. Minds as fine as yours have tried.

However, advertising is not strictly an expense, it is an *investment.* Understanding this is the first step in understanding how advertising works: *Advertising increases in value over time.* Depending on the quality of the advertising and the service itself, the increase may grow slowly, like a coral reef, or quickly, like an island from a volcanic eruption.

ADS CAN SECURE NEW CLIENTS

Lawyers are like most salespeople in this important way: They do not call on prospects until after they have inquired. Why? Because lawyers are spending their time servicing existing clients, who demand the most attention, contribute the most to the bottom line, and provide the most dependable source of income for the firm. But they retire, become absorbed by larger companies, fail, and turn the reins over to a less-loyal generation, thus requiring that new clients take their place. And so every firm needs a constant stream of new relationships. This is the opportunity advertising offers—over time.

Probably no in-house counsel will admit to being influenced in choosing law firms by ads. But studies prove that advertising seems to help in-house counsel *find* lawyers. Advertising increases awareness of law firms and their services. Although the referral network is the primary mode of finding legal talent, there are three times as many lawyers today as there were in 1970. The referral network cannot support the demand for increasing specificity in legal expertise. Advertising acts as a broadcast above the referral base. Getting called to the table starts with an awareness of your service offerings. So when you measure return, measure your investment against the number of new prospects with advertising and the number without it.

COMPETING FOR A PLACE IN MEMORY

"Advertisements are now so numerous that they are negligently perused," said Samuel Johnson in 1758. Imagine how much greater the challenge is to today's advertiser. We live in a society of overcommunication. We receive about 3,000 messages a day—from radio or television when we awake, from morning newspapers, from store signs on the way to work, from the mail in our in-boxes, and from e-mail messages—a day-long assault on our consciousness by businesses of all sorts promoting products and services. To protect ourselves from this rush of stimuli, we react the only way we can. We tune out. Of the thousands of messages, we select only a few in each category of product or service (usually only three or four) and rank them in precise order in our minds, like rungs on a ladder. Typically, the three or four we remember are the market leaders, which have won the battle for our minds.

This theory about the organization of consumer memory is called "positioning," a concept as fundamental to marketing as gravity is to physics. Positioning is a theory about human memory applied to consumer behavior. Businesses study positioning to learn how to influence consumers' minds, not only to recall their products or services, but to remember them in a positive light. It is at the heart of advertising and all marketing communications. Physiological research confirms this theory. Studies suggest that the eye is a relentless hunter, always scanning the scene before it. As it scans, the eye is also continuously focusing and discriminating, separating figure from ground. The scanning eye sends signals to the brain, where decisions are made about whether to linger on an object. Studies show the eye lingers most often on complex or new images, as it tries to sort out the complex or identify the new.

Web Sites and Other New Media

Brochures, seminars, and newsletters have for years been the favored means of promoting lawyers and law firms. However, new technologies have arrived to broaden the spectrum of law firm marketing. Now more than one-third of law firms have established Web sites—perhaps the least personal avenue of marketing communications. At the same time, the use of electronic sales presentations is rapidly increasing, a technological aid to the most personal moment in the marketing cycle. In between, fax and e-mail brochures are being developed. Technology has arrived at the center of business communications.

THE WORLD WIDE WEB

Whether you call it the Web, the World Wide Web, or W3, or distinguish it from the slightly older, wider Internet, it's the place your money, phone calls, and e-mail—as well as lawyers and clients—may soon live. (For more information, see Chapter 8.)

TURNING SWORDS INTO MARKET SHARES

The Internet evolved from a Department of Defense Cold War project that enabled computers connected by long-distance phone lines to share information independent of a central source. Today, the Internet is a global network of millions of computers linked by phone lines and microwave and satellite links. The Internet works because everyone speaks the same language (TCP/IP) when packaging and routing traffic through the network. But the Net is more than that. It's a cultural watershed. A network of networks, it connects countless newsgroups, online forums, and bulletin boards focusing on virtually every topic known to humankind. It is, as Julian Dibbel wrote in *Wired,* "the single most complex information entity since the emergence of the human brain."

THE WEB: THE INTERNET MADE VISUAL

The Net is also home to the World Wide Web, a come-one-come-all global repository of words and pictures. The Web is the Net brought to life—with colors, sounds, and intuitive navigation. It is the most graphic-intensive region of the Net. And, because its ease of use has attracted millions, the Web is now responsible for most of the traffic (and congestion) on the Net. The growth in Web use stuns the imagination. Today, "smart" houses are built wired for the Web. As technologies converge, familiar providers of local phone service, long-distance phone service, and cable television vie to improve your access to the Web.

Businesses have been paying attention. Many companies use the Web for e-mail connectivity, electronic securities trading, and research. And more companies of all sizes find the Web to be an inexpensive way to reach millions of potential customers through twenty-four-hour access. They have established "information storefronts," which they refresh constantly with new information and interactive features. More than half the Fortune 500 companies already advertise on the Web, according to WebTrack Information Services. Expect that to increase as Netscape, Microsoft, and others add features that attract ever-greater numbers of computer users to what is becoming the world's largest theme park, shopping mall, and public library.

HOW ARE LAWYERS USING THE WEB?

Unlike earlier waves of new technology, the legal community is embracing the Net with the same fervor as the general public. In 1996, more than 720,000 legal professionals were using the Internet, including 550,000 lawyers who logged on at least weekly from their offices and homes, according to an Internet Lawyer/Microsoft Corporation survey. The most common uses are legal research (traditional legal material such as court opinions and state and federal codes, as well as financial and business research), e-mail, and discussion groups.

ARE CLIENTS USING THE WEB TO FIND LAW FIRMS?

It may be too early to assess the value of Web pages as marketing tools. But as a starting point, note these remarks by a Fortune 500 general counsel in an online discussion group:

> I believe a good Web page can become part of the matrix of reasons I have for hiring a firm. I suspect that I will look at a firm's Web site

(and I will definitely check to see if there is a site) because I found the firm in *Martindale*, or someone has recommended it, or the firm's name is well known, or some other reason that has caused me to specifically look at the site.

One theory of chaos suggests there is a larger order to things we perceive as chaotic. For example, there is a larger order to the movement of clouds or the apparently random drip of a faucet. The results of a firm's marketing efforts often seem chaotic, too. No one really knows which impression or which contact will someday circle around and result in a call for business. So we give speeches, write articles, and volunteer in organizations that broaden the circle of those who know us. In that larger order, we take as a matter of faith that more impressions and greater frequency will reward the firm with more business. Extending the law firm's presence by broadening its contacts through the Web is just another step. Although little is understood about the impact of the Web on business, the potential is so staggering that law firms cannot afford to ignore its presence. Better to sign on and see where it takes you.

WHERE CAN THE WEB TAKE YOU?

Research tells us in-house counsel are looking for more specific information about law firm capabilities than brochures typically provide, yet most law firm Web sites are little more than brochures online. Simply transferring existing print materials to the Web is an understandable first step, but ignores the potential—and the character—of the new medium. Not only can a Web site be a repository of the firm's skills and experience, it can also preview what it's like to work with the firm; that is, a Web site can reflect the firm's personality. *Any tool that effectively previews the actual experience of working with you is a powerful marketing tool.*

WHERE DOES NEW LEGAL TALENT FIND YOU?

Law firms can introduce new lawyers to the firm's culture and practice through a Web site, cementing a positive feeling about the firm. Law students can confirm their impressions of your firm with visits to your Web site, in anticipation of their job searches or in preparation for interviews with your firm. Although no formal research has yet been done on this subject, anecdotal evidence suggests that students and laterals expect to preview the firm's capabilities via the World Wide Web.

WHO MANAGES WEB SITE DEVELOPMENT?

Requests to develop a law firm Web site often wind up on an executive director's desk. From there, the request typically funnels to an Information Services (IS) department before the project gets underway. The mechanics of constructing a Web site should not overshadow its marketing communication function. The IS function is certainly important—the site should operate flawlessly if it is to reflect the high standards of the firm. But technical design and programming should not begin until the site's information goals and graphic designs have been agreed upon. These are marketing and communications functions that demand leadership of the firm's marketing director, in partnership with IS and the firm's management, or with consultants, if in-house personnel are not available.

Successful Web sites are built with online behavior patterns in mind—what it takes to get visitors to a site, how they are motivated to go beyond the home page, and why they return to the same sites again and again. To keep visitors interested, follow these guidelines:

1. From the first moment, keep visitors involved.
   - When visitors get to your site, you have their attention. Don't lose it. Use headlines to confirm their interest. Involve them immediately in making choices about where to go next.
   - Make each visit an active experience. Use interactive questions and answers to identify visitors' needs and interests. Establish customized tours of the site and a suggestion box for improvements.
2. Make your site client oriented, not firm oriented.
   - Identify your target audiences. Focus on their needs. Guide them to those sections of the site where they can find answers. And provide hypertext links to other sites (such as government sites, libraries, or publications) that might provide more information.
3. Deliver a high return on time invested.
   - Design the site around features that address the concerns of key audiences. Of course, the site should include lawyer biographies and practice area descriptions, but the main event should be helping visitors find information they can use.
   - Visitors want answers to the problems on their desks. They also are attracted to features that offer interesting sidelights on their profession or background on some aspect of their jobs.
4. Think of your site as a magazine.
   - Successful magazines are not just attractive, they are architecturally sound. Movement through each issue is planned around reader behavior, from cover to cover. Web sites need that same clarity.
   - Design should begin with a "footprint" or birds-eye view of the site. Visitors must understand the icons and navigational aids that will guide them through the site. Seek input from visitors on the ease of the site's navigation. Site specifications should include graphic elements to be used consistently throughout the site.
5. Don't keep clients waiting.
   - Time weighs heavy in cyberspace. Some day, the Net will equal television's standards for speed. Meanwhile, site design must recognize the speed limitations of today's modems. Avoid graphics that take too long to download (but don't sacrifice good design).

6. Move clients closer to making the right decision.
    - Ask yourself, "What will give clients the confidence they need to retain our firm?" Then deliver as much evidence in those areas as possible: specific expertise, industry experience, technical backgrounds of your lawyers, languages, or alternative billing arrangements—and invite visitors to ask for more information.
    - The content of your Web site can educate readers about needs they may not even realize they have. Think of the site as a public-relations vehicle and publish, publish, publish.
7. Update the site regularly.
    - Like fish in the market, news gets old fast. Would you buy a copy of the January issue of your favorite magazine in February? News gets old even faster on the Web.
8. Promote your site—online and in print.
    - Linking your site with all the search engines is only the first step. Be certain that your Web address appears on print ads, business cards, stationery, and other printed materials about the firm.
    - Once the site has been tested, mail clients and prospects postcards or other promotions inviting them to visit. Over the next few days, track visits to the site to measure the results of the mailing.
9. Have a plan to bring them to the site, and to bring them back.
    - When you launch a Web site, you become a publisher. To maintain an editorial schedule, you'll need a firmwide commitment to gathering interesting cases, writing and adapting articles, and adding new features that attract visitors to the site.
10. Who does what in Web site development?
    - There is often confusion about who does what in designing and servicing a Web site. A useful metaphor is the division of responsibilities in building and maintaining an office building: the owner, architect, construction company, and building manager. Your law firm is the owner of the site. The marketing design firm is both architect and construction contractor, with responsibility for designing the site and subcontracting for its construction. The actual construction is done by programmers and engineers who write and test the code that brings your content to the Web. The marketing design firm renovates and expands the site as you add new features and functions to the site. Maintaining or "hosting" your Web site will be handled by an Internet service provider that may be the same company that constructs your site.

NEW MEDIA

New media, in the broadest sense, are methods of presenting information digitally. Books, brochures, and newspapers are old media. So are slides and overhead transparencies. Multimedia techniques, CDs, interactive kiosks, and the Internet are new media.

Research confirms a rising tide of RFPs. In addition to written responses, 28 percent of large companies ask for formal presentations and 13 percent of smaller companies do so. With increasing frequency, the decision to hire is made following a formal presentation. Thus the need for media that enhance presentations and extend their impact has increased.

OUTSHINE THE COMPETITION: BE PRESENTABLE

Improve your presentations by designing templates for software applications such as PowerPoint, Freelance Graphics, and Persuasion. In creating presentation screens, extend your firm's visual identity right through to the point-of-sale. Transfer the key messages from the firm brochure to build a framework for the entire presentation—creating standard introductory and concluding screens, and style guidelines for text, lists, charts, and graphs.

As for "low-tech" presentations, PowerPoint, Freelance Graphics, and Persuasion are designed to help create handouts that complement the presentation. Handouts can add value by allowing you to provide more in-depth information than can be put on a single screen. The best handouts include information you may not have had time to cover. They remind your audience of salient points in the presentation. Moreover, your handouts reflect your firm. How they look gives a nonverbal message about you, your firm, and your firm's commitment to quality.

CD-ROM AND OTHER PRESSING DEMANDS

Digital science has presented another communication tool having resources and capabilities that rival the Internet. For marketing purposes, CD-ROM offers practically unlimited storage; for example, it allows all of a firm's newsletters, white papers, and practice descriptions to be delivered on one disk—with room to spare for full-motion video, audio, animation, and lush illustration. Compared with the Web, disks are a static medium. Revision is expensive and far from immediate. But once the CD is in the hands of the client, the information is accessible in a trouble-free moment, in contrast to the long waits for access and pauses for downloading sometimes experienced by Web users.

With those advantages, it is surprising CDs are, as yet, used so little in the business. A recent survey asked management executives to rank their media preferences. Even when they need large volumes of complex data, three of four executives prefer printed material. Fewer than half would consider looking for the same material on the Net. And only 12 percent would use a CD. Nevertheless, acceptance of new media can come quickly. And CD-ROM may become the medium of choice for standard presentations, demonstrations of analytical tools and methods (such as trial techniques), leave-behind supplements to law firm brochures, and even court briefs.

SECTION 3

Implementing Marketing Strategies

CHAPTER 5

The Written Word

Roberta Montafia

Why Write?

The written word—arguably it's the most powerful marketing tool a lawyer can use. Why write? In short, to build credibility and to differentiate yourself in a highly competitive market. Writing is a logical first step in building a reputation, enhancing a résumé, developing name recognition, and establishing yourself as an expert in the eyes of your peers. Properly executed, it is a cost-effective use of your marketing time, as it allows you to reach a vast number of people with relatively little expenditure of money and time.

All lawyers face the challenge of breaking out of the pack to market their uniqueness. Marketing is not a "one size fits all" endeavor, and the written word can be a remarkably effective vehicle for achieving differentiation. A published article, whether the original or a reprint, sends a message to the reader that the writer has experience. It also carries an implied endorsement by the publisher that this person has credibility.

Perhaps the greatest attraction of the written word as a business development tool is that even the most reluctant marketer is generally comfortable with the activity—it is easy and familiar. The variety of formats and flexibility of the medium permits the harnessing and packaging of personal strengths in a way that client prospects seeking expertise will recognize. Even for a newly qualified lawyer who may feel he or she has little to offer, writing is a means to build relationships and communicate developing strengths.

Every time you write, you create a marketing opportunity. To build a practice, you need to create a connection in the buyer's eyes between you and the buyer's needs. If you want to be in a buyer's consciousness, you first need to get into the buyer's mind. Using written materials can be the least intimidating, most effective, and simplest means of achieving this goal.

How to Begin

Now that you've decided to use the written word as a marketing tool, you need to decide what to write and where to publish. On the surface, the answer to these questions may appear obvious. You should resist the temptation to "just jump in," nevertheless. The planning stage is often dismissed as unnecessary, or is neglected because of its tedious and time-consuming nature. But without a sense of direction, even the most disciplined writer is wasting time.

You also need to avoid the mind-set that one bylined article will lead to success. More than one lawyer has written an article (usually at the prodding of someone else) and had it published, and then sat back waiting for the telephone to ring. Such a singular effort is usually doomed to fail, because the lawyer's expectations were hardly realistic. Any isolated marketing effort—whether it's writing, speaking, or advertising—will seldom achieve results; it's numbers that count. Marketing and business development are the cumulative effect of consistent efforts. Success takes time and energy. Therefore, the first step is to create a plan—one that is simple, realistic, attainable, and sustainable, and that complements your overall marketing plan. The plan can be as uncomplicated as deciding to submit four articles to targeted publications in the coming year.

Steps in Creating a Plan

Initially, you need to identify the best audience for your marketing efforts. Examine your current client base, or, if you are just starting out, determine the type of clients you want to form your client base. Then ask yourself the following questions:

- What type of work have I enjoyed the most?
- What type of work would I like to do more of?
- Which clients have I enjoyed working with?
- What areas of my practice are growing?
- What areas of my practice are declining?
- What type of clients will I need in the next three years, and the next five years, to attain my goals?
- What trends can be detected in the legal and nonlegal sectors that may affect the growth or decline of my practice?

Finally, determine the referral source for each client and the potential referral sources for prospects. It is helpful to analyze referrals in a variety of ways, such as by geographical region, by industry, and by source (whether referrals came through third parties such as other lawyers or accountants, or from existing clients or in-house counsel). By categorizing your client base, you can group clients by common characteristics. Generally, clients who share common characteristics engage in related activities and have similar legal needs and interests.

Once you have gone through this exercise you will have a clear picture of the makeup of your target audience, as well as greater clarity about the direction of your business. A critical element of effective marketing is knowing to whom you are communicating. You can then turn your attention to what to write, and where you should appear in print.

What to Write

You have decided to write a bylined article and are ready to put pen to paper, but you need a topic. An obvious and efficient choice is to write about subjects that you know and that strongly interest you. Your own work product is a good source of ideas and is always an excellent starting point. If you have done an internal research memo or produced material for a seminar or speech, it probably can be turned into an article with relatively little effort. The leveraging of your existing work product is the most efficient use of marketing time. Also, once that work product has been turned into an article, it can be rewritten and updated for future use. Previous articles can be used to create a series or to form the basis for new articles tracing trends and examining patterns in developing areas.

Probably the most fertile and relevant ground for ideas can be found with your clients. Who better to ask what issues are important to them? If a client has asked you a particular question, or if there has been an unusual issue raised in a transaction, there is a good chance that a discussion of the issue will interest other people in similar circumstances.

One lawyer I know keeps an "idea" folder. When she has an idea for an article, she makes a few notes and puts them in a file. Then, when she finds additional pieces of relevant information from various sources, she adds them to her file. By the time she starts writing, she has accumulated the majority of her research and is able to eliminate the often painful and time-consuming process of preplanning and research. What began as a conscious effort for this lawyer is now an unconscious act—a habit. She benefits by being prepared when an opportunity arises and often finds herself with enough material for several articles.

Once you have selected a topic, take care to ensure that your writing is framed in terms of benefits to the audience. Though people perceive benefits in different ways, your research should have focused your writing to a selected group with identifiable common characteristics. There will always be issues that are client-specific, but by categorizing your clients you can address at least some common concerns.

The process of analyzing your client base, targeting a market segment, and focusing your efforts is demanding and time-consuming. It is easy to see why many lawyers opt to forego this exercise. Yet the process results in a strategic assessment, without which your marketing endeavor will probably be of little value.

How to Write—Your Style

Legal writing should be clear, concise, persuasive, and precise. But, in reality, much of it is strangled by use of the "legalese" that bombards lawyers throughout law school. To avoid confusing or alienating your reader, you should strive to simplify your writing and avoid using the obscure language and weighty sentences so typical of the profession.

The majority of lawyers' writing is intended to persuade. To be persuaded and convinced, the reader must understand your point of view. To be convincing, you need to organize and present issues in a logical fashion. The organization does not necessarily need to mirror a chronological sequence of events, but should run with a logical flow of ideas.

The constructive and informed use of metaphors or anecdotes from your clients' industries can be powerful tools of persuasion if applied sensitively. Clients generally warm to the "familiar"; it increases their comfort and thus assists them to "own" the ideas you try to sell. Clients may even take your ideas further and discover additional applications that, in turn, become business opportunities for you. Good legal writing is an art that needs to be cultivated, and because words are our primary method of communication, the development of that art is critical.

Where to Publish

USING RESEARCH TO CHOOSE PUBLICATIONS

Now that you have decided what to write, where will you look to get your work published? With the proliferation of newspapers, newsletters, trade journals, and electronic media, there is an almost inexhaustible supply of sources from which to choose. For those who already know the publications that are specific to their clients' interests, the selection of a publication may be an easy task. For others, it will involve research.

Here again, your clients can help. One of the most cost effective and foolproof research methods is simply to telephone your clients and ask which publications they regard as necessary reading for their industries. This is a straightforward request that has the added benefit of demonstrating to clients that you are interested in their businesses and value their input, and that they are important to you.

If you are just beginning to build a client base or targeting a new market, it is essential that you do the preliminary research. Do not rely on your instincts or another person's opinion, or select a publication because another lawyer has done so. Though your intuition or a third-party recommendation may be cause to consider a publication, only your research will determine if it is worth expending your effort on an article. It is not unusual for lawyers to begin writing without specific outlets for their products in mind. Generally speaking, this is not a good idea. By targeting a specific publication you have the advantage of reviewing previous editions and requesting a media kit, which will provide you with the publication's circulation numbers, demographics, advertising rates, and additional relevant information.

Reviewing previous issues of a publication allows you to see the style, format, and typical length of the articles. Also, don't overlook an evaluation of the quality of advertisers in a particular journal. Would the audience you are attempting to reach be consumers of the goods and services being offered in this publication? Are the advertisers leaders in their fields? Remember, no organization will allocate its advertising dollars to a publication that does not get results. And, finally, is this a publication with which you want your name associated? In sum, reviewing these materials will greatly assist you in determining the likely effectiveness of a particular outlet for reaching your targeted audience.

Moreover, the more you learn about a particular publication, the greater your chances of getting published. You would not want to devote your valuable marketing time to a written piece only to discover that you selected a publication that does not accept submissions from outside sources, or that has just published a similar story.

If an analysis of your client base reveals that most of your clients come through referrals from other lawyers, then the obvious objective is to set your sights on legal publications. Most lawyers, both in-house and in private practice, read legal trade publications as a means of keeping current with industry news. Your local bar association journal, as well as local, regional, and national newspapers, can be good starting places. Your goal should be to connect your name with an area of practice. Appearing in the legal trade publications helps establish you as an expert in the eyes of your peers.

For those whose search requires a broader scope, there are media directories that provide excellent references. They can be great time-savers, as they collect information from a wide variety of sources and produce it in a concise and easy-to-reference manner. They typically provide information on publications, trade shows, conventions, and mailing lists, as well as editorial profiles—all the information you need to help you target appropriate publications.

Nathan's Legal Markets is one such source, and because it is dedicated to the legal profession, it is a popular reference source for the legal community. The annual directory is available in hard copy and on CD-ROM.

Perhaps one of the most well-known and comprehensive media guides is *Bacon's Directories. Bacon's* is not limited to the legal industry but carries information on over 20,000 daily and weekly newspapers and business, trade, professional, and consumer publications in the United States and Canada. *Bacon's* also comes in CD-ROM form.

The ultimate goal should always be to get your name before the potential buyers of your services. Effective marketing with the written word begins with research that will ensure the placement of your writings in publications that will maximize your exposure to the appropriate audience. Because you have already done your analysis of your client base and chosen a publication, you have a good picture of the makeup of your audience, including its industries, interests, and needs. You understand the critical issues that face your targeted audience. This understanding allows you to focus your communication and market to the audience on the basis of its needs, not on the basis of your interests alone.

CONVINCING THE EDITOR TO ACCEPT YOUR ARTICLE

Once you are satisfied that a particular publication is appropriate for you to pursue, you need to persuade the editor that your article is worthy of publication. Write a letter and in a concise manner, introduce yourself and outline your proposed article. Make sure you provide sufficient information about your background and expertise, as well as the benefits the readers will gain from your article, so the editor can make an informed decision. Be mindful that editors are very busy people—keep the communication as short as possible and to the point. You should also follow up the letter with a quick phone call. You run the risk of reaching a harried editor scrambling to make a deadline, but you also may get the opportunity to "close the sale."

One comment about paying for placement of an article: *don't.* It is not necessary, and you certainly will not get good value for the expenditure. There are many reputable outlets for your work that are always appreciative of fresh ideas and well-written articles. This is particularly true for professional and industrial trade journals, which depend heavily on outside sources for editorial content.

Even if your article is turned down by your first-choice publication, don't assume the article will not be attractive to someone else. Perhaps you simply did not fit within the editorial calendar!

On a final note: remember your manners. Write a thank-you note to the editor after the article is published. It is yet another opportunity to put your name in front of the editor, and because it is far from standard practice, it also serves as another means of differentiation.

Leverage

Every time you complete a marketing exercise, you should look for ways to maximize the effort. An article that has been published has by no means outlived its usefulness. You spent effort in producing the initial publication—now capitalize on that effort by looking for additional audiences. How else can the article be used? The first consideration should be whether the same article could be offered, in whole or in part, to other publications. (A note of caution: Policies regarding the assignment of copyright vary among publications. Make sure you have a clear understanding of who retains the copyright.)

Reprints of articles will usually be supplied by, or can be purchased from, the publisher. If not, with the publisher's permission, you can have them produced at a local print shop or in house with a desktop publishing program. Reprints can be used in a variety of ways and generally have a long shelf life. They are a wonderful means of increasing exposure for little additional expense, other than postage and copying. In the first instance they should be sent to your clients with short notes. They should also be circulated throughout your firm with a request to your colleagues to distribute the article to their clients. The article can be mentioned in your newsletter, with an offer to send a reprint to interested readers. Articles can also be reproduced on your Web site, or you can link to the article on the publisher's Web site. This can make the shelf life continue for many years. Reprints should also be added to your portfolio as you progress through your career. They are very useful as introductions when a prospect has shown interest in your services, and should form part of your standard information package.

Reprints are excellent sources of writing samples. Being published in a reputable journal buys a level of credibility that can prove useful in "selling" yourself to another editor; your collection of prior articles can do the selling for you. They are an instant demonstration of your credibility and expertise.

Electronic media is a developing area—one that deserves its own chapter and is addressed more extensively elsewhere in this book. Do not neglect it as a potential outlet for your work.

Letters

Follow Up and Follow Through

Letters, both personal and business, can be one of the most efficient and cost-effective marketing tools, yet their impact is often overlooked. For example, a letter should be your final function after a presentation. If you have given a speech or been a presenter at a conference or seminar, don't think your job is done after the lights are turned off and everyone goes home. You need to follow up and follow through if you want to generate the most benefit from your efforts. If you used printed materials or overhead graphics for your presentation, offer to send copies to audience members who leave their business cards. This gives you yet another chance to get your name in front of them, and it will reinforce your message. It is particularly important to follow through when you make an offer to supply information. Otherwise, you greatly diminish any benefit you may have gained from your presentation.

Business and Personal Letters

Letters are particularly beneficial as supplements to more formal client communications, such as newsletters. If you take the time to know your clients and their businesses, you can capitalize on opportunities to demonstrate your interest and strengthen client relationships. When you see an article that a particular client may find interesting, take the time to write a short letter, or simply clip your business card and send it along with an "I thought you would find this of interest" note. Such communications keep your name in front of clients and demonstrate that they are important to you.

You should make it a habit to review your local and regional newspapers for news regarding your clients and be prepared to follow up with a note. Regardless of whether the note is sent in relation to a business matter or a personal matter (such as a congratulatory note for receiving a community or business award), it has the potential for generating numerous benefits. At the very least, a personal note sends a message that you care. It creates ongoing communication with the client, demonstrates your interest in—and knowledge of—the client's business, invites questions, and ultimately leads to better client relationships.

All lawyers should keep a supply of good-quality note cards in their desks, and develop the habit of handwriting brief personal notes.

Letters to the Editor and Op-Ed Pieces

Too busy to write an article? Then consider a letter to the editor—a simple, efficient, and effective variation of the personal letter. There is no doubt that you probably read several trade and business journals and have strong opinions or questions about many of the issues discussed. A well-considered letter that persuasively sets forth a different opinion or adds substance to a particular topic will generally find placement.

Similarly, an opinion piece that is placed opposite or near the publication's editorial page (hence, "op-ed") can provide good exposure. On the plus side, these pieces are typically short and therefore can be written quickly. However, they are generally about current issues, which makes them time-sensitive, and are highly sought-after opportunities. You will have a much better chance of getting an op-ed piece placed in a local or regional publication than in a national publication, where intense competition for placement leaves editors with the luxury of publishing mostly by invitation only.

The same rules of research discussed in connection with bylined articles apply to op-ed pieces. Study previous pieces to discover their common elements, and then structure your piece accordingly. The best op-ed writings cover a substantive issue in a timely fashion and provocative manner, and then provide possible solutions.

Firm Brochure and Collateral Materials

The Importance of Image

We work in a world of increasing choices in products and services. How you present yourself to the outside world is an important element of a marketing strategy. The objective of all printed materials should be to present the firm, practice group, or lawyer as possessing a coherent overall strategy and mission. The way to convey and reinforce that image is through the consistent application of guidelines that govern the design and presentation of everything that identifies the lawyer or firm—from letterheads and business cards to newsletters and brochures. Therefore, it is particularly important that every printed communication that goes out the door carries the same "signature." This is usually accomplished through the consistent use of an effective graphic layout. Once a strong identity is created and methodically applied, it should build and maintain a clear association in the minds of clients.

The objective is to develop an image that you will be comfortable presenting to the rest of the world for a very long time. Creating such a singular signature is a task that requires a great deal of soul searching, time, and yes, money. Yet it is an essential exercise that should be approached with diligence. At its most basic level, the intangible nature of services makes the creation difficult. The greatest chance for achieving the objective is through the advice and talents of a professional.

Image can be a particularly problematic matter for law firms for a variety of reasons. The individualism so fiercely protected by lawyers can make it very difficult to reach a consensus on how the firm should be portrayed to the outside world. Also, the organizational structure itself can hamper the ability to promote the firm as an entity. Yet, the benefit of a coherent signature is clear—it reinforces both the breadth and continuity of the firm.

Whether you are a single practitioner or part of a firm, care in the repetitive application of the signature is necessary to maximize its effectiveness. The real value of a signature depends on the extent to which the public recognizes it and identifies it with its owner. Making a success of your image is all about refusing to become complacent, and giving consistent attention to details.

Brochures and Practice Group Pieces

It is an accepted practice for law firms to produce printed brochures describing the firm's practice. Most law firms have concluded they need brochures because other firms have them and clients expect it. The first generation of brochures were mostly dry recitals of the practice, with the text chosen through committee compromise. This resulted in brochures that were too predictable, and too broad and generic to have marketing value. Although a brochure has a definite role to play in the marketing of a firm or practice, it will have relatively little value if it is an unfocused stand-alone piece written in an attempt to reach every audience.

The brochure is the most expensive, visible, and widely distributed communications document used by most firms. To have the most impact, it should flow from a uniform firm signature, created as a result of the firm's image and not in a vacuum. It should be written by a professional who has the talent to translate the firm's philosophy in a manner that celebrates the firm's uniqueness. The task of developing a firm brochure is not simply a writing exercise; it should instead be viewed as a process that will fully articulate the firm's strategy. If well written and produced with care as part of the larger marketing effort, a brochure can capture and convey the culture and vitality of a firm, communicate the benefits the firm brings to clients, and serve as the key tool for presenting an overall picture of the firm's capabilities. Even with the increasingly sophisticated use and importance of digital publications, the printed brochure has not outlived its usefulness.

Individual brochures for practice groups, departments, or industry groups are a good complement to the general firm brochure. They are particularly useful for providing supplemental information about large firms with multiple practice areas. A good practice brochure should have a narrow focus, describing the services and capabilities of the area in detail, stressing competitive advantages, and providing adequate information to assist in the buying decision. The practice brochure can be used in concert with a firm brochure, yet should contain sufficient substance and information about the particular practice area to be used as a stand-alone piece.

Fortunately, law firms have matured in their design and use of brochures. Today you can see any number of brochures that artistically convey distinct images of firms. Many firms are following the practice of other industries and producing pieces along the lines of "annual reports," providing information that answers the question, "Just what exactly does your law firm do?" They are adopting a concept that effectively communicates the firm's strengths, range of services, past successes, current issues and projects, and short- and long-term plans. They understand that the use of vignettes and "mini" case studies has memorable illustrative value.

The objective of the brochure is to convey the message that this is a successful, dynamic, forward-looking, and innovative law firm with which the client or prospect should be working. If you decide to produce an "annual report" to clients, make sure you have the resources and support to commit to the yearly production. Consistency will greatly enhance effectiveness.

Résumés

The last time you gave your résumé serious thought was probably when you were looking for a job. Though this is not uncommon, keep in mind that a résumé is a good self-marketing vehicle that should be approached as a sales tool. The intent is to generate a response from the reader. To be most effective, résumés—like all other written pieces—must be drafted with the audience in mind. Before distributing your résumé, you need to define the purpose for doing so. Is it going to a potential buyer of your services? To an editor of a journal you are targeting for publication? To a conference organizer to promote yourself as a potential speaker?

Before you begin drafting, ask yourself, "What information do I need to include to make myself more attractive for marketing or business development purposes?" If you create your résumé in sections, it can be easily accessed and customized for a particular need. This also allows you to store up-to-date information about your publications, speaking engagements, community involvement, associations, and memberships.

A good résumé is not merely a list of positions and experience. Instead, you should use language that will connect your skills with the readers' needs. What about the inclusion of personal information and photographs? For those who believe you should include only results-oriented elements and professional-accomplishment material, and save the personal information for the cocktail hour, an exception should be made if the information demonstrates a unique skill, attribute, or experience that would be attractive to the audience, especially if the message is not otherwise apparent.

Some general guidelines apply. If the résumé is to be included as part of a proposal, you should highlight like-kind transactions with which you have been involved, as you want the résumé to be a showcase for your professional experience and expertise. If you are marketing to a prospect and the purpose is introductory, you should emphasize previous industry experience and the types of services the target may require. You also need to ask yourself, "What else would a prospective client need to know?" Here is where more personal information may be beneficial. It could be used to describe yourself beyond the terms of your practice.

Providing information about personal achievements and community involvements can be effective. If you have raised a significant amount of money for a charity, or perhaps run an ultra-marathon, consider how including that information could demonstrate your level of perseverance, commitment, ability to focus, and character, all of which could be very attractive to potential clients. You should also consider adding personal information if you are using your résumé to promote yourself as a speaker, or are attempting to sell an editor on a particular story.

Requests for Proposals

In recent years, buyers of legal services have increasingly used Requests for Proposals (RFPs) as a method to evaluate legal services—an intimidating thought to most lawyers. However, technology allows the process to be automated and routinized, while also allowing you to customize for client-specific needs. A checklist of the most frequently asked questions and firm-specific material can be prepared, along with guidelines and procedures to streamline the process.

This is an opportunity to be exploited, so make the most of it. You should view this as a means of differentiating you and your firm.

When you receive an RFP, you should learn as much as you can about the client, the project or issue, and the decision makers in the company. The necessity for this may not seem obvious when the RFP comes from an existing client, but do not assume you already know all there is to know. There are many sources of information available, particularly for public companies. Begin with the company's Web site, if it has one. It will probably provide information about the company's direction, products or services, and activities, all of which will greatly enhance your understanding of the company. Even if the information is unrelated to the particular legal issue, the Web site still can be of enormous value in adding to your overall understanding of the organization, and this will be reflected in your response.

The Internet provides numerous Web sites containing a wealth of information for company research. For specific information on public companies, one of the best places to begin is the U.S. government's EDGAR database. It allows free access to Securities and Exchange Commission filings and can be accessed through the Internet at *www.sec.gov.*

Once you complete the client research and are well informed about the issues, call the client. Review your understanding of the particular issue, clarify any ambiguities, get information about the mechanics and timing of the decision-making process, and identify any areas that may not have been articulated in the RFP. The more information you gather, the greater your ability to respond with clarity.

The written response should mirror the format of the RFP, address every issue, and, most important, be written in a persuasive manner. Incorporate the information you learned in your research to demonstrate your knowledge of the client's business. All clients want to believe you have a genuine interest in their businesses and successes. Clearly outline the benefits that will accrue to the client by virtue of your representation. Also, although a response will always require a certain amount of background information about your firm and its capabilities, this should not be your focus. The client issued the RFP because it has a problem and wants to hear specifically how you plan to address that problem. Though biographies of lawyers and descriptions of firm capabilities are logical components of the response, the focus needs to remain on the client, not the firm. The response should be submitted to the client along with a short cover letter containing a straightforward expression that you want its business. The cover letter is also a good place for succinctly stating the benefits to the client.

You should be able to create a template for your proposals, which allows you to lay out proposed text in a uniform fashion and access portions for other proposals. This will give you control of the process, create uniformity, ensure a better product, help "brand" your image, and generally make your marketing life easier. Good internal organization eliminates the need to reinvent the wheel each time you need an RFP response, and allows you to respond in a timely manner.

Newsletters and Client-Focused Bulletins

Newsletters can add a great deal of value to a practice. They are a proven method of enhancing relations with existing clients, stimulating referrals for new business, building and maintaining name recognition, and providing a vehicle for lawyers to display their talents. However, though it may be easy to persuade lawyers of the importance of a newsletter in the overall marketing strategy, there are many inhibitors to regular production. As with other non-billable activities, the pressures of the practice often frustrate the ability to produce client newsletters in a consistent and timely fashion. Unfortunately, the effectiveness of a newsletter is greatly diminished if it is not produced on a regular basis.

To avoid the problems of production, some firms and lawyers have turned to outsourcing. The marketplace contains many organizations and consultants that provide production services for newsletters. They offer services with varying degrees of participation and control, thereby allowing the firm to structure a program with which it can be comfortable. If you want to take advantage of the benefits of outsourcing, you need to decide what type of service will work best for your practice.

Some organizations maintain staff lawyers to produce articles, which are then mixed with your available copy. At the other end of the spectrum are organizations that provide completely prepackaged pieces. They may simply put the firm's logo on the top and retain complete control of every detail, from inception to mailing. Be aware, however, that with canned newsletters you run the risk of your clients getting the same articles in a newsletter from another lawyer or firm. If you choose to use a canned newsletter, make sure you get an agreement giving you geographic exclusivity, and make sure you are familiar with all the content of the newsletter, as clients may present you with questions at a later date.

A client newsletter need not be limited to substantive topics, but it should be viewed as a service to the clients. It can include photographs and details about the lawyers and administrative personnel. This serves not only to make the newsletter more "personal" and convey a sense of the firm's culture, but also to provide information to clients on areas of responsibility and who to call with questions regarding billing or other administrative issues. Also, many firms have successfully utilized Internet-based client newsletters, at a healthy profit. There is no postage or printing expenditure, greater ease of mailing-list management, and much shorter turnaround time between writing and publication.

One area that is routinely treated as a secondary matter is the firm's mailing list. Although it might be viewed as just another mundane administrative process, it is critical to the success of many marketing efforts. Once you spend your valuable time, effort, and resources on producing a good newsletter, you greatly diminish these efforts and the effectiveness of the piece by having a mailing list that is untargeted, incomplete, or out-of-date. Don't waste your effort. There are too many good, inexpensive software packages on the market that have the ability to manage mailing lists.

For more in-depth information on developing client newsletters, read Milton Zwicker's book—*Successful Client Newsletters: The Complete Guide to Creating Powerful Newsletters* (ABA Section of Law Practice Management, 1998).

Client alerts or bulletins can be an alternative or a supplement to newsletters. Because they are only one-page documents, are best suited to dealing with a very focused issue, and are sent to a targeted audience, they can be produced quickly and efficiently. Minimal production time allows the lawyer to deal with breaking news—which may have a profound impact on a segment of clients—in a timely manner. Newsletters can then be saved for further in-depth coverage of the issues discussed in a client alert or bulletin.

Announcements

Lawyers apparently feel an intense need to send costly announcements about new partners. If you believe they are essential, then at least get a scintilla of value by sending them only to people who may have an interest, and by giving the recipient some additional information that may have some benefit. You can do this by describing the uniqueness of the individual or the service that he or she brings to the firm, especially if it is the addition of a specialty or creation of a new practice area.

Press Releases

Press releases are often considered by lawyers to be the most efficient and effective means of communication with the media. However, they have their limitations and should be used cautiously. To be considered for publication, a press release must contain information that is timely, important, helpful, and concise yet thorough. Lawyers commonly send press releases for the addition of new partners. Let's be honest. For all but the legal trades and family members, very few people care about the rise of an associate to partner, or that the firm changed its name or location. Remember, it's not your perception of what is newsworthy that counts.

Press releases do have a place and can be effective if they deal with subjects that are newsworthy and appealing to a wide audience. For example, a press release could be used as an alert to the community regarding a controversial change in the law that may have an adverse impact on a segment of society, or as an announcement of the firm's involvement in formation of a much-needed new business or industrial development project.

One very important thought—a press release is a discretionary matter. Before you write, ask yourself, "Is this something that would interest anyone else? If yes, then who?" Send it only to a targeted audience. And, don't let your ego get in the way. Take an honest look at whether the dissemination of the information benefits the reader, enhances your reputation, raises your profile, and generally reflects upon you in a positive manner. If it does not meet those criteria, then don't issue the release.

A press release can give you an element of control and be particularly effective in dealing with an event that may receive negative publicity. For example, if your firm has a seemingly sudden departure of a group of lawyers, or if you have a client who lost a particularly controversial case, a press release offers an opportunity to structure the story in a way that lessens negative speculation.

An accepted "rule" is that a press release should never exceed two pages. To grab the reader's attention, the first paragraph should contain the relevant information, and the release must tell a complete story. Write in clear, concise language; stay away from sophisticated legal terms or you will lose your audience. Don't forget to mail copies to your clients.

As with bylined articles, different publications will have different audiences. To maximize the attractiveness of the press release, tailor it to the individual audience. Though a press release may go to a number of sources, it does not need to be identical for each source.

Additional Resources

If you are associated with a law firm, then you may have the good fortune of working with a marketing director, librarian, or knowledge manager. Don't overlook this resource. These professionals can play an invaluable advisory role in your efforts; they have a wealth of experience and expertise that can be tapped for every aspect of your marketing efforts, and they will know how to leverage your efforts. Their suggestions will probably include the use of your own corporate intranet, which can be a gold mine as a market research tool. Firms with strong information-sharing cultures will have one in place. You can gain useful information and, in turn, the marketing know-how you accumulate can be fed back into the intranet for the benefit of other users. This saves time in future research projects you may undertake.

Putting It All Together—One Lawyer's Story

Michael C. Fondo is a tax lawyer in Boston. He clearly understands the business development benefits of the written word, and has used this to his advantage as part of his overall marketing efforts. Mike is also an avid golfer. While reading an issue of *Golf Digest* magazine, he came across a blurb about the Internal Revenue Service (IRS) and its proposed treatment of caddies as employees and not independent contractors. Mike was familiar with the issue of independent contractors, and immediately thought the IRS was wrong. A little research proved not only that the IRS was wrong, but also that it had issued a revenue ruling about thirty years ago that looked at the issue and concluded that caddies were independent contractors. Mike was indignant that the IRS could now take a position against the taxpayer, contrary to its own publicly announced position.

Mike immediately thought of the *Wall Street Journal* (*WSJ*) as an appropriate outlet to express his views. He believed the *WSJ* to be a bastion of truth and a defender of capitalism, and that it generally held a dim view of the IRS; therefore he thought it would be interested in the story. He was also astute enough to recognize that the issue was timely, as it was the beginning of golf season and shortly before the U.S. Open. Though he viewed this as a marketing effort, Mike also had an underlying concern and feeling of empathy for the caddies. It was clear to him that the success of the IRS in this matter would not have been felt by the golf clubs, but by the caddies themselves, the majority of them being teenagers.

Mike began his research by contacting the Western Golf Association to get some background information on caddies in the United States. He then drafted a piece and sent it by e-mail to the *WSJ* editor, asking if this was something the *WSJ* would consider publishing. The *WSJ* jumped on the story, immediately contacting Mike and asking if he could have it ready to run for the next day. He spent some time working with the *WSJ* copy editor, and *IRS Bogey-Man Threatens Caddies,* by Michael C. Fondo, was published on June 3, 1997. All told, Mike's efforts, research, and writing took five hours. As you will see, he made a small investment for a very large return.

On the day the story ran, Mike received about a half-dozen telephone calls from people who shared his concern. One of the calls was from an organization that lobbies on behalf of golf clubs. It had been disturbed by the issue and had already been working with Congress, trying to get the IRS Code amended. The organization was thrilled, as Mike's article focused national attention on the issue and was a huge boost to its effort.

The story was quickly picked up by Bill Littlefield of National Public Radio for his *It's Only a Game* broadcast, for which Mike was interviewed. CNN also interviewed Mike for background information on a story it was running. The print media responded as well. *Sports Illustrated* asked him to write a column, which resulted in a similar request from *Golf Journal.*

However, the most significant contact came from Congressman Dan Burton. Congressman Burton saw the *WSJ* story and as a direct result introduced H.R. 2321, the Caddie Relief Act of 1997, to amend the Internal Revenue Code to provide that nontouring caddies are independent contractors and not employees. In a press release announcing the filing of the bill, Congressperson Burton noted that he became aware of the IRS's efforts to reclassify caddies after reading Mike Fondo's column in the *WSJ.* (The bill has been filed and will probably be attached to a tax bill that is currently working its way through Congress.)

The name recognition and business contacts that Mike received as a result of this effort are immeasurable. The National Association of Touring Caddies, as well as several prominent business people, contacted him. The article has been distributed to the boards of various caddie scholarship funds, all of which are large organizations with very impressive board members. And the benefits keep coming. Mike was recently featured as one of the up-and-coming lawyers in his home state of Massachusetts by *Mass Lawyers Weekly*. He credits the article as being an instrumental factor in his selection. He has also received some very positive feedback from existing clients. A published article goes a long way to legitimize you in the eyes of your clients. This is particularly true with a publication such as the *WSJ*.

What did Mike do right? Just about everything. He recognized an issue of importance, wrote about a subject for which he had a passion, did his research, targeted a publication, knew his audience, leveraged the work, and provided a valuable service to a distinct business sector. What were the benefits he received? He increased his profile both inside and outside the legal community, gained name recognition, significantly added to his business contacts, enhanced his reputation with his peers, and has the satisfaction of knowing that he helped thousands of caddies. A lot of profit for five hours' work—not a bad return on the investment of time.

The success of this effort was not due to luck on Mike's part. Early in his career, Mike recognized that the day would come when he would need to justify his existence by proving he has the ability to produce clients. He has a clear idea of where he wants to be, and recognizes the necessity for business development and the importance that the written word can play in achieving his goals. Writing is just one tool Mike uses as part of his marketing plan.

Conclusion

Building a career in the law used to be a great deal simpler. It didn't matter if you were pursuing a career as a sole practitioner, within a law firm, as in-house counsel, in government, or in academia—the paths to success were well known. If you worked hard and became a good legal technician, you could reasonably expect to prosper and remain in your selected environment for your entire career. It isn't that simple anymore. Today's lawyers face increased competition and are entering a more diverse, complex, and global environment than ever before. There can be no doubt that hard work and legal competence remain critical elements of success, but they constitute only the foundation. To shore up that foundation, you need to develop other talents that will help you find your way to stand out from the pack. The written word is a user-friendly business development tool that can be used by everyone in a bid for differentiation.

CHAPTER 6

Marketing Through the Spoken Word: Conversations and Public Speaking

Robert N. Kohn
Lawrence M. Kohn

The vast majority of your marketing efforts will be dependent upon the spoken word. Though the written word plays an essential part, the spoken word has many distinguishing qualities. First is its interactive nature: Conversations provide opportunities to receive immediate feedback. Prospects can ask questions and express concerns and lawyers can immediately respond. This rapid exchange of information expedites the sales cycle. The spoken word also is multisensory: It allows lawyers to use body language, intonation, volume, rhythm, and energy. These added qualities help give depth, meaning, and motivation to marketing communications.

Marketing through the spoken word comprises two components: Sales dialogue and public speaking.

Sales Dialogue for Lawyers

Most lawyers feel uncomfortable with—and even hostile to—the idea of sales dialogue. There is a strong anti-sales sentiment, which is constantly reinforced by exposure to obnoxious, pushy, and unknowledgeable salespeople. This negative stereotype of selling is prevalent in industries where the consummation of a sale represents the *end* of the interaction. For example, when someone buys a car, the salesperson doesn't handle the ongoing service. By contrast, for most lawyers, closing the sale means *continuing* the relationship. Pushy, abusive sales dialogue cannot work for lawyers, whose clients expect trusting, supportive, and loyal service. This chapter's goal is to prove that sales dialogue can be appropriate and effective. In fact, after exposure to the techniques discussed in this chapter, many lawyers learn to appreciate that sales dialogue is emotionally gratifying, in that it develops friendships and financial security, and intellectually stimulating, in that it requires clear thinking and sophisticated strategies.

The first step in selling is initiating sales dialogue. Most lawyers feel relatively comfortable when explaining their services to prospects who have expressed needs, but much more uneasy when doing so with prospects who have not yet expressed needs. Initiating sales dialogue exposes lawyers to the risk of feeling rejected and embarrassed, and of being perceived as pushy or needy. As a result, many lawyers simply prefer to wait until business comes in the door. But this approach may be too slow. You may have to be more proactive in pursuing new prospects.

There are two groups of prospects you can pursue: people you know, and strangers. Your most immediate marketing opportunities are probably with the people you already know—your clients, friends, family, and business and social acquaintances. You have greater access to these contacts.

Sales Dialogue with Clients

Obviously, your best marketing opportunities are with your existing clients. Satisfied clients can give you more work and they can introduce you to their contacts. However, your clients may not be thinking about these issues, in which case you must initiate the subject.

EXPANDING CLIENT RELATIONSHIPS

You may have clients with needs that could be served by either you or other members of your firm. The key to feeling comfortable in discussing additional services with a client is confirming that a need exists. If in fact there is a need, then initiating the subject is not only appropriate, it's obligatory.

However, if you cannot anticipate client needs, there are two techniques for doing research. (See Chapter 3, *Marketing Intelligence for Intelligent Marketing: Using Research to Get and Keep Clients.*) One is the client survey. A survey can be informal, such as asking for feedback on the work you are doing, or it can be a formal questionnaire. In either case, you could ask the question, "Are there other legal needs where the firm can be of assistance?" Another approach is to provide a detailed list of services so clients can learn what is available.

The other technique for identifying client needs is an annual legal review. The purpose of the review is to help your clients look into the future. Ask them about future plans and other issues about which you may be unaware. As you help clients look into the future, you may identify areas where you can assist them.

LEVERAGING RELATIONSHIPS

Another marketing opportunity clients offer is their ability to introduce you to their contacts. For example, you should consider meeting their accountants, bankers, and other advisors. This is not a problem if you need to meet them in the normal course of your work; if not, it is still appropriate to request an introduction. Another technique for meeting client contacts is to ask clients about the organizations they support, such as trade organizations or charities. Getting involved in these organizations is a way of becoming familiar with issues that affect clients' lives, and it will help you meet their contacts.

As you initiate sales dialogue with clients, be sensitive to the concern of selling when you are practicing law. You don't want to upset clients by selling to them on billable time.

Sales Dialogue with Friends

Another group of potential prospects are friends (and family). However, many lawyers feel uncomfortable discussing the availability of their legal services with friends. One concern is the risk of losing the relationship by either imposing on it or failing to meet expectations. Another problem is not wanting to discuss sensitive personal matters. Though these are valid concerns, it would be unfortunate if you categorically dismissed the opportunity of doing business with friends, as they can be a significant marketing resource. Many lawyers regularly represent and receive referrals from their friends. In fact, some friendships are significantly enhanced by a business relationship. You should analyze each friendship individually, carefully looking at the opportunities and risks. You may discover that doing business with a select group is the most appropriate choice.

Once a friend is identified as a prospect, the next question is how you appropriately raise the subject of providing legal services. Some indirect and direct methods follow.

DESCRIBING DAILY ACTIVITIES

One method is to increase your dialogue about the daily activities in your practice. For example, a common lost opportunity may be your response to the question, "What's new?" Instead of saying, "Not much, what's new with you?," consider talking about an interesting case or legal issue. You might also encourage your friends to discuss their own concerns, and then discuss your work if it is relevant.

You can also transition from social dialogue to business dialogue by identifying issues appearing in current events that also appear in your practice. For example, in talking about a current issue, you could say, "I experienced something like that in my practice." Another technique is to invite your friends to law-related programs they may find interesting. When using any of these techniques, focus on whether the friend would generally be interested in the matter. All these indirect techniques help paint a picture of you as a lawyer, as well as a friend.

"FULL DISCLOSURE" TECHNIQUE

A much more direct approach for initiating the subject of business with friends is a technique called "full disclosure." Full disclosure is the process of introducing a sensitive topic by first fully disclosing your feelings and concerns.

For example, assume you have a close friend who owns a business, and you think you could do a good job as the friend's lawyer. But you are uncomfortable suggesting it, because you worry that it might be perceived as an unwelcome offer. You could say something along the following lines: "I'd like to discuss something that is really important to me. I think it would be of great value to both of us. But before bringing it up, I want you to know that I feel a little uncomfortable mentioning it. I really value our friendship and I don't want you to feel that I'm imposing on it in any way. If you are not comfortable with my suggestion, just let me know and I won't bring it up again. With that in mind, I'd like to express my interest in the possibility of becoming your lawyer." This dialogue allows you to raise a sensitive issue without placing your friend in an awkward position.

Of course, doing business with friends is a personal decision. Friendships are too valuable to be taken lightly. But make sure your concern about doing business with friends does not eliminate the possibility of harvesting this potentially valuable resource. In fact, you may find it helpful to remember the following poem:

Business with Friends

Business with friends offers great dividends.
In addition to cash, it's relaxing.
Dinner out is a night off, as well as a write-off.
That's why business with friends is less taxing.

—Lawrence M. Kohn, 1985

Sales Dialogue with Strangers

Though much business comes from people you already know, you may not know enough people to build your practice. This means you need to initiate dialogue with strangers.

A common opportunity for initiating sales dialogue with strangers is at a social gathering, such as a wedding or cocktail party. You learn that the person you just met is a quality prospect. The question is whether it is appropriate to talk about your practice. And, if so, how do you bring up the subject?

A rule of thumb is to refrain from discussing your practice until someone asks you what you do for a living. Once you have been asked, it is socially appropriate to respond. However, it may be a long time, if ever, before you are asked that question. So, if prospects fail to ask what *you* do, ask what *they* do. Generally, if given an opportunity to describe their own businesses, prospects will return the favor. If they still don't ask what you do, comment on how the issues they describe in their businesses apply to your practice as well.

GOALS WHEN NETWORKING IN A BUSINESS ENVIRONMENT

In the process of marketing, lawyers inevitably find themselves at social functions designed specifically for the purpose of meeting prospects. Although these events—if well targeted—are extremely beneficial, lawyers may find them to be distasteful experiences. It is common to feel insecure in a room filled with strangers. The solution for many is to look for a familiar face, and then visit with that person for the rest of the meeting. Following are some techniques that will minimize the unpleasantness and maximize the effectiveness of "working a room."

One of the reasons lawyers find "working a room" so distasteful is that they often do not have a clear understanding of their goals. They make the mistake of assuming the goal is to be entertaining, providing witty remarks and quick repartee. This myth imposes pressure on lawyers who feel shy. Another mistake is desiring to close the deal in the first meeting. Meeting someone for the first time and convincing that person to hire you on the spot is unrealistic. Potential prospects may not have immediate needs for your services, or they may already have relationships with other lawyers. When lawyers "go for the close" too quickly, they come across as being pushy.

At networking events, focus on the following goals: (1) meeting new prospects, (2) qualifying prospects, (3) maintaining open lines of communication, and (4) creating opportunities for follow-through.

MEETING NEW PROSPECTS

When you go to an event and find yourself in a sea of strangers, follow these tips to navigate the situation. First, arrive early. You will find it much easier to make acquaintances when the room is relatively empty. Meeting people after they have already formed small groups is more difficult. Furthermore, if you arrive late, you may miss valuable marketing opportunities. Next, upon arrival, introduce yourself to the organization's staff persons. They will know many of the organization's members and will gladly introduce you to appropriate contacts.

Another tip for meeting new prospects is to go with a friend, which can ease the pressure of being alone in a room full of strangers. You can work as a team to meet people, but avoid the temptation of sticking together. If the function involves a meal, do not sit at the same table. Your goal is to meet others, not socialize with your teammate. (With this concept in mind, it is fascinating that some law firms reserve whole tables at networking events and stick together the entire time!)

One of the difficulties lawyers have with working a room, especially those who are new to networking, is the fear of introducing themselves to complete strangers. One technique for overcoming this obstacle is to realize that many people at the networking activities share the same fear, and that you do them a favor by taking the initiative to introduce yourself.

Begin by establishing eye contact. This helps you determine whether someone is approachable. The easiest technique for breaking the ice is simply to ask,

"Hello, may I introduce myself?" You can then talk about the organization sponsoring the event. For example, you could say, "I'm new to this group. Are you active in this organization?" Your goal at this early stage is merely to establish enough rapport to begin qualifying the person as a potential prospect.

QUALIFYING PROSPECTS

After establishing some rapport, your next objective is to determine whether the person is a *qualified* prospect. This requires asking in-depth questions. Instead of engaging in small talk, ask questions that invite answers that help you in the selling process. Some samples follow:

- "What do you do for a living?" This is one of the first questions to ask, as it helps you determine whether the person fits your client demographic.
- "Who are the kinds of people you do business with?" This helps you discover whether the person is a potential referral source.
- "What obstacles does your industry face?" and "How are you planning to deal with those obstacles?" These questions reveal something about the person's needs.
- "What trade organizations are you involved with?" This helps you explore other marketing opportunities.

The answers to these questions help you determine whether a prospect is worthy of your marketing attention. If so, then your next goal is to make sure you have the ability to maintain an open line of communication.

MAINTAINING OPEN LINES OF COMMUNICATION

One technique is to communicate that you have some things in common, such as interests, values, or contacts. These similarities are called "connectables," because they create connections between you and your prospects. The technique for verbalizing connectables is to listen for similarities and then point them out. For example, try to identify common interests, such as hobbies or organizations, or similar values, such as the importance of family and charity. Look for common experiences in your past, such as having gone to the same school or lived in the same city. Identifying connectables will increase the feeling of safety in working with you, create a bond between you and your prospect, build trust, and create opportunities for doing things together.

Another technique for maintaining open lines of communication is to respond effectively to the question, "What you do for a living?" Keep in mind that when someone asks this question, he or she is really asking, "How can you help me?" Instead of simply answering, "I'm a lawyer. What do you do?," structure the answer to respond to the underlying value you offer. For example, a tax lawyer ultimately will help a client save tax dollars. Therefore, the answer to the question should be, "I help people save tax dollars—I'm a tax lawyer." The goal is to keep the door open by quickly communicating that there is a *reason* to build the relationship. However, keeping in mind that telling prospects what you do for a living is not nearly as important as learning whether you can help *them,* you should quickly shift the focus back to them after explaining what you do. As you learn about their needs, you will be in a better position to describe how your services can help them.

CREATING OPPORTUNITIES FOR FOLLOW-THROUGH

Always request the prospect's business card. Often, instead of asking for a card, lawyers say, "Here is my card. Give me a call." The problem with this approach is that the prospect may lose your card or forget to call you. If *you* get the *prospect's* card, then you are in control of the ability to further the relationship. Also, even when lawyers ask for a business card, they often intend to follow up but never do. To insure follow-through, you should—as you engage in conversations—make a commitment to implement some future activity. This technique is called "marketing at the moment." For example, making a commitment to mail something or to call and schedule a future meeting forces you to take action and further the relationship. Write your commitment on the prospect's business card so you will remember it later. Add the information to your database or contacts-management program. Then, when you do follow through, it will demonstrate to your prospect that you are someone who honors commitments.

After you leave an event, take a moment to review the cards you collected. On each card, write whatever you can remember about each good contact and make sure that person gets added to your mailing list. Remember, your goal is to build relationships. If you fail to put a prospect on your mailing list for follow-up, you have rendered the effort of meeting people virtually meaningless.

ENDING THE CONVERSATION WITH A NONQUALIFIED PROSPECT

One of the challenges at networking events is not knowing how to extricate yourself tactfully from a conversation with a nonqualified prospect. One universal signal that brings closure to a conversation is the question, "May I have your card?" Another technique is to spot someone else in the room you want to meet and say, "I hope you don't mind, but I see someone over there I'd like to visit." Always comment that you enjoyed meeting the person before you leave—*never burn bridges.*

Sales Dialogue with Qualified Prospects

As you follow through with qualified prospects, it is important to understand that prospects use varying criteria in deciding who they should hire. Some have only a few requirements, such as adequate skills and affordable fees. Others have more elaborate criteria, such as graduation from a particular school or connection to a certain social group. Before attempting to close the sale, you should make certain you understand your prospect's criteria. This requires active listening. You then need to communicate that you can satisfy those criteria (that is, reveal your worth), discuss fees, and accelerate the "close." Finally, you can use voice mail as an effective tool in furthering your relationships with your prospect. A discussion of these steps follows.

ACTIVE LISTENING

Active listening means focusing on the statements of your prospects and encouraging their continued communication. Asking meaningful and insightful questions can help stimulate conversation. Obviously, you should ask questions concerning legal needs. In addition, however, you should ask prospects about any past experiences with lawyers, their expectations in working with you, and, if possible, their interests and personal background. The more you know about your prospects, the easier it will be to satisfy their criteria.

Make sure you maintain consistent eye contact. Wandering eyes communicate boredom and disrespect. If you are uncomfortable with maintaining eye contact, try looking at the speaker's mouth or the bridge of his or her nose. You can also provide supportive sounds and gestures such as, "Uh huh," or "Hmm," as you nod your head and smile, and use supportive words such as, "That's interesting," or "I hear what you're saying." It is no secret that people enjoy talking about themselves, and will do it freely if you show genuine interest in what they are saying.

Finally, confirm your understanding of what the person has said. Ask questions such as, "Are we on target regarding your needs?," and wait for a response. Don't assume you understand the situation until the prospect acknowledges that you do.

REVEALING WORTH

Once you understand your prospect's criteria, the next step is revealing that you possess the qualities that satisfy those criteria. These usually include expertise, quality of service, and personality.

EXPERTISE

Most prospects want to be convinced you have the expertise to handle their matters, so you must be able to discuss your knowledge, skills, and experience. Though you could simply give prospects brochures or biographies, don't be surprised if they never read them. And because many prospects will not know how to interview you, they may not ask necessary and specific questions. To communicate your expertise during conversations with prospects, make sure you weave in facts about your background and credentials, such as the law school you attended, awards or honors you may have received, articles you've written, and speeches you've given. Describe bar association committees on which you have participated, and other important legal organizations in which you are involved. When you are discussing a particular problem, cite cases that support your position and explain your track record with similar situations. And, if possible, provide the names of satisfied clients.

QUALITY OF SERVICE

Sales dialogue about the quality of your service involves information about your responsiveness, fees, procedures, partners, support staff, and other valuable resources. Most lawyers say they offer good service. But claiming to offer good service has little impact on prospects, because every lawyer claims the same thing. Merely *saying* you offer good service has no meaning unless you can *support* it. One way is to mention specific details about your practice such as, "I carry a beeper," or "We always return phone calls by 5:00," or "We offer to take calls at home," or "We are acquainted with contacts who would be valuable for you to meet." (Of course, you need to be careful about name dropping; mention only those people who will unquestionably take your call.)

PERSONALITY

Another important goal in sales dialogue is differentiating yourself from the competition. Legal expertise and quality of service alone are often not enough to position you as unique. In fact, many prospects are not sufficiently knowledgeable in legal issues to even appreciate expertise or service. One of the most important qualities that will distinguish you from the competition is your personality. The following list identifies several personality traits; take a moment to consider which traits will be important for you to reveal to your prospects.

Aggressive
Conscientious
Courageous
Creative
Empathic
Energetic
Enthusiastic
Ethical
Honest
Intelligent
Loyal
Patient
Persistent
Reasonable
Responsible
Self-confident
Supportive
Trustworthy

Although these personality traits are some of the most important criteria prospects rely upon in hiring lawyers, they can also be the most difficult qualities to reveal. For example, let's say you are proud of your creativity. Saying that you are creative may seem like bragging. And also, as with describing the quality of your practice, simply stating it has little meaning unless you can support it. The solution to revealing positive personality traits effectively is finding indirect methods of communicating that you possess them.

EXAMPLES AND WAR STORIES

One way of indirectly revealing personality traits is by giving examples or telling stories in which these qualities were operative. Some call these "war stories," because they often are depicted in environments of conflict. For example, if you wanted to indirectly reveal your creativity, you could tell a story about a personal experience in which you faced a significant obstacle, but then came up with a creative solution. Or, let's say you wanted to show that you are reasonable. You could give an example of a transaction in which you were able to balance the business needs of the client with your legal concerns and still close the deal. Using the above list, or other traits you would like to reveal, think of examples or war stories in which those characteristics were operative. This will give you the ability to plan your dialogue in advance, so that you will be more likely to incorporate these stories in your sales dialogue.

HOW TO AVOID REVEALING NEGATIVE QUALITIES

If you don't make an effort to reveal specific personality traits, the risk is great that your prospects will not perceive or appreciate those qualities. If you are not clear about your personal qualities, an even greater risk is that you may inadvertently reveal qualities that make you *undesirable.*

Lawyers regularly speak in ways that do not accurately reflect their true personalities. We recently coached a lawyer who consistently decorated his dialogue with phrases like, "Sort of . . . ," "Kind of . . . ," "I'm not sure but . . . ," and "I'm afraid that . . . ." Interestingly enough, he thought of himself as being decisive and self-assured. Yet his dialogue made him appear apologetic and insecure.

Some other common mistakes to avoid:

- Don't deliver too much technical information in a social conversation. An overabundance of it will be boring and position you as an intellectual elitist.
- Eliminate off-color jokes and cultural slurs. Though this should be obvious, people regularly make these mistakes. Be aware of bad habits that may be acceptable in your social dialogue, but disastrous with prospects. Even minor infractions of this rule can be incredibly insulting.
- Be careful not to show disrespect for clients. Lawyers sometimes forget that their clients are not supposed to know legal issues, and they make light of the clients' lack of knowledge. This hurts you in your sales dialogue because your prospects logically assume you feel the same way toward them.

There are, of course, many more negative qualities that you should be careful to avoid. Maintain constant vigilance to reveal characteristics that position you positively.

TALKING ABOUT MONEY

Once you are satisfied that you understand your prospect's criteria and adequately communicated your worth, you need to discuss your fees. It is important not to be defensive about any aspect of your terms. A lack of confidence in discussing your fees could easily be misinterpreted as a lack of confidence in your legal skills.

OBSTACLES TO TALKING ABOUT MONEY

One reason many lawyers are not confident in discussing their fees is that they are defensive about the subject of money. It is interesting that lawyers can be so effective in discussing the financial needs of their clients, but when it comes to talking about money for themselves, they feel uncomfortable. This attitude may stem from prevalent beliefs that money is tainted. After all, a well-known proverb holds that "the love of money is the root of all evil." Negative attitudes about money may also stem from fear of being greedy, lack of confidence in self-worth, and lack of familiarity with the competition. Some ideas for alleviating this anxiety follow.

REMEMBER THAT LAW IS A BUSINESS

Talking about money requires that you look at law as a business. You should have a clear understanding of all the costs of doing business, including depreciation, write-offs, and marketing. Similarly, you should be aware of what the competition is charging. Thinking of your practice as a business will help you quote fees with confidence.

FOCUS ON BENEFITS IN COMPARISON WITH FEES

Another technique is to remain mindful of all the benefits you bring to your prospects. Most lawyers underestimate their value, especially those who feel they are not living up to their own standards. Regardless of their talent, some lawyers minimize their worth by judging themselves too harshly.

When you quote your rates, always do so in relation to benefits. The first type of benefit is your ability to help your prospects make more money. Virtually every transaction makes money by either increasing the client's profits or minimizing liabilities. In quoting fees, you should explain to your prospect the financial impact of your service. It is easier to quote fees when they are smaller than the benefits. Also, remember all the other ways you bring value to your prospects, such as your ability to reduce their anxiety and introduce them to other contacts. Though these qualities may be difficult to appraise, an awareness of them makes it easier for you to quote—and for your prospects to appreciate—your fees.

ACCELERATING THE CLOSE

The goal in sales dialogue is to receive and reveal enough information that prospects will ask to get started. If they don't ask, and you believe you've invested enough time in the process, it is time to accelerate the close.

For certain prospects, such as large institutions who are accustomed to using many lawyers, an effective approach is to ask, "What are the procedures for becoming an approved provider?" Usually, a large institution will have written procedures for becoming part of its approved-provider list. For prospects without written procedures, the best way of accelerating the close is simply to start solving the prospect's problems and begin doing the work. For example, you might offer to do some research or make a phone call on the prospect's behalf. By starting, you "assume the close," and hopefully the prospect will consider the relationship established.

If you can't just get started, the second best technique for accelerating the close is to be forthright and state, "I'd like very much to represent you. Are you ready to proceed?" If the prospect is not ready, then you need to discover and address the prospect's objections.

OVERCOMING OBJECTIONS

When prospects express objections, it is important not to respond negatively or defensively. You want to avoid confrontation or weakness with prospects. Negative communication about one small point could cloud the entire sales process. Instead, try using a technique called "agree and clarify." This technique requires that you find some aspect of the objection with which you can agree. For example, if a prospect objects to your fees, you can agree that it is important to be cost-conscious. Then, you can clarify your position by explaining the value you offer.

Don't be surprised if it takes a long time to win a client. Many lawyers give up too easily when prospects are slow to hire them. Keep in mind that in sales, a "No" means "No, not now." Just because you are unable to close prospects today does not necessarily mean they are no longer prospects. The key in sales dialogue is follow-through. The goal is to maintain a positive presence in the lives of your prospects until they ultimately have the need for your services. As stated before, never burn bridges. Circumstances can change dramatically. There are many amazing stories of nonprospects who convert to clients!

USING VOICE MAIL

In furthering relationships, you will inevitably swap voice mail messages with prospects. It's often difficult to reach people during the day, and voice mail is an effective communication tool. Without it, busy schedules could result in weeks of missing calls. Although some lawyers see voice mail as a barrier to the sales process, others see it as an advantage. Using voice mail is superior to leaving messages with a secretary or receptionist; humans are rushed, and they make mistakes. And others cannot deliver your message with the same power and authority that can be communicated through your voice. Following are some techniques for using voice mail to further relationships.

USE HELPFUL OUTGOING MESSAGES

First, make it easy for prospects to leave messages. Make your outgoing message brief, and leave good instructions for getting the caller's name and phone number. Also, if you have a voice mail system that allows callers to press the "pound" key at any time to leave a message, make sure you say so at the *beginning* of your outgoing message. Prospects may become very annoyed if they must listen to lengthy messages before learning they could press the pound key to stop your message and begin recording.

LEAVE VOICE MAIL MESSAGES THAT INVITE A RESPONSE

Lawyers regularly complain that their messages to prospects are not returned. To encourage a return call, you must leave a message that invites a response. For example, if you have something of value to communicate, leave a message that says, "Please call me when you get a chance. I have something that I believe will be helpful to you." If you want to have lunch, leave a message suggesting it, and offer some potential dates. Then ask the person to get back to you as soon as possible, either selecting one of the dates you offered or suggesting alternatives. This approach allows you to schedule a meeting without having live contact. Or, you may want to schedule a telephone appointment instead of a face-to-face meeting. If so, leave a message saying that you are going to call on a certain date and time, and if that is not convenient, to please call with some alternatives. You can also use voice mail to invite people to events, asking them to respond by a certain date.

If you want to use voice mail to communicate with the press, you can call editors and reporters and pitch your ideas for articles or offer your expertise as a quotable source right on their voice mail systems. Many editors and reporters respond promptly.

Also, to encourage responses, you may find it helpful to use voice mail and e-mail together. For example, you could leave a brief voice mail message, and follow it with a more detailed e-mail message on the same subject.

Conclusion

As you understand and experiment with the foregoing sales dialogue techniques, you—like every other rainmaker—will learn that selling is not only appropriate (within ethical constraints), but also sophisticated, exciting, and fun. One limitation to sales dialogue is that it is usually restricted to small numbers of prospects at any given time. If you want to communicate with larger numbers, you should consider public speaking as a marketing technique.

Public Speaking as a Marketing Technique

Of all the marketing techniques available to lawyers, public speaking stands out as one of the most effective. Well-targeted public speaking provides exposure to large numbers of quality prospects and referral sources. Members of the audience, by virtue of attendance, have demonstrated an interest in the topic and are more likely to perceive the need for the speaker's services. Even speaking to groups of lawyers can be an excellent marketing opportunity, due to specialty areas or conflicts of interest. Another benefit of public speaking comes with the effort of *preparing* the speech. The research, organization, and scripting for a speech helps you clarify your thinking about a topic and thus creates not only the speech, but also valuable dialogue. Also, once implemented, a quality speech will increase your self-esteem and self-confidence. It will position you as a leader in your field and enhance your résumé.

Most lawyers think that the best way to use public speaking as a marketing technique is to educate the audience. This is based on the belief that if the audience finds the information helpful, they will, in turn, be more inclined to hire the lawyer. However, though education is an important motivational element of your speech, it is not enough. As with sales dialogue, you want to communicate to prospects that you are the right person to help them with their needs. You want to reveal *all* the qualities that will help the audience feel connected to you. And finally, you want to create opportunities for follow-through.

But, unlike sales dialogue, speeches are primarily monologues and so present additional challenges. Greater distance between you and the audience makes it more difficult to keep the audience's attention. Subtle expressions and gestures will not be noticed. There is less opportunity for eye contact. There is less opportunity to ask and respond to specific questions. There is uninterrupted speaking for a prolonged period of time. You have to be more general so you can appeal to a more diverse audience. Because of these differences, speeches require some additional selling techniques.

Meet the Audience

Before the program begins, try to meet members of the audience. Introduce yourself as the speaker and ask if they have any specific issues they would like you to address during your presentation. This allows you to personalize your presentation, which in turn will help you gain and keep the audience's attention.

Prepare Your Introduction for the Host

Often, the host's introduction of the speaker does not stimulate the audience, especially if the host simply recites material from the speaker's biography. Ideally, the host should prepare the audience in a way that generates optimism and enthusiasm about the upcoming presentation. You can help in this effort by preparing your introduction for the host. Consider the following example:

> I'm pleased to introduce someone who is a close friend of our organization. Many of us already know him as a great asset to us. Here are a few of his achievements [from biography]. His topic today will help

us in our ability to earn a living. Please join me in giving a warm welcome to [speaker].

Additionally, you can ask the host to share a personal experience: "I have personally worked with [speaker], and found him to be very helpful."

Prepare Your Speech

The more effort you put into the preparation and delivery of your speech, the greater the return. And although it's true that preparation is time-consuming, keep in mind that acquiring one good client as a result of your speech could more than compensate you for your efforts.

THE OPEN

An important part of a speech is making a good first impression. Because you don't have a lot of time to make your first impression, everything you do and say in the first moments of your speech should position you as someone worthy of the audience's attention.

To help communicate self-confidence, be sure to have good posture, try to establish eye contact with as many people as you can, and smile. Remember the following phrase as you walk up to the lectern: "Tall, focused, and happy."

A common dilemma is not knowing whether to open with a joke. Because this can be very risky, you should not do it unless you are extremely skilled in telling jokes. Jokes are often insulting or not funny. In either of these cases, it takes a lot of time to recover, if you ever can. Similarly, you should be especially cautious about using self-deprecating humor. Although this may seem like a good way to entertain the audience, it usually positions the speaker as being weak or deficient in some area. We recently coached a lawyer who wanted to prove to his audience that he was an exceptional negotiator. Unfortunately, he decorated his speech with self-deprecating stories and examples that inadvertently positioned him as being a poor negotiator. Though his comments made the audience laugh, his failure to communicate his worth was anything but funny.

An alternative method for starting a speech is to tell a story that has the same main point as your speech. A story makes the issue more interesting and memorable. It creates drama, and gives the speech direction. The story could be about the history of your topic, or about why you became interested. Personal stories are the easiest to tell, and audiences often relate well to them.

Another effective technique for opening a speech is to state your goals and objectives clearly. This helps the audience members pay attention, because they know how they will benefit from your speech.

CONTENT

In our role as coaches in public-speaking skills, we have observed that some trainers focus primarily on delivery skills rather than content. Though delivery skills are important, we have found that superior content produces superior delivery. When you are confident that your speech contains valuable and easy-to-understand material, you will naturally be more expressive in your delivery. A simple technique to insure that your speech is informative and understandable is to provide lots of tips. Audiences regularly comment on how much they appreciate tips. In fact, we often hear comments such as, "If I can leave a program with one new tip, I'm satisfied the program was worthwhile." With this in mind, here is our tip: Offer a dozen.

SOUND BITES

A technique for making points that are both understandable and memorable is using "sound bites." A sound bite is a small number of words revealing a great deal of meaning. An example in the advertising industry is the famous question, "Where's the beef?" This sound bite captures the concept of a competitor's inferiority, making it understandable and memorable. The strategy of using sound bites is appropriately and easily applied to legal issues.

NOTES AND MEMORIZATION

It is perfectly appropriate to use notes when you speak. Your audience will be pleased with useful information and not concerned that you did not memorize it. However, the risk in using notes is that you will refer to them too frequently and lose contact with the audience. Consider these tips for using notes:

- Try using notes as a reminder, not a script.
- Use a large font size, such as 20 points or more. A large font will help you see your notes, and still allow you to maintain contact with the audience.
- Use colored markers to identify important points.
- Write your notes in narrow columns, similar to a newspaper or magazine. By stacking the words in narrow columns, you can see the entire thought at a glance more easily than reading across a full page.

Memorizing material also has its benefits. If you are not dependent on notes, you will find it easier to be animated and to focus on the audience. One technique is to memorize both the introductory and last sentences of each main point. This approach is similar to the structure of a joke. The opening line and punch line are delivered as written, while the rest of the content can be less structured. It is not necessary to remember the entire text word-for-word, as long as you communicate the main ideas. Memorizing the closing statement guarantees delivering it with power.

ENHANCEMENTS

A technique for improving a speech is to "decorate" the main points. This is done with examples, metaphors, stories, and quotes. Try to select these enhancements from unusual environments that may not directly relate to the topic at hand. For example, you could quote from a popular song, take an example from science, or tell a personal anecdote about your family. By drawing on information outside the legal topic, you bring life to your presentation.

AUDIO/VISUAL EQUIPMENT

The purpose of audio/visual equipment is to increase interest and enhance meaning. However, most speakers who use it do so in a way that actually detracts from the presentation. Too often, using overhead projectors gives an audience the opportunity to daydream. And, if you turn down the lights, you might provide a nap-taking opportunity. Another risk in using audio/visual equipment is that it may not function. So, if you use audio/visual equipment, make sure it adds value to the presentation (which could even be accomplished with music, or a film clip), and be sure to either have a backup or be prepared to speak without it.

HANDOUTS

According to conventional wisdom, speakers should provide the audience with reams of written material. Though in some cases this may be a requirement, such as for continuing education programs, extensive handouts do not necessarily serve your best interests. If the purpose of the speech is to sell yourself, you want the audience to focus on you and not the written materials. Extensive materials create the impression that your entire content could be read at a later time. This allows the audience to be distracted. One of the best ways to increase interest and enhance learning is to use the "fill-in handout." Unlike conventional handouts, which provide printed information, fill-in handouts are predominantly blank, with spaces that allow audience members to take notes. The speaker provides verbal information and instructs the audience on how to fill in the blanks. This approach forces audiences to pay attention, and it allows them to feel greater "ownership" of the material.

AUDIENCE PARTICIPATION

Another way to improve your speech is to promote audience participation. Try to ask questions and stimulate discussion. This maintains interest. To maximize the effectiveness of this approach, be sure that you are supportive of the audience's remarks. Be careful not to criticize or embarrass anyone. Even subtle negativity will discourage continued participation.

If you plan to ask questions to stimulate audience participation, make sure you ask questions the audience will be motivated to answer. A common mistake speakers make is asking questions that require a specific answer. It is a technique many of us learned from our teachers and professors. However, instead of stimulating a response, this approach actually inhibits audience participation. Audience members feel embarrassed for not knowing the answer, or worse, for giving the wrong answer. A superior approach is to ask about attitudes and experiences concerning the issues being discussed. Ask the audience members what problems they have encountered and how they solved them. If given the opportunity, audiences are enthusiastic about sharing feelings and opinions, and, in turn, you gain greater insight into their needs.

TIMING

As you write your speech, make sure you identify specific time slots for your main points, and even annotate your notes with time markers. You don't want to make the mistake of focusing too long on one point, at the expense of the rest of the presentation. The timing issue becomes even more challenging when you encourage audience participation. Make sure you don't stray too far from the main point and remember to check the time frequently. Consider putting a small clock on the lectern.

OPPORTUNITIES FOR FOLLOW-THROUGH

Throughout the speech, one of your goals is to create mechanisms for furthering the relationship with prospects in the audience. The standard approach is to give information and hope someone will be motivated to hire you. The reality is that the sales cycle for closing a deal with someone in the audience could be years. Therefore, as in sales dialogue, you should be looking for ways to maintain communication with your prospects over an extended period of time. The following techniques will significantly increase the likelihood of your staying in touch.

CALL TO ACTION

One of the ways you open the door to future interaction with your prospects is to make a call to action. At the end of your speech, you can offer some activity in which you invite them to participate. For example, you could invite them to join organizations in which you are involved. You could enlist their assistance on some project you may be implementing. Or, you could suggest that they participate in roundtables or brainstorming sessions you are coordinating. The more interesting the offer, the more likely you will find eager participants, which will enhance the likelihood of developing an alliance and ultimately acquiring a client.

REQUESTING BUSINESS CARDS

Another effective technique for furthering interaction is to motivate members of the audience to give you their business cards. During your speech, offer to add interested prospects to your mailing list by promising to send them newsletters, articles, surveys, reports, or other informative correspondence. Offer to send them invitations to programs such as seminars or workshops. Experience has demonstrated that after a speech, when members of the audience return to their offices, the pressures of their lives take over. Even if they intend to call you, they are likely to procrastinate or forget. A successful marketing speech always provides many reasons for prospects to give you their cards.

PRACTICING

Finish writing your speech well before the date of delivery. Busy lawyers often procrastinate and destroy the opportunity to practice. As you practice, stand in front of a mirror. Repeat your introductory and closing sentences and sound bites dozens of times until they flow naturally. Try recording your speech on audio or video, and then review it to identify weaknesses in content and delivery.

Another helpful tip is to speak in front of audiences frequently. Not every speech you give has to be in front of prospects. In fact, you may want to join a speakers group such as Toastmasters International. This well-known organization provides a remarkable network of individuals throughout the world who share the desire to practice and improve their public-speaking skills. Practicing not only improves delivery, it is the only way to overcome the fear of speaking.

Arranging Speaking Engagements

If the purpose of your speech is lead generation, and not just practice, then make sure your audience is well targeted. There are many ways of reaching out to audiences with quality prospects. Consider the trade organizations that serve your existing clients. Many of these organizations regularly seek speakers. Consider obtaining speaking opportunities through people you already know. For example, a lawyer serving the banking industry could, through an existing contact at a bank, arrange to speak to all the loan officers of that bank. And finally, consider implementing joint-venture seminars with noncompeting professionals who share the same client demographic; this gives you an opportunity to reach your joint-venture partners' contacts.

Conclusion

Lawyers have a high level of verbal skills. But, because of prejudices about selling, they typically do not invest their energies and talents in this important area. With confidence in the propriety of selling, any lawyer can learn how to market through the spoken word and improve the ability to communicate his or her worth. In addition to helping build a practice, this ability enhances self-esteem, self-confidence, and the quality of relationships with clients, prospects, and referral sources.

CHAPTER 7

Proposals and Responding to RFPs

Stephen D. Barrett

Introduction

Rare is the month that goes by when a law firm is not invited to compete either for its "own" clients' ongoing business, or for the business that another law firm has failed to retain—in some cases clients a firm has controlled since time immemorial.

Many clients have grown tired of the seller-focused "hours times dollars" billing formulas and are looking for creative fee and service structures; some are undertaking "convergence," which is a movement toward better relationships with far fewer firms; some are looking for specific new expertise; and still others are going through the proposal process just to ensure they are getting the best deal possible from their existing counsel. Whatever the reason, more and more law firms are being asked to respond to Requests for Proposals (RFPs) or so-called "Beauty Contests." Smart firms realize that it is critical to spend time and money developing effective, creative responses to these very *real* opportunities for new business. That is what this chapter will focus upon.

Why Are Proposals/Responses So Important?

In a recent survey of the law departments of *Fortune*'s top 500 corporations, some 40 percent reported that within the past two years they conducted organized competitions for all or major portions of their outside legal work, and another 40 percent indicated that they planned to conduct such competitions in the next two years! This has ominous implications for those law firms that do not know how to compete.

Getting the opportunity to compete for the business of another law firm is a low-cost way to add to your firm's business. Beauty contests also provide you a chance to participate in a unique "benchmarking" exercise, in which you can see how well your firm "stacks up" against the competition. When law firms depend solely upon seminars, newsletters, brochures, and advertisements to compete for new-business opportunities, they usually spend more money, produce less traceable business, and have an inherently less-effective means of determining the comparative success of each activity.

For example, a large-format seminar could cost between $50,000 and $100,000 to produce. Even very large ones with 500–1,000 attendees rarely produce direct new client relationships, although they often stimulate individual matters or inquiries. A major ad campaign could cost between $250,000 and $1 million to produce and place, and may never yield any directly discernable business. On the other hand, a response to an RFP, or an open competition for a prospective client's business, could cost as little as a few hundred or few thousand dollars in staff time, production expenses, audio/visual costs, and travel/lodging charges; and the effort could yield hundreds of thousands—even millions—of dollars in revenues in the years following a "win."

Thus, if your law firm participates in a large number of competitions per year, measures the effort, and maintains a "positive" win/loss ratio, few other marketing activities will surpass it in effectiveness or produce comparable "bang for the bucks." Before you can compete, however, your firm must get invited to compete. In the words of hockey's great Wayne Gretsky, "You miss 100 percent of the shots you never take," or those you never get the chance to take.

Getting on the Prospect's RFP "Radar Screen"

If a case can be made for a firm to spend money on advertising, media relations, seminars, newsletters, brochures, and the like, it is that these tools generate sufficient awareness to get the firm invited to compete for more business. Most service marketing gurus, however, place greater emphasis on relationship building, as it is a more effective means to gaining chances to compete. These other activities likely contribute to the process, but they will not typically be directly responsible for acquiring invitations to compete for work. Make no mistake, a well-placed article in a trade publication occasionally generates an opportunity to compete for a prospective client's transaction. And, if funds were unlimited, most marketing directors would love to be supported by massive literature, advertising, seminars, and public-relations campaigns. But even the most prosperous law firms cannot spend limitless funds on marketing. Most expect their marketing departments to justify their existence and prove that what they do produces results. Many marketing professionals prefer making "expenditure versus results" reports, rather than trying to prove that their expenditures actually produce results.

Warning: If most of the RFPs in which your firm participates are conducted by your existing clients, you better seek immediate help in repairing your client relations. Better yet, ask your accounting department to run a "lost business" report to determine what business you have lost, or what business is in serious decline. Stopping that erosion should be a first order of business; it should precede all efforts to attract new business.

There seem to be several ways to "get on the RFP screen" or, to put it another way, to be asked to compete for business:

- Make sure that all your firm's partners and senior associates are trained in recognizing opportunities, and in converting those opportunities to business.
- Have an active media-relations program that reaches out to the trade press in each of the firm's practice specialties. Articles and speaking engagements before industry specialty groups can produce business expansion opportunities. Organizing and promoting the firm's practice groups, whether vertically or horizontally, should be a component of any marketing program.
- Communicate internally your firm's eagerness to compete for new business from existing and prospective clients. Also, tracking and communicating your win/loss record within the firm reminds lawyers of the importance of RFPs to the firm's success.
- Your compensation system should reward not only new business origination but also the effort to proliferate existing client business across new areas of specialty.
- Provide direct mailings to existing clients—suggesting new legal issues or areas of concern—by letter, newsletter, client alerts, facsimile, or e-mail. These can initiate inquires from present clients and prospects. Small-format, topical seminars, perhaps even presented at client facilities, can accomplish the same end, as can specialty areas on your firm's Internet home page, or a subject-matter-specific extranet. This could be called "selling by educating."
- Just ask! At any given time, some of your clients have law firm assessment and evaluation programs under way, whether or not they involve a formal competitive process, and others are preparing formal RFPs. Your firm often can arrange to be invited to participate, simply by calling the corporations' legal departments or their outside consultants and asking to be included. (These beauty contests often are produced and run by outside consulting firms under contracts to the clients, just like advertising agency selection competitions.) There might be an extra prescreening step to go through, but with seven to eight figures in annual revenue at stake, the cost to submit a prequalifying package should not be a deterrent.
- Simply get "out there." It is essential that the firm's lawyers make contacts and expand their social and business networks with the aim of

seeking opportunities for your firm to originate work or participate in competitions for legal business. To encounter these opportunities, lawyers must get out of the office and get involved with industry, community, business, social, and civic groups.

What to Do When Asked to Participate in an RFP or Beauty Contest

Determine Scope of Required Response

First, you must determine the scope of the required response. Is the target asking for an entirely new approach to a relationship, or just legal services within one specialty? Is the request national, international, or regional in scope? Is it simply a specific one-matter opportunity, such as the defense of a litigation matter because the company's outside counsel has been conflicted out? These questions should be considered in determining whether to respond at all.

Check for Conflicts

It is also essential that you check for conflicts with your existing clients. Whenever your firm responds to an RFP, or seeks any new business, you should first pass the prospective client through your firm's conflicts system. Checking can save some embarrassment further into the process.

Checklist of Considerations

There are a number of considerations that should be explored before responding to an RFP.

- Are there any legal, industry, internal, or marketing reasons *not* to represent this prospect or client in this particular matter?
- Are there any issue conflicts, or present firm clients for whom taking on this prospective new client would pose a serious problem? For example, hospitals and health maintenance organizations often proscribe their law firms from representing tobacco interests, and Big-Three auto manufacturers may prefer that your firm never represent their competitors.
- Would winning the engagement be profitable for the firm?
- What level of commitment is required to sustain a mutually beneficial relationship with this client? Is the firm prepared to commit such resources?
- Is the size and scope of the matter compatible with the firm's capabilities?
- Is alternative pricing absolutely necessary to obtain the work? Is the firm's management willing to consider such pricing arrangements?

- Is the competition "wired" (that is, merely a pro-forma exercise for the issuer) to produce a predetermined winner? Even public/government agency bids—often required every several years under public purchasing regulations—can be "tilted" or merely "for show" exercises necessary to reassign the work to the incumbent firms.
- What other firms are likely to compete, and how do your firm's capabilities measure up to the competition? If you are presenting a comparatively weak specialty of your firm against that practice area's national niche leader, it may be better to pass.
- If the chances of winning the competition are slim, are there other valid reasons to compete nevertheless? Even losing can lead to fractional business opportunities later, if the winners should encounter conflicts or disappoint the buyers down the road. Debriefing after a loss (see "Conduct Post-Presentation Follow-Up" later in this chapter) can be the platform from which you can "win" the next time. But it is most important that you make a great impression in your response.

If you choose not to compete, notify the buyer with a cogent and valid business reason, and express interest in being considered again. Then be sure you add that organization to all your mailing lists so you can "stay in touch" through seminar invitations, newsletters, client advisories, and announcements. *You should compete to win, or decline to compete.* Winning efforts require hard work and "doing the homework," not just mailing in a boilerplate response package. If you are willing to work hard and do your homework, however, the process of winning is quite straightforward.

Winning RFPs

Start by Identifying Client Needs

1. What does the RFP tell you?
2. Has the firm done work for this company in the past?
   - Seek information from your conflicts or accounting departments.
   - Canvass the firm's lawyers.
3. Does someone in the firm have an inside contact who can provide information that will help in preparing the response?
4. Call the person for whom you are preparing the RFP and either arrange an in-person meeting (best) or ask on the phone:
   - What are the important issues in the resolution of this matter?
   - What is most important in your relationships with outside counsel?
   - Why have you decided to use a competition to select outside counsel for this work or matter?
   - Who within the company (individual, committee, board) will make the final hiring decision?

- How do you want this matter staffed?
- Are there other people with whom we should speak regarding this matter?
- Which other firms are being considered?
- What are your expectations and preferences regarding budgeting, billing rates, alternative pricing arrangements, and the like?
- Can you provide written policies/guidelines regarding dealing with outside counsel?
- Is there any other relevant information about this particular competition that you can share?

Often lawyers are reluctant, or even unwilling, to seek this type of added information. But this simple process of "due diligence" not only avoids embarrassment and wasted effort, it flatters prospective clients by showing that you care enough to try to understand their business challenges (just like a caring family physician—"Tell me where it hurts").

Conduct Industry and Company Research

All other things being equal (that is, all firms responding have generally comparable rates and capabilities), the responding firm that wins most is the one that displays the greatest understanding of the company's business and the issues it must resolve. Getting this information demonstrates that your firm is interested enough in the business to do the necessary preparation, and that your firm is farther up the "learning curve" than the competition. The advance analysis and preliminary diagnosis you offer are clear examples of the care with which your firm approaches the delivery of its services. It gives the prospect a "preview" of your firm's service-delivery attitude even before it hires you.

When doing industry research, use trade journals and publications to do the following:

1. Determine major issues facing the industry (such as trends, relevant legislation, community developments, and recent, pending, or potential litigation).
2. Develop an understanding of industry-specific terminology.
3. Gain insights into the prospective legal issues that this understanding and analysis permit.

When you conduct company research, you should seek to obtain the following information about the company:

- Ownership and organization
- Current and future products/services
- Current locations and future expansion/contraction plans
- Financial condition
- Technology capabilities

- Primary competitors
- Primary contractors/vendors
- Other legal activities
- Size and capabilities of legal staff
- Names and backgrounds of key personnel

Prepare the Presentation

Once the research is done, you need to prepare the presentation. For your presentation to be "first rate," you should make certain that you accomplish the following tasks:

1. Start early—determine a proposal production schedule and assign responsibilities.
2. Identify the lawyers with the necessary expertise and qualifications and assemble the team.
3. Check the availability of the team members for an in-person presentation.
4. Determine who will lead the team.
5. Seek targeted, in-person advance meetings to both gain information and begin building personal relationships. (Personal relationships should be examined to determine if internal target company *coaches* can be identified—they can provide guidance and feedback throughout the process.)
6. Download or assemble relevant experience examples. Canvass the lawyers in your firm to gather examples of relevant experience and capabilities. (If you do not already have this information assembled, compiling this data often is the hardest part of the process.)

Prepare the Written Proposal

With the wealth of knowledge you now have, you can create the written proposal response. The keys to ensuring an effective written document include the following:

- Check whether the RFP specifies a particular format, word processing file, or diskette for submission along with the hard copy.
- First impressions are critical, though cosmetic "packaging" should be only a secondary factor. Focus on content first, and then enhancement through inclusion of graphics, the prospect's logotype(s), a custom desktop-published look, and the like.
- The cover letter should be a one- or two-page synopsis of the firm's experience and qualifications for the work, and your expressed desire to be selected.

- Include a table of contents.
- The executive summary should make all the summary points you want the audience to take away; this may be the *only* section that is read completely.
- The practice area descriptions should feature recent, relevant experience. To demonstrate expertise, this section must contain specifics and describe any innovative projects or work.
- If no specifics about budgeting and billing are requested in the RFP, the proposal should include an outline of hourly rates, available alternative billing arrangements, a description of billing format and frequency, alternative service-delivery vehicles, and the like. If the RFP mandates alternative billing configurations, or if you believe an innovative approach might create appeal, then describe new billing or account management approaches that might interest the prospect.
- Describe a staffing plan.
- Include lawyer/paralegal biographies, tailored as necessary to fit the situation or the prospect's expressed needs.
- Include a specific client service plan.
- Describe your technology capabilities.
- Provide general information about the firm, such as office locations and contact information.
- Include (but only as exhibits) relevant firm newsletters, articles, or speech reprints.
- If possible, beat the deadline.

At the risk of giving away my secrets, it must be said that the proposal that includes one or more significant service innovations, or creative solutions to the prospect's expressed needs, often gains a critical competitive edge in the evaluation process.

Market the Presentation

When it is time to market the presentation, you should take care to do the following:

- Check the logistics—including the size, shape, and style of the interview or meeting room.
- Ensure that appropriate audio/visual capabilities are available.
- Decide on a presentation format with a team leader, who will handle specific portions of the presentation. Can all team members attend? If not, can some participate via conference call (audio or video)?
- Provide all presentation team members with a company/industry research dossier.
- Anticipate questions/objections, and prepare and rehearse responses—especially to the toughest expected questions.

- Rehearse the entire presentation. Make sure it can be completed within the allotted time with enough time left for "Q & A."
- Be on time. Schedule conservatively to avoid delayed flights or traffic problems that would undermine the impression that you are prompt, organized, and considerate.
- Bring extra copies of the proposal, your slides, and the presentation diskettes.
- Confirm whether those in attendance have had an opportunity to review your written proposal.
- Let the prospective client take the lead, but supply a proposed agenda in case the client is leaving it up to you.
- Create a dialogue about the client's issues; remember, *listening is more important than talking* in an effective presentation.
- Respect the prospect's "time contract" and end on time, or arrange a convenient time to continue or reconvene.

Conduct Post-Presentation Follow-Up

After you complete the presentation, you should conduct post-presentation follow-up. This includes taking the following steps:

1. Hold a "debriefing" session with the presentation team.
2. Send a follow-up letter to the prospect, asking if there are any questions, and thanking the prospect for the opportunity to compete and be considered for the business.
3. If your firm is not chosen, ask for the opportunity for in-person feedback from the prospect.

With this overview of the process as a guide, you should be able to take your responses to a whole new level. Now let's look at a couple further components of the process in more detail.

Developing a Proposal Database

Although the legal industry is probably the most paper- and information-intensive industry in modern economies, it is considered by many to be the least automated. Law firms that take the process of competing for business seriously have recognized the need for a central repository of proposal-building information. These proposal databases, proposal "engines," or proposal "toolboxes," as they may be called, are a critical component of a "rapid response" capability. Moreover, even if a rapid response is not necessary, having the standard portions of the proposal documents available for easy assembly into well-crafted templates takes much of the time pressure out of the production process. The team can use this time to focus on developing and analyzing client and industry information, as well as assembling the customized portion of the response. The best databases are those that are updated and maintained centrally, yet are available for use on a decentralized basis (for firms with multiple offices).

There simply is no way that any but the largest marketing staffs can assist in the production of more than a few dozen proposal responses per year without a proposal database. Some large-firm marketing departments are asked to handle several hundred proposal responses per year. Doing so without a proposal development system is folly.

Establishing a proposal database involves creating, "harvesting," and updating all relevant documents that may exist within the firm, and getting them online in a central location. This is a laborious process, even if you have the staff available to handle it, but it is nonetheless essential. These documents should share one archive dataset or library, and be accessible to all computers over the firmwide network, as well as being text-searchable. Assuming your firm uses any of the major contemporary document archiving systems, you can organize descriptions of your firm into a system that makes sense and is available to all users in the firm, on a text-searchable basis. An index to this archive also should be at the fingertips of everyone in the firm.

The descriptive information in the database should include (at a minimum) the following:

- An overall firm description
- Descriptions of each of the firm's principle departments and practice groups
- One or more biographies of every lawyer within the firm (many now include a digital rendering of the lawyer's photograph)
- "Special" or "horizontal" capabilities descriptions, such as class-action defense, mass-tort coordinating counsel capabilities, and the like
- Office addresses, phone numbers, Internet contacts, and the like
- Copies of all proposals done by the firm for the past several years

Through the deployment of necessary documents via digital forms, a firm can "mass customize" its RFP responses quite easily. Various document-organizing programs also are commercially available. You feed these with the same information described above, and they help you assemble responses using prompts.

This "centralized" versus "decentralized" issue should be addressed, because you definitely do not want out-of-date or inconsistent information retained on a local office's server. This could result in understating your firm's talents or size (lawyer headcounts, for instance) or, even worse, claiming some specialty that your firm has failed to maintain or that has left the firm. Also, "old" proposals (if archived) should include hidden notes that point out the areas in which outdated information could survive, such as listings of lawyers that may include those no longer with the firm. In an evolved firm-marketing culture, one in which most of the firm's senior lawyers have been trained in marketing techniques, decentralized production of proposals should be encouraged, as it arithmetically increases the number that the firm can issue. Issues of centralized versus decentralized control can be addressed by management policies that encourage the involvement of the marketing department in the process, and that require the lawyers to provide the marketing department with copies of each proposal upon issuance, for archival and updating purposes.

To test whether the marketing department is being notified, "hidden characters" can be included in all proposal database documents (in the comment boxes). This can simplify the chore of periodically seeking out all proposals created throughout the firm. In cases of dispersed offices, scheduled all-server text searches (they can be run overnight) can locate and list all documents that were produced since the last search (we do ours quarterly) and that have included the "hidden character." Other document management systems can provide logs of user accesses, which can guide you to people accessing the marketing documents.

Determining the Firm's "Batting Average" in Competitions

There are a host of ways to track how many "at bats" a firm gets each year. Start by tracking those responses that involved the marketing department and follow the "success rate" of these efforts. Assuming your marketing department is involved in all the firm's competitive new-business efforts (or at least gets copies of all proposals), it is simple to build a table to track frequency and success. Simply list them in either a database or a text-searchable word-processed table or spreadsheet, as they occur.

Our table's column headings include the date, the prospect (with responsible marketing department representative), the "lead" and team lawyers, the type of presentation (for example, RFP or contested proposal), status (pending, or targeted decision date), and comments, such as the level of support provided by the marketing department (full research, team counseling and support, document production, or rehearsal, for example). The table is summarized on a monthly and running annual basis, with the summary including the number issued, the number pending, wins, losses, subtotals, and "success rate" (wins as a percentage of total decisions, expressed as a percent).

Although informal notifications are nice ("Hey Steve, we got the XYZ Company's business!"), it is best to develop or make use of a system that tracks new matters and clients on intake. New client matters opened as a result of the competitive presentation process can be noted in your proposal outcomes table, and the new client/matter numbers can be uploaded to the accounting department for periodic reports on collections from the new business intakes.

If the new matters are in a new area of law, such as adding employment work for a previous litigation client of the firm, the report can track the collections just in this new area of law from the onset date forward. If the client is entirely new to the firm, then all collections from that entity, from the date of origination onward, should be tracked. Armed with this information, it becomes easy to ascertain collections that have been produced from new business generated with the support of the marketing department. These figures should be useful in justifying the existence of the marketing function. Several years of such data is particularly useful in comparing the performance of different offices and departments, detecting trends, measuring progress, and noting whether any areas of the firm have been deficient in pursuing new business.

If your firm is an active advertiser, produces newsletters and brochures, and hosts a lot of seminars and receptions, then these efforts should be systematically tracked as well. Many firms are installing integrated marketing databases to capture client contact information, maintain mailing lists centrally, track attendees at firm functions, and the like, so they can derive implicit or explicit information to tie new business to types of firm marketing activities. Although I have not yet heard hard dollar or success-rate results from any sophisticated users of such systems, I suspect that proposals and RFP responses will remain one of the most trackable, most affordable, and most effective activities in which a law firm can engage for developing new business.

Nothing discussed here is "rocket science," yet woefully few law firms closely track their results in the area of new-business development, or accurately understand which marketing activities produce favorable outcomes. I hope this discussion about RFPs, and all the other terrific information in this book, motivate you to take this entire process more seriously.

CHAPTER 8

Internet Marketing

Gregory H. Siskind

In the spring of 1994, the first law firms began premiering Web sites. In December 1995, when I was writing the ABA book *The Lawyer's Guide to Marketing on the Internet,* only 334 law firms were listed in the *Yahoo!* directory. And in only the few years since then, law firm marketing has been revolutionized by the Internet. Nearly 3,000 firms are now listed in the *Yahoo!* directory alone, and about two-thirds of the *National Law Journal*'s top 250 law firms have launched Web sites. Yet the number of firms on the Web still represents only a small portion of the nearly 800,000 practicing lawyers in the country—many have been slow to embrace marketing through this medium.

Perhaps the firms that have been most successful are the ones who have not forgotten core principals of marketing—understanding the audience, using Web sites to build image and name recognition, and knowing the limits and advantages of the medium, for example. After more than four years of law firms using the Web, there are many successful models to follow.

Reasons to Consider Internet Marketing

There are a number of good reasons why a law firm should consider Internet marketing, including these: (1) it can reach untapped client bases; (2) it is cost-effective; (3) it delivers information effectively; (4) it provides an excellent marketing complement; (5) it can enhance the firm's image; (6) it reduces geographic barriers; and (7) it can used as a recruitment tool.

Reach Untapped Client Base

Over the last several years the number of Internet users has increased dramatically, to the extent that Internet use is nearly on a par with established media such as television, newspapers, and radio. In October 1995, CommerceNet and Nielsen Media Research released their first major study of Internet usage. The study found that 37 million people in North America had Internet access. Two and a half years later, in March 1998, a new CommerceNet/Nielsen study showed 52 million users in North America. And the predictions on Internet growth remain strong. Internet access has become cheaper and connection speeds have increased steadily, making the Internet a reliable, convenient means of accessing information for a substantial portion of the American public.

As the Internet draws people closer together by eliminating communication and expense barriers between those separated by geographical barriers, law firms interested in expanding into new geographic markets will be presented with new opportunities for client-base expansion.

Benefit from Cost-Effective Marketing

Compared with the costs of marketing in the Yellow Pages, television, and radio, advertising expenses connected with the Internet are quite reasonable. Marketing via e-mail and on Usenet newsgroups (the Internet's bulletin board discussion groups), for example, can cost just a few cents a day. And the major expenses associated with developing a Web site—server space and Web design—can cost as little as a few hundred dollars a year. The lawyer looking for both services can save considerably without skimping on quality by shopping around and by learning to design some or all of the site in-house.

Distributing information by and about a law firm via the Internet is also considerably less expensive than the traditional methods used for creating client newsletters and firm brochures. For example, a newsletter distributed by e-mail can be created without incurring typesetting, printing, or postage expenses. Compared with a firm brochure, a Web site can look just as attractive yet contain much more information, and it can be updated regularly without major new expenses for printing and design.

Deliver Information More Effectively

By using the Internet, a lawyer wishing to distribute information on developments in the law can reach a virtually unlimited audience within a few hours, in contrast to the days or weeks required to communicate the same news through traditional marketing. Information can be distributed in a number of ways, and on the very day the news breaks. An announcement similar to a press release can be made in appropriate Usenet newsgroups. The same announcement can be distributed to subscribers of a firm's electronic newsletter mailing list. And, with very little effort, the announcement or article can be posted in a "What's New" section of a firm's Web page.

World Wide Web viewers can also customize the way they see information. On a Web site, an Internet user can jump from one location to another with a click of the mouse. The user can also jump from one site to a Web site stored on a computer anywhere else in the world. A well-designed Web site that is laid out in a succinct and attractive manner, with logically organized links to a large amount of information important to the site's viewers, demonstrates the firm's expertise.

And on Web sites, firms can allow readers to sign up for placement on automated mailing lists, which allows them to receive requested information regularly without returning to the Web site.

Take Advantage of an Excellent Marketing Complement

Most people who are considering using your firm are going to hear about you somewhere other than the Internet. Even as the phenomenal growth of the Internet continues, you can expect it will not become your primary marketing mechanism for some time. Where the Internet can really help many firms today is by providing more in-depth information to someone already considering the firm. Your Internet site can provide more firm information than a brochure and demonstrate your expertise in a way that no other media can approach. The Web site can help "close the sale" after initial marketing has opened the door.

Enhance the Firm's Image

Even if a firm does not expect that it can measure a substantial, direct increase in its client base by establishing an Internet presence, being online conveys a number of positive messages to existing and potential clients.

First, it tells the public that a firm is on the "cutting edge" and keeps up with the latest technology. Clients want to believe their lawyers have the best tools available to help solve problems and get results.

Second, on the Internet, a newer, smaller firm can convey an image every bit as sophisticated as a larger, more established firm, without expending the same financial and personnel resources. A keen eye for design and a continuous commitment to developing high-quality content can help a one- or two-person firm get as many "hits" on a site as a five-hundred-lawyer firm. For example, the small law firm of Siskind, Susser, Haas & Devine (the law firm of this chapter's author) receives an average of 175,000 hits per week, perhaps more than any large firm's Web site in the country.

This is not to say that a large firm cannot take advantage of its size and resources to give it a "step up" on the Internet. A large firm could perhaps hire a top Web designer or Internet marketing consultant to assist the firm not only in creating a technically attractive site, but also in developing content and publicizing the site effectively. A larger firm can also tap into a greater number of internal resources when developing content. The firm may already be producing several newsletters and its lawyers may be writing articles regularly, all of which can be incorporated on the Web site.

Reduce Geographic Barriers

For many people in small and rural areas, and for people residing great distances from locations where they need lawyers, the Internet can make finding qualified lawyers considerably easier and faster. In addition, the Internet offers considerably greater choice in choosing counsel.

Use as Recruitment Tool

Online marketing does not necessarily need to focus strictly on bringing in new business, even if that is a primary goal. An Internet presence can also greatly benefit firms trying to recruit high-quality lawyers, paralegals, and support staff. Most law students, for example, have Internet access through their law schools and are usually quite comfortable with the medium. Most of them, as well as many practicing lawyers, now use the Internet in their job-searching efforts. Consider the following:

- Typically, law school graduates are much more technologically savvy than lawyers at the firms where the graduates interview. Recruits who believe they must take a major step backward and revert to an antiquated computer system (or worse, no system at all!) will not be impressed. Being active on the Internet sends the message that your firm cares about the quality of the lawyer's work environment. More important, it sends the message that the firm is interested in staying ahead of the competition.
- The more firm information a job candidate can access easily, the greater the likelihood the candidate will pursue the job opportunity. A top job candidate will no doubt have several job opportunities. Why should the candidate lose valuable time traveling around the country to interview with firms only to learn those firms are not appealing? By the same token, why should a firm spend time interviewing a job candidate who has nothing in common with the firm's philosophy? A good Web site can help maximize the chances that better matches are made early in the process.

Reasons to Approach Internet Marketing Carefully

As much potential as the Internet holds as a marketing tool, there are, of course, reasons to approach Internet marketing carefully and thoughtfully.

Significant Time Investment

Without having a lawyer or consultant who really understands the Internet culture, a law firm that undertakes Internet marketing risks not only sinking a potentially large amount of resources into a totally ineffective effort, but actually presenting a negative image to the public. A number of well-respected firms have established amateurish, billboard-like Web sites that will probably attract few new clients and will certainly not impress the firms' existing Internet-savvy clients. And many lawyers have been guilty of serious Internet etiquette ("netiquette") violations. Even if the breach is unintentional, the damage will be done. Unless a firm has both the resources and the commitment to undertake such responsibilities, the effort to establish an Internet presence may not be worth it.

Rapidly Changing Medium

Technological changes involving the Internet are measured in months, not years. Five years ago, few knew about e-mail and Usenet newsgroups. Three years ago, the World Wide Web was recognized by few. Now, new Internet technologies—such as real-time audio and video broadcasting, teleconferencing, executing programs on distant computers, and virtual reality—are maturing. In practical terms, this means that a law firm should expect to revisit its Internet marketing plan frequently, and should be prepared to make rapid decisions if it wants to move at the same pace as its audience.

Unlawful Practice of Law and Other Ethical Issues

Ethical issues related to marketing cannot be ignored when touting one's services on the Internet. Are Web sites subject to the same regulations as any other form of law firm advertising? Is a lawyer liable for practicing law without a license if a firm's home page reaches citizens of a state where the lawyer is not licensed? Is a lawyer liable for information he or she provides via e-mail or in a newsgroup? And what are the lawyer's confidentiality obligations in connection with communications sent and received via e-mail and Usenet newsgroups? Unfortunately, the rules are still not always clear, and appropriate cautions need to be observed when engaging in such communications.

Nonuser Markets

Firms should examine their targeted client bases to determine the likelihood that a significant number of potential clients would use the Internet to seek legal services. A firm's practice might be strictly oriented to a client base that uses personal computers at a lower rate than the general population. Demographic studies show, not surprisingly, that the wealthier and more educated people are, the more likely they have Internet access. Thus, if your practice focuses on serving indigent or less-educated people, you might not see the same return on your marketing investment in the Internet as another lawyer. But the growth in sales of personal computers and in the number of Internet accounts demonstrates that computer use is rapidly working its way into all segments of our population, and that most firms will realize at least some benefit from an Internet presence.

No Personal Contact

Regardless of how much the Internet is praised for reducing barriers between people, many still feel very uncomfortable with a process in which they never meet face-to-face with a lawyer before establishing a client relationship. This obstacle is bound to become less of a problem as people become accustomed to communicating and conducting routine business activities over the Internet. Furthermore, face-to-face communication over the Internet will become more common as video teleconferencing becomes practical. Nevertheless, firms that want to engage in Internet marketing should recognize this obstacle and do what they can to address it. For instance, a firm can encourage follow-up communication via e-mail and telephone, and include photographs of the firm's lawyers—as well as voice and video clips—in a Web site.

Integrating Internet Marketing with a General Marketing Plan

In the minds of much of the legal profession, the benefits of the Internet seem to outweigh the negatives. If you come to the same conclusion, the next step you need to take is the development of an Internet marketing plan that is part of a general marketing effort. Before jumping right into developing a Web site or engaging in other types of online marketing, take the time to outline your strategy clearly.

Analysis Needed for a Successful Marketing Plan

Just knowing a lot about the Internet and having a big budget to set up an Internet presence will not get you very far in Internet marketing. If you want to achieve online success, a plan for marketing your law practice on the Internet should be integrated into your firm's general marketing and business plans. This blueprint for establishing an online presence should resemble a conventional marketing plan in its basic structure. Jane Rectenwald, in the book *The ABA Guide to Legal Marketing: A Collection of the Best Ideas, Approaches, and Success Stories* (published by the ABA Section of Law Practice Management, 1995, at pp. 17–28), notes that a successful marketing plan should begin with an analysis of your firm's market, services, clients, and competition. (Refer also to Chapter 2 of this book, *Strategic Marketing Planning.*) Thoroughly understanding these subjects will provide the necessary foundation to develop an effective online marketing plan.

YOUR MARKET

When evaluating your firm's market, you should address several basic questions:

1. In what types of industries are your clients?
   - Break down your client base according to industry.
   - Do you want to target your Internet marketing efforts to the same types of clients you currently serve, or do you want to focus on a different industry or market area?
2. Are these existing and potential clients on the Internet?
   - Run searches and sift through directories to get an idea of how many are on the Internet.
   - Check back periodically to see if new sites are listed and if the sites are changing substantially.
3. How do these potential clients use the Internet?
   - What newsgroups do they read?
   - Which mailing lists do they receive?
   - Do they have their own Web sites?
4. What types of information are online potential clients seeking?
5. Can your online information complement traditional promotional information that is being distributed to potential clients?

YOUR SERVICES

Before developing the content for your Internet presence, you should carefully analyze the areas in which members of your firm have expertise. These are the areas in which your firm should consider developing Web sites and e-mail newsletters and articles. Focus on offering added value to your clients by providing useful information in your practice area. Gather previously published public-relations materials that document your firm's expertise in these areas and plan to incorporate them in your Web site.

YOUR CLIENTS

Analyze how you can better serve existing clients via the Internet. The first items to consider are how your clients use the Internet. Do they use e-mail? If so, do they send documents via e-mail, participate in mailing lists, or encrypt confidential information? Do your clients use the World Wide Web? For what purposes are they using the Web? Some obvious examples of ways you can use a Web site to serve clients include the following.

IMPROVING COMMUNICATIONS VIA E-MAIL

The Internet provides an incredibly convenient way to facilitate communications between a client and a lawyer. Rather than trying to pass messages via phone, letters, or in-person communications, e-mail lets a client communicate a detailed message or transmit a document to your computer when it is convenient for the client. Sometimes clients simply want to pass on quick messages to you but do not have the time to track you down. An additional benefit of e-mail is that it allows a person to send back a reply instantly, with the text of the earlier messages included in the reply message.

REDUCING THE COST TO CLIENTS OF LEGAL RESEARCH BY MAKING VALUABLE INFORMATION AVAILABLE AND EASILY ACCESSIBLE ON YOUR WEB SITE

You can link sites that interest your clients. You can provide information more quickly regarding legal developments. For example, you can easily keep clients updated on developments that interest them by providing an online newsletter that covers items such as pending legislation that may affect them or important cases affecting their industries.

EDUCATING CLIENTS ABOUT YOUR FIRM'S STRUCTURE AND AREAS OF EXPERTISE

A client may have contact with a single lawyer in a large firm, but what if the client needs the services of a lawyer in a different specialty area? The ability to learn about a firm's different lawyers and departments could significantly benefit the client, especially if it lets the client find a lawyer with whom he or she will be most comfortable, or if it shows the client that the firm provides the type of assistance being sought. Your Web site can be a natural part of "cross-selling" other lawyers and services in your firm. Some argue that providing rich content such as articles and newsletters is the only important element of a good law firm Web site. But providing quality information on the firm itself can be just as critical to success. Most law firm marketing experts agree that emphasizing cross-selling in a firm's marketing plan is just as important as most, if not all, other types of marketing the firm conducts. And providing an "electronic brochure" on a Web site can be a significant tool in cross-selling.

PROMOTING EXISTING CLIENTS BY LINKING YOUR WEB PAGE TO YOUR CLIENTS' SITES

One way to build client loyalty and trust is to try to help the client's business. Aside from patronizing the client's business, a law firm also can refer business to the client. And linking your clients' Web sites or e-mail addresses gives you one more tool to refer potential business to your clients.

YOUR COMPETITION

Find out what your competitors on the Internet are doing. Address the following types of questions:

1. What Internet tools are your competitors using?
    - Do they have e-mail links for each of their lawyers?
    - Do their lawyers participate in newsgroups? If so, which ones?

- What type of content are your competitors including in their Web sites?
- Are they providing services or information that you should be offering as well?
- Do they distribute information via an e-mail mailing list?

2. What percentage of your competitors is online?
   - Is that number rapidly increasing?
   - How much lead time do you have over other firms getting onto the Internet?
   - Are you keeping pace with your online competitors, or are you leading the pack?
3. How are your clients publicizing their Web sites?
   - In which directories are they listed?
   - Do they use traditional marketing tools, such as print advertising, for their sites?
   - Have they sent announcements to the bar and press releases to the media?

After you have analyzed your market, your services, your clients, and your competition, you should be able to set clear goals for your Internet marketing. When developing your marketing plan, you should also consider a number of special Internet issues.

Focus on Information, Not Self-Promotion

A surefire recipe for failure on the Internet is to design an Internet advertisement that mimics print, television, or radio advertising. Conventional advertising is designed to get a clear, brief message across in a limited amount of space or time. The ads often need to be attention-getting devices, because readers, viewers, or listeners are normally not seeking the advertisement's information, or because the advertiser is competing to grab attention from competitors' ads. In contrast, Web users choose to visit a site. The quality and accessibility of the site's content will determine whether people visit regularly. Users of the Internet typically seek information, not blatant advertising. This may be information on a particular legal subject. It may be detailed information about your practice that can be used to help someone decide to hire your firm. Users will skip Web sites and newsgroup messages lacking useful information, or will certainly not seek further information. Firms offering in-demand information will attract much more attention in the unstructured Internet environment. But do not forget to also focus on the presentation of your site. The look of your page will shape your firm's public image. Make sure your site is clearly organized and attractive. Make it interesting and easy to navigate. Even if you provide great content, you will lose potential clients if the site is too difficult to find.

Make Your Firm Accessible

The Internet makes attracting clients outside your geographic area much more realistic. But nonlocal prospective clients or referring lawyers are naturally inclined to favor local firms that offer personal contact. The potential client may prefer face-to-face contact, or fear expenses will be higher with an out-of-town lawyer.

Your Internet marketing plan should address overcoming these potential barriers. Consider offering a toll-free telephone line to encourage people to follow up their Internet contact with a phone call to discuss their matters. Offer consultations via telephone, Internet phone, or another Internet voice-conferencing program (though both the lawyer and the client should have a high-speed Internet connection if this option is used) or, better yet, video teleconferencing over the Internet. Consider accepting credit cards—they are convenient to some clients and can also significantly reduce your collection problems, especially for out-of-town clients (but make sure to shop around for a bank that will offer you a competitive merchant rate for credit card transactions).

Follow up quickly with people who contact the firm after seeing your Web site. Answering an e-mail inquiry quickly is as important to attracting a potential client as responding to a telephone call quickly. Prepare form responses to common inquiries so you can offer a speedier reply. Some of the newer e-mail programs (such as Netscape E-mail and Eudora) let you create stock responses to common inquiries so you can send replies with a few clicks of the mouse.

And, most important, make your Web site more personal. Include photographs of members of the firm and consider using voice and video clips.

Integrate the Different Tools of the Internet

To maximize the benefits of using the Internet, your marketing plan should use all the tools of the Internet, both separately and in conjunction with each other. Examples of using multiple tools in an integrated communication include the following:

- Promote your Web site and electronic mailing list in your e-mail and newsgroup signature blocks.
- Use your Web site to subscribe people to your electronic mailing list.
- Let readers of your Web site know that you offer voice and video teleconferencing over the Internet.
- Link your lawyers' e-mail addresses in your Web site.
- Issue public-relations releases to various Usenet newsgroups that publicize your e-mail newsletter's contents.

Market Your Internet Presence Both Online and in Traditional Media

Producing a top-notch newsletter for the Internet and maintaining an incredibly informative Web site will not translate into marketing success unless people know about your Internet presence. The adage "If you build it, they will come" may work in the movies, but it will not work on the Internet. Your Internet marketing plan should be bilateral: Develop an excellent Internet presence and effectively publicize it both on the Internet and offline.

On the Internet, link your Web page in as many places as possible. List your Web site and newsletter in a range of Internet directories and search engines (Internet sites that allow you to search the Internet by entering key words). Though some directories charge a fee to be listed, most are free and welcome additions. Link your page to other sites that may target the same clientele but do not compete. Most people are happy to link to your page if you, in turn, link to theirs. Sponsor other Web sites and link your advertisement or logo to your Web site.

Offline, promote your e-mail and Web addresses in your traditional marketing materials. Those addresses should be listed on your business cards, letterhead, brochures, and print advertisements. In other words, anywhere you list your phone number, list your Web site and e-mail address as well. List your site in several of the books on the market that provide directories of the Internet.

Promote your Internet presence via press releases and contacts with the print and broadcast media. Commerce on the Internet is still fresh news and reporters are looking for real-life examples of firms and companies that take advantage of the new medium. Finally, do not forget to let your existing clients know about your new use of the Internet.

Keep Pace with the Medium

It's a pretty safe bet that the Internet will continue to evolve rapidly. Firms that have been able to react quickly to these changes have planted the seeds for long-term success. Firms that treat the Internet like a relatively static medium, such as television or newspapers, will find that their Internet presence seems dated after months, not years.

One thing a lawyer interested in online marketing can do to keep pace with change is to read Internet-oriented publications, both online and in print. Several excellent resources address the general subject of Internet marketing. One is the Internet Marketing Mailing List. Maintained by Glenn Fleishman, this discussion group focuses on a wide range of subjects—such as appropriate and ethical marketing practices, new software, choosing a Web developer, and analyzing Web site "ratings." To subscribe to this list, send an e-mail communication to *listproc@einet.net* with the message "subscribe INET-MARKETING."

Among several new magazines addressing the Internet, one standout is *Internet World*. The magazine is well written, attractively laid out, and very timely. You can also find a variety of new periodicals on the Internet at your nearest bookstore.

A number of resources are tailored specifically to the legal profession. The following are all quite helpful:

- One of the best online resources aimed at lawyers is the Net-Lawyers mailing list. This online discussion group, comprising nearly 2,000 individuals, is maintained by lawyer Lew Rose of the Arent Fox law firm in Washington, D.C., and addresses just about every issue that confronts lawyers using the Internet in day-to-day practice. In addition to thorough discussions on marketing issues, the list is an excellent resource for finding out about new research resources, ethical issues unique to the Internet, and new software. The discussion group is also an excellent place to contact other lawyers. To subscribe to the list, go to the home page for Net-Lawyers at *http://www.net-lawyers.org/* and click on the "subscribe" button. The messages posted in Net-Lawyers are archived on the World Wide Web at *http://www.kentlaw.edu/cgi-bin/ldn_news/-D+law.listserv.net-lawyers.*
- The ABA's Law Practice Management Section produces a number of very helpful resources, including *Law Practice Management,* an excellent magazine that covers, among other topics, computers in the law office. Be sure to check out the column by G. Burgess Allison, author of *The Lawyer's Guide to the Internet.* And consider purchasing my book, *The Lawyer's Guide to Marketing on the Internet.* Go to http://www.abanet.org/lpm/catalog to find additional useful books on legal technology.
- Every March in Chicago, the Law Practice Management Section puts on the outstanding ABA TECHSHOW™ conference. This annual conference, now the premier event that deals with technology and the law office, offers a multiday track of seminars about the Internet in the law office. The phone number for more information on TECHSHOW is 312-988-5619, and the Web address is *http://www.techshow.com.*
- The Law Practice Management Section's Web page (*http://www.abanet.org/lpm*) also provides extensive information on TECHSHOW, as well as an excellent list of law-related Internet publications, including the following (the Web address is *http://www.abanet.org/lpm/magazine/booklist.html*):
    - *Law Office Computing* is a magazine that covers a range of issues relating to the use of computers in the law office, and includes extensive coverage of the Internet. To subscribe, call 714-755-5450.
    - *The Internet Lawyer,* a print newsletter whose name says it all, is published by Andrew Adkins of GoAhead Productions in Gainesville, Florida. The publication costs $149 a year. To subscribe, send an e-mail communication to *aadkins@freenet.ufl.edu.*
    - Another very useful print newsletter is *legal.online.* Recent articles have provided in-depth coverage of marketing issues, case decisions, and regulatory developments of interest to lawyers on the Internet and research resources available online. The newsletter is

edited by lawyer Robert J. Ambrogi and is published by Legal Communications Ltd. A one-year (twelve-issue) subscription to the publication costs $99. To subscribe, call 800-722-7670.

- *Counsel Connect* (*http://www.counsel.com*), maintained by American Lawyer Media, is an excellent Web source for lawyers. It has a very helpful marketing forum, as well as periodic Internet-related, online continuing legal education programs.

CHAPTER 9

Technology Tools and Techniques for Client Development

Kelly Kiernan Largey

Technology is a valuable tool for every lawyer who has felt there is "simply no time for business development." Technology enables lawyers to communicate better with clients, work more efficiently, and set themselves apart from their competitors. Sometimes technology enables lawyers to offer clients a new service: For example, an extranet enables clients to have twenty-four-hour, seven-day-a-week access to information about cases, docketing, billing, and research. Other times, technology can change the way a service is provided: For example, an electronic newsletter can be delivered to a client's computer rather than printed and mailed. And investing in the right technology is just as important for small firms as for large firms. In many ways, technology levels the playing field, allowing the solo practitioner to compete with larger firms. Technology enables a sole practitioner to manage large amounts of information and be more accessible.

Technology's tools seem to change daily. Rather than offering detailed descriptions of various types of technological products, this chapter instead includes practical advice on how technology can be applied to business development and client service. Technology enables lawyers to deliver better client service because it helps organize information, improves communications, and enhances lawyers' work product.

Organizing Information

Client and Contact Databases

Problem: How do I keep track of my clients? I have a mailing list for sending invoices and holiday cards, but I don't have any way to keep track of the type of work I do for each client. As my client list has grown, I find it difficult to remember personal details about each client. I also want to keep track of people I meet at association meetings, from whom I often get referrals.

Every lawyer has a client mailing list, even if it is used only for sending invoices. Turning your client mailing list into a marketing database requires time and effort, but yields many benefits.

A marketing database is a central place where you can store information about your clients, prospects, and referral sources. You can also keep a record of marketing activities for each, for example, the newsletters they have received, the seminars to which they have been invited, the seminars they have attended, or the ball games they have attended with lawyers from your firm. A good marketing database enables you to customize mailing lists so that, for example, you can send information about changes in tax laws to probate clients, or information about expected changes in food and drug regulations to biotechnology and medical-device clients. Including information about how each client came to you will help you generate reports about which of your marketing efforts are most successful. You can even do something as simple as remembering your clients' spouses' names by including personal information about your clients in your database.

CHOOSING SOFTWARE

Although some firms have successfully developed custom marketing databases in house,[1] it is generally better to purchase database software than it is to create your own.[2] Several database software programs are designed specifically for law firm marketing.[3] These programs require a substantial investment in both software costs and training, but they provide any type of sorting or reporting that a law firm would need. Some of these law firm marketing databases are modules of law firm time and billing programs.

Not all marketing database programs can be linked to all time and billing programs. If you are not buying the marketing module of your time and billing program, be sure to ask whether your time and billing program can be linked to the marketing database you are considering. Linking your database to your time and billing program enables you to analyze your client base to determine which types of legal work generate the most fee income, and to target client retention efforts toward your largest clients. Other benefits to linking time and billing information to your marketing database include these: the ability to sort client lists by fees billed (for example, all clients generating more than $X thousand per year); the ability to analyze the largest fee generators by industry group; and the ability to track business development efforts, especially cross-selling efforts, according to trends in the level of fee income generated by targeted industry groups or specific legal services.

Off-the-shelf contact-management software, designed for salespeople to keep track of leads, can provide a useful marketing database for a fraction of the investment required for a database designed especially for law firms.[4] You should look for a relational database, rather than a flat database. From a user's perspective, a relational database lets you slice and sort your information in more ways than a flat database. Some off-the-shelf programs cannot easily organize records for corporate clients for which the firm may have many individual contact names, or clients for whom the client team includes a large number of firm lawyers. You should determine whether the limitations of an off-the-shelf program are material to your database needs.

Before deciding which type of database you need, you should consider the following matters: (1) the number of records you plan to track, (2) your hardware capabilities (and whether you are willing to invest in more hardware), (3) who is going to gather the information for the database, and keep it up to date, and (4) what you want to do with all the information you record. The size of your firm is not the only factor to consider. Even a large firm may find that an off-the-shelf contact manager suits the firm's needs. If you know that you will want to print personalized letters, mailing labels, envelopes, and name tags from the database, evaluate how easy it is to perform each of these tasks using the database and your firm's word processing software. If your firm's management requires reporting of financial information in spreadsheet format, find a program that can create tracking reports in spreadsheets. You should also consider whether you want to give more than one person the ability to add, or edit, information for the database. This will distribute the labor, but increase the likelihood that information will be added in an inconsistent manner. Even if you centralize data entry, you may want to make the database available in read-only format to everyone at your firm. Keep in mind that increasing the number of users will increase the cost of most software programs.[5]

DECIDING WHAT DATA TO COMPILE

The kinds of information you track in your database will depend on both your marketing goals and the strategies and tactics you have identified in your marketing plan. For example, if your goal is to cross-sell additional services to your current Fortune 500 clients for whom you are billing less than a certain dollar amount each year, you will want your database to identify—for each client—the type of work you do, the Fortune 500 rank, and the billing history. If your tactics include sending a variety of newsletters to promote your knowledge base in a new practice area, and you want to track whether your newsletters bring in new work in those areas, you will want to keep track of which clients have received which publications. If you plan to introduce new firm lawyers to a client at the next association meeting the client attends, you will want to keep track of the associations to which the client belongs. A probate lawyer who wants to send periodic reminders to clients to update their wills will want to include information about the date of each client's most recent will.

At a minimum, a good client database should include the following items for each client:

- Name, mailing address, phone number, facsimile number, and e-mail address
- For institutional clients, the names of all the firm's contacts with the client
- The title for each client contact (including designations such as Esq., Ph.D., or M.D., if applicable), and the appropriate salutation (such as Mr., Ms., or Dr.)
- The name of the primary lawyer handling the client's work, along with the names of other lawyers who do any substantial amount of work for that client
- The date the firm first started working for the client
- The type of work the firm does for the client
- How the client heard about the firm (the source or marketing efforts that contributed to bringing in the client)
- The firm's client/matter numbers (for cross-referencing to time and billing information)
- Whether the client uses a PC or Macintosh computer system
- The client's industry

Standard Industry Codes (SICs) are one way to classify clients, but the system is complicated and probably slices industries more finely than most firms need. You can create your own simplified classification system based on Fortune 500 industry segments or the firm's industry-related practice groups. Your database should allow more than one industry code for clients with diversified businesses. It should also link client records to any other clients that are corporate parents or subsidiaries. Organize the database so you can track not only the marketing activity that initially brought the client to your firm, but any activity that prompted a current client to seek additional services from the firm. This will help you track cross-selling efforts.

As noted previously, you should keep track of the associations to which the client contacts belong, the meetings they attend, and a history of all the interactions they have with the firm's business development efforts (such as lists of firm mailings to the client, interviews or surveys in which the client participated, and seminars the client attended). You should also keep track of, and link to the records for, other clients that the client referred to the firm.

PROSPECTS AND REFERRALS

In addition to clients, prospective clients should be tracked in a marketing database. Prospects can include companies for whom the firm has prepared a proposal or made a presentation, the names of people who have attended firm seminars, and those who have subscribed to firm newsletters. Many firms also keep track of information about firm alumni in their marketing database, because alumni are often a rich source of referral work. All referral sources should receive firm mailings and invitations to client appreciation functions, and be remembered in client entertainment plans. The same efforts that contribute to maintaining good client relationships apply to maintaining good relationships with lawyers and others who send work to the firm.

Staff or Skills Databases

Problem: Sometimes clients call and ask me whether we have anyone at the firm with a particular expertise. I want to be able to answer those kinds of questions immediately, but the firm has become too big for me to do this from memory.

A good staff database enables everyone at the firm who has access to a computer to search electronically for personnel with particular expertise, language ability, education, or experience. Some database software packages include programs designed to keep track of lawyer information.[6] If you have a marketing database that does not include a staff-skills database, or have chosen not to make the firm marketing database available at all desktops, you need to select a different software platform for your staff-skills database. Putting your skills database in a program like Lotus Notes, or on your intranet, is a good way to make information about skills available to everyone, especially in firms with multiple offices.

The skills database should include information about all staff persons, including administrative personnel. A secretary who speaks a foreign language may be able to help with an emergency translation and the comptroller who is also a notary may be able to assist with late-night document preparation. The database should include information that is useful internally, such as internal telephone extensions, office locations, and home telephone numbers. That information can be hidden when biographies are printed for promotional purposes. Printable information should include education, bar admissions, areas of expertise, specific case or matter examples, leadership and teaching positions, and publications. Your database should give you the option to print a standard lawyer biography, or to create a customized biography with selected case examples relevant to a particular client or matter. You should store lawyer photographs in the database, and configure the print options to generate a biography with or without a photograph. (No matter what the quality of your laser printer, printing on coated paper will improve the look of photographs.)

Marketing-Materials Databases

Problem: My firm has a variety of printed, standard marketing materials, but we get many Requests for Proposals (RFPs) that require customized replies. I don't want to reinvent the wheel with every proposal, but I do want to be sure that I include current information.

Many firms find that it makes sense to create a database for all firm promotional materials, such as firm brochures and practice group descriptions, lawyer biographies, and all RFP responses. Converting all your marketing materials to electronic form makes them easily searchable, and also provides a format from which your materials can be readily e-mailed or faxed. A marketing-materials database is especially useful for firms with offices overseas or in several time zones, which rely on the services of a marketing staff in a distant office. The database gives everyone immediate access to everything needed to convince a prospect to hire the firm.[7]

The marketing-materials database should include nonconfidential information about significant cases or matters the firm has handled in the past. This information should reference the lawyers, client, industry, practice area, subject matter, and dates, so examples of prior experience in a particular area can be easily retrieved.

Some firms have automated the production of proposals with word processing macros. Using macros, initial draft proposals can be generated by individual lawyers, who choose proposal text from a menu of options. There is now at least one software package designed specifically for generating proposals.[8] When the production of basic background and capabilities information needed for a proposal is automated, you have more time to analyze the potential client's particular needs, and to propose solutions that are bound to set your proposal apart from the rest.

Communicating with Clients

Problem: I understand that in a service industry, accessibility is crucial. How can I use technology to be more accessible to my clients?

From a client services perspective, the most important benefit of technology is that it increases your accessibility by creating new ways for clients to get in touch with you.

Exchanging Documents by E-mail

E-mail is a terrific way to keep in touch with clients, and it has become essential for firms that serve corporate clients. A 1997 survey of in-house counsel at Fortune 150 companies revealed that 87 percent had the ability to communicate through e-mail.[9] Although many of those who use e-mail deviate from rules of grammar, spelling, and punctuation, lawyers are judged by their ability to communicate clearly and should proofread and spell check e-mail communications as if they were printed letters.

From a client services perspective, one of the dangers of e-mail is that it carries with it the assumption of an instant response.[10] You must read and reply to your e-mail daily. When using e-mail, don't miss the opportunity to communicate your address and phone number, and your firm's URL if you have a Web site, through a signature line on your e-mail communication.

The value of e-mail lies not just in its ability to send messages, but in an ability to attach and exchange documents in electronic form, almost instantaneously. You can send a client an entire word processing document, a spreadsheet, or even a document formatted in a desktop-publishing program with same-day (usually same-hour) delivery. The e-mail recipient can open and edit the document, and attach revisions to a return e-mail communication.

Two important considerations in exchanging documents by e-mail are confidentiality and compatibility. If the document contains confidential or privileged information, it is prudent to use a direct e-mail link or an encryption program to safeguard your communication. To use encryption, the recipient of your e-mail must have the same encryption program and a key to decode your message. Many users find encryption too time consuming and difficult to use. There is currently disagreement about whether encryption of e-mail is necessary to protect the attorney-client privilege. At least one state ethics opinion has held that it is not.[11]

Before you send a client a word processing document by e-mail, be sure you know which word processing software the client uses, and which version. Most of the newer word processing programs enable you to save a document in other word processing formats and older versions, and as PC or Macintosh documents. Save your document in a format that your client can open without difficulty, or save documents using Adobe Acrobat, a format for Macintosh systems or PCs.

You can also use e-mail to send newsletters. E-mail newsletters cost substantially less than printed versions, and are far easier to mail in a timely fashion.

In a recent survey by the Legal Marketing Association (LMA) (formerly National Law Firm Marketing Association, or NALFMA), 75 percent of in-house counsel said they preferred receiving printed newsletters to faxed or e-mail versions.[12] The survey's authors attributed this preference to in-house counsel's lack of familiarity with e-mail, and lack of access to laser printers on which to print electronic newsletters. This will change. In-house law departments are investing in technology at a brisk clip, reporting an 18.3 percent increase in spending in 1997 over 1996 rates.[13] Take advantage of the anticipated future demand for electronic newsletters by having yours ready now. You can send a text-only newsletter, or one in the same format as your printed newsletter—complete with masthead and graphics—by sending it in "portable document format" (pdf) using Adobe Acrobat. Many Web sites post long documents, such as corporate annual reports, as pdf files because the pdf format preserves the columns, page breaks, and fonts of the original. Anyone who has Adobe Acrobat can then read and print your newsletter in its typeset format. The Adobe Acrobat reader can be downloaded for free from Adobe's Web site.[14]

Intranets

An intranet is an internal network that uses Internet technology to make information available within the firm. Intranets use the same browsers and hypertext markup language (HTML) that the Internet uses, but the material on an intranet cannot be accessed from outside the firm. Some firms use databases like Lotus Notes to simulate an intranet.[15]

As noted earlier, an intranet enables you to make lawyer biographies and marketing materials accessible to everyone in the firm. Many firms find it useful to post human resources information, firm phone directories, and firm policies and procedures on an intranet.[16] Distributing information over an intranet is cost-effective; corporations estimate that by posting information in an easily accessible manner on an intranet, they save their employees twelve minutes each day. For law firms, this translates into more billable time.[17] An intranet is also an excellent way to post news about the firm's business development efforts, and tips on how to do everything from creating a slide show to working a room. Some firms, like Fish & Richardson, post their business development newsletters on an intranet. An intranet newsletter shares the benefits of an e-mail newsletter—it can be distributed instantly to multiple offices at little cost. But an intranet newsletter can include photos and other graphics, features that make the newsletter more interesting to read. An intranet newsletter that describes the firm's promotional materials can link to electronic versions of those materials, or to sites on the Internet. Some firms, like Steptoe & Johnson in Washington, D.C., use their intranets for marketing databases that include information about firm alumni, indices of firm-authored articles and speeches, cites to news clippings about the firm, and information about resources available from marketing departments.

Extranets

An extranet uses Internet technology but creates private sites accessible only to clients you select. The beauty of this technology is that a client can access your extranet even if it uses a Macintosh system and you use a PC. All the client needs is an Internet browser—there are no other special software requirements. Some firms have used extranets to make docketing and case status information available to clients, or to give clients access to firm research memoranda. One firm gives its clients access to a virtual law library, a centralized database of links to research sites available on the Internet and through paid online services.[18]

Some commentators believe that extranets will be the next "big thing" for law firms, especially those that work with corporate clients.[19] An extranet brings the client into the law firm's "network," enabling real collaboration and partnering. For example, a law firm could create an extranet with checklists and training information for a client's human resources department, which the client's managers could access when making hiring and firing decisions. Or, a firm could monitor legislation in the client's industry, posting summaries of legislation that affects the client and generating a "head's up" e-mail to the client whenever something new is added to the site.[20]

Extranets also offer a way to enhance information firms provide to the public on an Internet site. For example, a firm that offers case commentaries to the public on its Internet site might offer a topical index to those commentaries only to its clients through an extranet. Or, the firm might invite clients to participate in a discussion group covering selected topics on the site. That way, while the site provides the general public with useful information, clients get something extra.

Voice Mail

Voice mail is affordable for law firms of any size. Local phone companies now offer voice messaging services for those who do not want to invest in a voice mail system. This system has an advantage over an answering machine, as it will answer your line if you are on the telephone and offer callers the option of listening to and editing a message before finalizing it.

Some believe that voice mail offers a way to duck callers. Used correctly, however, it is an excellent way to be more—not less—responsive. Many clients prefer voice mail, which allows for messages filled with verbal shorthand and eliminates the need to spell out terms that the client and lawyer will understand but a message taker may not. The key is to use voice mail in a way that makes leaving messages easier for clients. For example, when it is not possible to have your telephone answered by a person, be sure that callers go automatically to voice mail after only a few rings, and that your system provides the option to go to an operator if the caller does not wish to use voice mail. The best way to use voice mail is to change your greeting to reflect your schedule. If you will be out of the office and unable to return any telephone calls, say so in your greeting. A caller who does not expect your return call until the next day will not be disappointed when you return the call as soon as you are able. A caller who expects an immediate reply, but receives a return call the following day, will assume the call was not important to you.

Videoconferencing

In-person meetings and travel have historically been necessary components of providing legal services, and are typically charged to clients. As clients seek to reduce their legal expenses, however, videoconferencing has become an excellent lower-cost substitute for in-person meetings. One advantage of conducting a meeting by videoconference rather than telephone is that the participants can look at documents, slides, or other graphics together. Users should know that the videotape used in videoconferencing has fewer frames than videotape seen on television, and movement looks awkward on the screen. There is also a delay between the time a party speaks and the time the other party hears what was said, and this delay can interfere with discussion for those who are not familiar with it.

In the past, videoconferencing equipment was expensive. Room systems, which have cameras that can transmit images of large groups of people or entire conference rooms, cost in the $20,000 to $40,000 range. More recently, smaller desktop camera systems, which are appropriate for a two-party meeting, have become available at a cost of between $1,000 and $2,000. Because all videoconferencing systems require investment in a network or ISDN to transmit video images, many firms find that it is easier to use either a service provider's videoconferencing equipment, which can be rented by the hour, or a video camera over the Internet, which is affordable and does not require long-distance charges.

As with most investments in technology, your decision about whether to invest in videoconferencing equipment should be based on whether your clients would like to communicate with you using videoconferencing. Clients who have videoconferencing equipment will likely ask you to use it with them. In the 1997 survey of in-house counsel mentioned earlier, just over half the law departments said they had videoconferencing capability.[21]

Client Presentations

Problem: How can I make a really great presentation without spending a bundle?

Slide presentation software and less-expensive, color ink-jet printers have made it possible to prepare professional-looking overheads at very little cost. Even simple color transparencies can create a polished, professional presentation if done correctly. Choose a standard slide background and use it consistently in every client presentation. Add your firm's logo or wordmark to the bottom of each slide, and prepare paper copies, in color if possible, to give to the client. Any extra effort you undertake to customize your slide presentation will make a favorable impression. If the client has a Web site, copy the client's logo and add the client's name and logo to the cover slide of your presentation.

A basic rule for slides is to keep them simple. Your overheads will look best if you limit the number of words and ideas you express on each one. Slides should be an outline of your remarks, not the full text. All presentation software programs have good graphing capabilities. Use them. Expressing your thoughts graphically will enrich your presentation.

The next "step up" from using color overheads is projecting slides to a screen directly from a laptop computer. Some laptop computers have a special monitor that can be placed on top of an overhead projector. The monitors of standard laptop computers can be projected directly from the laptop to a screen using a video graphics array (VGA) or super VGA video projector. When you project your slides directly from your laptop, you can—with just a click of your mouse—use the "special effects" built into presentation software. These include lines of text that fly or fade in, cumulatively, as bullet points on a slide. Projectors are not inexpensive. If you decide to rent a projector, or use your client's projector, check ahead to make sure the equipment is compatible. Not all laptops work with all projectors.

Many law firms differentiate themselves by creating multimedia presentations—that is, presentations that include not only slides, but audio and video as well. Multimedia presentations are saved on CD-ROMs and are usually organized so that the presenter need not follow the presentation in any linear fashion, but can navigate among its parts. In-house production of multimedia presentations is not advised, as it requires extensive specialized equipment, as well as a good photographer, a capable narrator, and the technical expertise to compile the whole presentation in a navigable format. It makes more sense to use an outside company to produce a standard, multimedia presentation CD-ROM that can be used with all clients and prospects.

Enhancing Work Product and Standing Out

Technology can be applied to almost any area of law practice to make work more efficient. Sometimes a technological innovation can also produce good publicity for you and your firm. Such was the case when the Fish & Richardson firm used hypertext markup language (HTML) in an appellate brief.

HTML, the language of the World Wide Web, enables you to jump from one section of a Web site to other text or graphics within that site, or to another Web site, with a fingertip command to your computer. HTML offers many potential applications in legal documents, which are generally full of references. Appellate briefs are particularly well suited to this technology.[22] In January 1997, Fish & Richardson submitted an appellate brief written in HTML along with a traditional paper brief in an appeal in a patent-infringement case, which was then pending in the Court of Appeals for the Federal Circuit. The 25-page brief, 300 pages of references, and three videotaped clips were assembled on a single CD-ROM that could be read with any Internet browser software. Although the appellate court noted that the HTML brief had much to commend it, the CD-ROM was stricken from the record at the request of opposing counsel, who complained that he did not have a CD-ROM drive or browser software. Later that year, Fish & Richardson and opposing counsel Merchant & Gould, in another case pending in the Court of Appeals for the Federal Circuit, worked together to file all their briefs and their joint appendix on a single CD-ROM. In that case, the court accepted the HTML briefs. Fish & Richardson posted the briefs and joint appendix on its Web site while the appeal was pending.

The greatest benefit of using HTML in the appellate setting is that it makes the court's job much easier. Giving the judge the ability to view all the evidence in the record with a simple mouse click at the appropriate point in the argument also contributes to a stronger, more convincing argument. But putting the appellate documents onto a CD-ROM had the added benefit of enabling Fish & Richardson to involve the client. Sending large stacks of paper trial transcripts and appendix materials to a client is cumbersome. Sending background documents on a CD-ROM allows the client to have direct input in preparing the appellate argument.

Fish & Richardson was able to stand out by writing about the HTML brief, because it was the first such brief of its kind. Its filing was reported in both general and legal publications,[23] and the lawyer who supervised the project wrote many articles about the experience, including a piece on the appropriate use of this technology for the "At Issue" column of the *ABA Journal*.[24] Many other legal documents could benefit from effective use of HTML technology. Patent applications, complicated contracts, lease agreements, and Securities and Exchange Commission filings may one day be prepared in HTML format. Opportunities exist for other lawyers and firms to be the first to set new standards for preparing other types of documents in HTML, or another format that adds value to the paper document.

Conclusion

Whether to invest in technology and what to buy depends on what you want to do. Before you decide whether you need a marketing database, an electronic newsletter, or the ability to prepare documents in HTML, look at the information you would like to manage, to whom you want to be accessible, and the nature of your work product. Most important, look at how other industries use technology. This will give you ideas about how to apply technology to the delivery of legal services, as well as to the practice of law. In the fast-changing world of technology, there are limitless opportunities to be first.

Notes

1. Arent, Fox, Kintner, Plotkin & Kahn was one of the first firms to develop a computerized marketing database. Marketing director Vicki Schieber described that database at a National Law Firm Marketing Association (NALFMA) (now Legal Marketing Association, or LMA) conference in 1991. Vicki Schieber, Tracking Results, Presentation at NALFMA Regional Conference, Boston, Massachusetts (October 1991).
2. At Fish & Richardson, we created a contact-management database in Lotus Notes. We chose this database because it was familiar and accessible to everyone at the firm. Other relational database software programs that can be used to create a marketing database include dBASE and Paradox, both from Borland (800-457-9527) and Microsoft's FoxPro.
3. Elite (310-398-4900), LegalEase (415-759-8878), CMS Marketsense (904-224-2200), and APS Marketecture (415-495-4710) are all designed specifically for law firms.

4. Contact-management software includes Goldmine (800-654-3526), InterAction (888-572-1400), Symantec Corp.'s ACT! (408-253-9600), CogniTech's Sharkware (800-947-5075), and Microsoft Outlook.
5. For help in analyzing marketing database options, see Kelly B. Newcomb, *Proper Selection and Utilization: How to Shop for a Marketing Database,* Marketing for Law, July 1997, at 1.
6. LegalEase has a staff database, Elite does not.
7. Wren Harris Batterton, *Steptoe and Johnson Uses Technology to Manage, Share Marketing Information,* Marketing for Law, Oct. 1996, at 6.
8. The RFP Machine, Pramatech Software (212-626-6877).
9. Alicia Philley, *In-House Goes High Tech,* Corp. Couns. Mag., Oct. 1997, at 47, 51.
10. Nancy Roberts Linder, *Be Aware of Your On-line Persona,* Law Marketing Exchange, Aug. 1997, at 10.
11. The Legalethics.com Web site tracks ethics opinions dealing with this issue. <http://www.legalethics.com/e-mail.htm>.
12. National Law Firm Mktg. Ass'n, *Hot off the Press: Measuring the Effectiveness of Newsletters as Business Development Tools,* Legal Directions: supp. L. Marketing Exchange, 1997, at 6.
13. Alicia Philley, *In-House Goes High Tech,* Corp. Couns. Mag., Oct. 1997, at 47.
14. <http://www.adobe.com>.
15. Wren Harris Batterton, *Steptoe and Johnson Uses Technology to Manage, Share Marketing Information,* Marketing for Law, Oct. 1996, at 6.
16. Nigel Armitage, *Net Gains,* Legal Abacus, Autumn 1997.
17. G. Scott Davis, *The Intranet for Law Firms: Why Every Firm Should Implement an Intranet,* Internet Legal Prac. Newsl., Mar. 24, 1997; <http://www.collegehill.com/ilp-news/ilpn9.txt>.
18. Carol Todd Thomas, *The Virtual Law Library,* Law Marketing Exchange, Aug. 1997, at 4–5 (describing virtual law library of Brouse & McDowell).
19. Richard S. Granat & David Levine, *Extranets: Creating the Collaborative Law Practice,* Internet Legal Prac. Newsl., Sept. 27, 1997; <http://www.collegehill.com/ilp-news/granat2.html>.
20. See Granat & Levine, *supra* note 20 (describing both of these hypothetical uses of extranets).
21. Alicia Philley, *In-House Goes High Tech,* Corp. Couns. Mag., Oct. 1997, at 47, 51.
22. By the end of 1997, two briefs written in HTML had been filed in the U.S. Supreme Court. The first HTML brief was filed in 1995 in a shareholder class-action lawsuit, and was posted on the World Wide Web. It was intended to demonstrate the use of the Web to disseminate public filings in class-action lawsuits to the general public. Another HTML brief was filed in the spring of 1997 in a case that addressed the constitutionality of the Communications Decency Act of 1996. That act criminalizes indecent

and offensive speech on the Internet. One of the most interesting things about that brief is that it had hot links to various medical and artistic Web sites that included images that might be considered indecent under the act. By reviewing the brief, and the hot links, the justices could see first-hand the breadth of the communication that the act would suppress.

23. *See, e.g.,* Wendy R. Leibowitz, *When High-Tech Is Over the Top: Is a CD-ROM Brief Fair or Foul?,* Nat'l L.J., Mar. 3, 1997, at B8.
24. *High-Tech Appeals,* A.B.A. J., July 1997.

CHAPTER 10

Using Win-Win Pricing As a Marketing Advantage

Peter D. Zeughauser

Because so much of successful law firm marketing is based on extraordinary client service, client relationships (repeat business), and partnering concepts, it is important to look at ways in which firms can compete for business by moving away from the traditional hourly rate fee structure and toward aligned incentives.

About Fee Arrangements

All fee arrangements should achieve two goals—the generation of profit and increased client satisfaction. In doing so, they should strengthen and build the relationship between the law firm and the client. As simple as this seems, law firms and clients have endured the fidelity of a twenty-five-year marriage to the hourly rate, a fee arrangement that serves neither goal spectacularly well. The hourly rate is far from the most profitable fee arrangement available to firms. Indeed, with the increased importance of technology and depth of expertise in the profession, its profitability is diminishing rapidly. (The best that can be said about the hourly rate is that its "cost-plus" underpinnings ensure some profit, although the margins are often small and realization rates unacceptably low in an increasingly competitive environment for law firms.)

And, although many clients are resistant to, and fearful of, experimentation with alternatives to the hourly rate, they harbor deep suspicion and distrust of the system due to the wrong incentives it provides. The system survives, though, because the readily apparent alternatives appear fraught with the same, if not worse, problems that are endemic to the hourly rate. They don't ensure profit and they pose great risks to relationships. Firms need to explore new hybrid fee arrangements that will align the interests of law firms and clients, build relationships, and ensure profitability.

I experienced my first alternative pricing arrangement as an in-house counsel involved in a dispute in which I switched from an hourly rate lawyer to a contingent-fee lawyer after two frustrating years of attempting to negotiate a precomplaint settlement. From that time forward, I often engaged plaintiffs' contingent-fee lawyers to help resolve disputes. I learned several important lessons about the powerful incentives fee arrangements provide. I also learned a lot about the impact of fee arrangements on relationships. There is amazing structural parallelism between the two.

Risk/Reward Allocation

Most lawyers would agree that the earnings hierarchy in the profession places contingent-fee lawyers at the top. They make the most money. Taking a look at the Am Law 100 list, one would conclude that lawyers at the big Wall Street firms come in a tidy second. Interestingly, third place seems to fall to the many other lawyers who populate the bottom 80 percent or so of the Am Law 100 firms. These are the big hourly rate firms.

Let me hypothesize that this is significant because of the striking manner in which profit potential parallels risk taking and relationship building in the fee arrangement. From the point of view of a client and its law firm, there are three principal risks one faces in every engagement: The risk of a cost overrun, the risk of a bad outcome, and the risk that quality might be compromised because of the fee arrangement. Reward-based incentives may be used to allocate or shift these risks. The following chart depicts how these risks are allocated in the three basic fee structures: The hourly rate, the flat or fixed-fee structures, and the contingent-fee arrangements.

THREE BASIC FEE STRUCTURES—RISK/REWARD ALLOCATION

Risks	Risk of cost overrun	Risk of bad outcome
Hourly fee	Client bears entire risk	Client bears entire risk
Flat/fixed fee	Law firm bears entire risk	Client bears entire risk
Contingent fee	Law firm bears entire risk	Shared risk

This chart graphically demonstrates the relationship between risk and reward. Contingent-fee lawyers make the most money because they take the most risk. Flat-fee lawyers (for instance, in mergers and acquisitions work) make the next greatest amount of money because they take the next greatest amount of risk. And lawyers who work by the hour, on a cost-plus basis, rank third because they take no risk.

Relationship-Building Fee Arrangements

The chart also demonstrates why none of the three basic fee arrangements is particularly well suited for relationship building. That is because they fail to *allocate* risk and reward effectively between the law firm and the client. Instead, they shift risk and reward absolutely. This absolute shifting of risk and reward, as opposed to a fair allocation of the two, creates great danger of disrupting relationships. Even with the successful contingent-fee lawyers I often used, I frequently felt like I was overpaying them because of the windfall they experienced if they got great results with little effort. I could have more smartly gone to an hourly fee structure if I knew the dispute would have been quickly resolved. This feeling that I was overpaying was disruptive to my relationship with counsel.

Although contingent-fee lawyers may get a lot of referrals, they seldom see repeat business, so ongoing relationships are less important in the same sense that they are important for the corporate client. Contingent-fee lawyers are in a business in which the results rule over all else. Relationships between business law firms and their clients, for whom the firms handle portfolios of litigation, for example, couldn't survive the friction that would build after repeated windfalls. Results are a very high priority, but there are other important priorities, too, like predictability of cost and intimate knowledge of the client.

Tiering fee arrangements and creating hybrids, like flat fees with bonuses, is likely the key for structuring a fee that increases profitability and client satisfaction. In successful relationship-building fee arrangements, one of the tiers should be the "blow-out" or "re-opener" tier. This tier kicks in when the fee arrangement, however carefully structured, isn't working for one side or the other because of events that were not reasonably foreseeable at the time the arrangement was agreed upon.

In addition to allocating risk, as opposed to shifting it completely, another lesson I learned as a client that attracted me to further use win-win pricing is that there is more than one source of funds from which the reward for a great result can be paid. Most lawyers think of bonuses and premiums as coming from the result achieved by the law firm. Indeed, in recent years contingent fees have increased dramatically in popularity with the corporate bar. Defense contingencies are the fastest growing type of alternative fee structures. But, another important source of bonus funds is cost savings. In the end, as much as business clients want quality and results, they also want efficiency and predictability. Thus, a fee arrangement that provides incentives for saving the client legal fees is a fee arrangement that builds a stronger relationship. And, bonuses and premiums paid out of money saved can be equally or more satisfying than money paid out of results, if one of the client's top priorities was to save money.

Assuming these suggestions make sense, the other tool needed to allocate risk and reward properly in a creative fee arrangement is "work segmentation."

This follows because the risk of windfalls is greatest from the unknown. Thus, if a fee arrangement is based upon discrete pieces of work, you should be willing to revisit the budget when the work is required; for instance, negotiating a mini-fee structure for a motion at the time the decision to file the motion is being made (when, presumably, more is known about the likelihood of its success than at an earlier time). This reduces the likelihood of a windfall for either the lawyer or the client. The key here is to build a budget plan for the matter that anticipates discussion of different fee arrangements at important junctures.

These basic principles illustrate how fee structures can be used to increase profitability and strengthen client relationships at the same time. The key is in allocating risk rather than shifting it, identifying a source for the payment of the premium or bonus that is aligned with the client's interests, and segmenting the work so the fee structure is agreed upon at a time when the unforeseeable can be best avoided.

The Impact of Fee Structures on Quality

In recent years the legal press has been rife with reports of high-profile flat-fee arrangements between corporate clients and their law firms. ABA and other industry surveys over the past several years indicate that somewhere between 40 and 60 percent of corporate clients are using flat fees today. Still more *plan* to increase their usage of them. These surveys also indicate that clients are willing to pay significant premiums, in the neighborhood of 50 percent, when using flat fees. When paying premiums to shift the risk of cost overruns to their law firms, clients are paying premiums for predictability. The willingness to pay premiums stems in large part from what is nearly a corporate obsession for meeting budgets. In a free marketplace, rewards incentivize behavior, and if you take away a reward, the behavior it incentivizes likewise goes away. I believe that quality is likely to decline when flat fees replace hourly rates.

This proposition will undoubtedly be denied and debated by major law firms and reputable legal departments alike, because *quality is the Holy Grail* of all the practice paradigms. And, though it is true that clients often want a Chevrolet, not a Rolls Royce, the Chevy better be well built and run properly. For all its foibles, the hourly rate incentivizes quality more greatly than it incentivizes anything else. After all, if you take a lot of smart people, which lawyers tend to be, and tell them you will pay them by the hour to solve difficult problems correctly, they will get it right. But the incentive for quality under a flat fee is as indirect or nonexistent as is the incentive for efficiency under the hourly rate.

Although many clients and big law firm lawyers share the belief that quality is an *untouchable,* my experience is otherwise. I believed that quality was not at risk because the big-firm marketplace was overrun with quality. Quality had become the commodity of big-firm work product—an integral component of what they all offered. I often stated that if you were worried about quality dissipating or disappearing because of the fee structure, then your problem was not fee structure; you had the wrong lawyer. I learned this was incorrect. In a free marketplace, when you squeeze profits, you may also squeeze quality. Quality is rampant only because clients pay handsomely for it under the hourly rate.

In a very big flat-fee deal I did, I learned that when the fee was exhausted, morale and enthusiasm for winning began to wane as economic pressure from within the firm forced my lawyer to reevaluate strategy and resources. Yes, this bred some good results, like staffing consistency (to avoid learning time) and looking for ways to go for the jugular. But as the investment of time became unprofitable, my case looked more and more like a disease, with no one in the firm wanting to go near it. I had the same problem arise with a small firm. The case was on a contingent fee, but it suffered the same plight as the promise of punitive damages faded and the ability of the lawyers to earn a profit on the case, much less a bonus, evaporated with their growing investment of time. In both cases, the lawyers were forced to look for shortcuts so they could remain profitable. Creative strategies were posited, but they did not include thoroughness and exhaustive preparation, the hallmark of most winners in litigation.

Because of this failure, just like when clients ultimately became disenchanted with hourly rates, I suspect the same will come to pass should flat fees dominate the marketplace as hourly fees have done in the past. On the other hand, flat-fee arrangements allow clients to compare "apples to apples" on price. You can get a quote on a summary judgment motion, a research project, or an initial public offering. This facilitates shopping for legal services and allows more effective competitive pricing than is allowed by the hourly rate. With the cost cutting that accompanies predatory pricing, there will also come, in all likelihood, corner cutting. And when you cut corners, you raise quality issues.

The truth is that strange things happen on the frontier of change. Often, things don't happen as one would expect. The profession is clearly at the frontier of change when it comes to alternative billing. It needs to take a very hard look at how it will avoid quality failures as risk and reward shift.

When confronted with the basic question of whether to make money or die, most law firms will choose to make money. They will find a way to remain competitive, by cutting costs and providing predictability. Fee structures must reward the behavior the client desires for the matter at hand. If clients want predictability, cost cutting, quality, *and* improved results, then firms better build in rewards for all three, because flat fees don't reward results.

My own experience with alternative fee arrangements has led me to the conclusion that no single fee structure is appropriate for all legal work. Indeed, each of the three basic fee structures—the hourly rate, the flat fee, and the contingency—provide serious incentives for behavior that is often adverse to the client's interests. My experience and premise is that the structuring of fee arrangements is akin to the structuring of a commercial transaction or the development of a strategy for a dispute: There are few "one size fits all" alternatives. The appropriate fee structure for a significant matter will be tailored to the client's interests and priorities, and requires thought and knowledge to develop. Every successful fee structure needs to reward desired behavior. Although flat fees incentivize efficiency and disincentivize process, they speak little to results. In this sense they are strangely akin to the hourly rate. They work some of the time, for some matters and portfolios of work, but they are not a panacea.

The Proper Role of Discounting

Generally, I advocate that law firms not discount. They spend umpteen years developing brand-name equity. Why diminish it by selling top-line service and quality on the cheap? But, discounting worked wonders in many of my relationships with outside lawyers and, although I firmly believe that law firms should not discount *indiscriminately,* when employed effectively, discounting can be an important tool for improving client relationships and law firm profitability. Let's take a look at a few good reasons to discount.

Effective, win-win pricing should be the glue for a strong relationship between a client and its law firm. After all, the right price is the *sine qua non* of value in any client's mind. Defining and producing value is often difficult when the seller is selling something that is invisible, like legal services. Ensuring that value is perceived in the client's mind is likewise difficult. And, when it comes to value, like many other things in life, perception is reality.

When a law firm charges by the hour, its interest in selling hours is often inapposite to what a buyer wants to buy. The problem with *indiscriminate* discounting is that it doesn't address this fundamental flaw of the hourly rate.

Before one can align interests one must first discover interests. Clients and law firms actually share several interests. They both want to manage legal work in a way that makes each of them more profitable. They both want a fee arrangement that incentivizes great results and high levels of expertise brought to bear on the work at hand. They both want cost-effective fees. And, they both want robust and trusting relationships. Discounting is an effective tool for aligning all these interests.

Discounting can be used to incentivize results. The simplest example of this is discounting the hourly rate or a flat fee with a contingency, so the discount is recaptured if an agreed-upon result is achieved. This fee structure can be used for an entire matter or a discrete piece of work. When a client seeks to obtain a result and the lawyer has confidence in his or her ability to achieve the result, this fee structure aligns interests and influences the perception of value by conditioning the payment of the full fee on achieving what the client wants and what the lawyer thinks is possible.

Clients also want to incentivize cost savings. A discount can be employed to incentivize cost savings just as it can be employed to incentivize a certain result. In this fee structure, the law firm and the client agree on an anticipated cost for a matter or a discrete portion of a matter. For example, a client and law firm may agree that the reasonable cost of documenting, negotiating, and closing a transaction is $50,000. Posit that the client closes five of these transactions a year, and has paid its law firm $250,000 a year for the past five years to do this work. The client wants to reduce its fees by 5 percent, or $12,500. It is "shopping" the work to other firms. In this instance, the law firm offers a 5-percent discount, but has the ability to recapture the discount if it can reduce the fees beyond $12,500. Thus, if the law firm can close the five transactions for $200,000 at full rates by pushing the work to a lower level or through technology, knowledge management, or other techniques, the law firm and the client split the difference between $237,500 and $200,000. The law firm would recapture its $12,500 discount first from the savings, and the client and firm would split the balance of the savings, with the firm being paid a total of $225,000 for the $200,000 in work, or a 112.5-percent realization rate (which for most firms would improve profitability by 20 percent or more). And the client has achieved a 10-percent discount as opposed to the 5 percent it sought. Will clients pay extra for these kinds of savings? Well, they frequently do when they hire contractors to construct buildings. Perhaps the most commonly used construction contract is one with a guaranteed maximum cost and a clause that provides for a sharing of any savings.

Even when a relationship is already strong and the client develops a need for services in a practice area outside the law firm's areas of expertise, the client usually has reservations about "paying for the education" of a lawyer in the firm. This is especially true if the client can buy the expertise "off the shelf" at another law firm. In this instance, the firm can offer a deep discount equivalent to its profit margin while a lawyer develops expertise. The firm not only prevents incursion into the relationship by another firm, but also expands the relationship.

Fulfilling client needs is not the only reason to discount. In slow times, when a firm experiences low lawyer-utilization rates, discounting may make sense if it improves lawyer utilization or, more simply put, allows a firm to sell more hours. The utilization rate (busy lawyers) is a key element of profitability. Just as it does not make sense to discount in a heated market for legal services, it does make sense to discount in a flat market if this will, in fact, keep lawyers busy.

Likewise, building market share may be a legitimate reason to discount. Market share can be measured not just by the amount of the geographic market a law firm dominates, but also by the amount of a specific client's budget for legal services the firm wins each year. Offering a discount as part of a cross-selling strategy, thus allowing the client to consolidate its legal work and achieve efficiencies and perhaps other benefits (like better opportunities to practice preventive law), may prove worthwhile. Similarly, a discount can be an effective way to develop a dominant market position or to win a new marquis client, both of which can be the prelude to raising rates.

It does not follow that discounting always makes sense. In a free market, buyers and sellers will perform best where and when the greatest rewards can be earned. Indiscriminate discounting can cause a law firm to lose interest in quality and clients, and may even provide greater incentives for excessive hourly billing than the straight hourly rate. But, when deployed as a strategy for achieving shared goals and allocating risks and rewards, discounting is an effective tool for building client satisfaction and law firm profitability.

Addressing the Whole Picture

So, if win-win pricing can be used by firms to make more money and build stronger client relationships, why is there not greater use of creative, alternative pricing structures? The answer to this question is not mysterious. Although there are great incentives in corporations for in-house counsel to budget predictably and achieve great results, there are few, if any incentives for lawyers in law firms to do so, even if a fee structure results in great benefits for the firm. For example, how can law firms increase client satisfaction *and* cash in on the action by promoting the use of alternative dispute resolution (ADR) to settle litigation? The answer is simple: It must reward the use of ADR by its lawyers. Typical law firm compensation models, however, do not reward the early truncation of litigation.

Impediments to Using ADR to Achieve Early Dispute Resolution

It seems fairly clear that there are significant impediments to the proliferation of the early use of ADR in litigation practices in law firms. At least five jump off the page: Law firm pricing, products, compensation, staffing, and training. Training is a two-edged sword. If you take a lot of very smart people, as lawyers in the best firms are, teach them for three years in law school that litigation is the chief—and probably only—dispute resolution technique, put them in a firm's litigation department, call them litigators and teach them how to ply their trade, pay them by the hour to litigate, and, finally, reward them for racking up hours, they will, not surprisingly, do one thing best: *litigate.*

What clients want is to get their disputes resolved. Litigation is a process for resolving disputes. But, clients paying by the hour are distrustful of process; they want resolution. This is where pricing and product, the second and third impediments to early dispute resolution through ADR, enter the equation. When law firms sell hours, it is in their interest to sell process, not results. If the "follow the money" adage of our generation is true, for as long as the billable hour is king, law firms will have a direct financial interest inapposite to their clients' in selling litigation as opposed to selling results. Mindful of and resistant to this, clients force an unwelcome reality on law firms: Clients settle 90 percent of their disputes. This is not welcomed by law firms because it limits revenue and results in very few trial opportunities for most lawyers. Although the latter problem is difficult to solve, the former problem could be solved with a pricing scheme that rewards ADR.

The fourth impediment is compensation. Even if law firms devise a pricing scheme that results in greater profits from ADR than litigation, a compensation system that formally or informally rewards lawyers for hours billed (or sold), as opposed to results, will create a significant impediment to proliferating an ADR practice. This flows, again, from the "follow the money" maxim. When you tell very smart people who have chosen a high-earnings profession that they will be paid for selling hours, they will do one thing: *rack up hours*. On the other hand, if you tell them they will be paid to resolve disputes quickly, they will figure out how to get that done.

The ADR Model As an Example of Creative Fee Structuring

Having addressed the impediments to ADR, the question is this: What might work? What follows is intended to spark discussion and consideration of what the appropriate factors might be in structuring a pricing, product, compensation, and staffing scheme that would proliferate the profitable use of ADR in a litigation practice within a law firm, *on the assumption that early dispute resolution is what clients want.* The ADR example can be used to extrapolate ideas for creatively addressing other client preferences.

Devising a pricing, product, compensation, and staffing structure that would proliferate an ADR practice would require the lawyers to develop a dispute resolution strategy and budget for each dispute. Clients have come to expect, but often don't get, suitable budgets from their law firms. The strategy would involve a litigation as well as an ADR component. Because so many unpredictable events occur in dispute resolution, many of which are beyond the control of one party or the other, the budget should have high- and low-side parameters.

For the staffing component, litigators in the firm would pursue the litigation strategy while at the same time an ADR lawyer/ombudsperson or department within the firm would pursue resolution through ADR on a parallel track. The litigators would continue to bill and charge by the hour, perhaps subject to a collar and/or an incentive for achieving agreed-upon results. The ADR lawyer would keep track of hours (for management and realization-rate computation purposes), but the client would not be charged unless the ADR person successfully settled the dispute.

If the ADR lawyer is successful, the reward component of the fee could be structured in a number of different ways. For instance, the firm's fee could equal the difference between the total budget for the matter (high, low, or something in between) and the amount actually paid to date by the client (that is, the unspent litigation budget, which is the amount of unspent legal fees saved by the client by settling) or some portion thereof. This pricing structure would incentivize the firm to use ADR to resolve the dispute as early as possible to earn the "cost savings premium." Or, the firm's fee could be tied to how well the settlement outcome compares with what was agreed upon by the firm and the client as a reasonable expectation. Tiered results could provide for greater and lesser rewards depending on the degree to which expectations were met.

Law firms will likely worry at the prospect of not being paid for the ADR lawyer's time if the case doesn't settle. This concern should be allayed for two reasons: First, 90 percent of cases do settle, and second, under this model, trial lawyers can charge a premium (discussed below) for the truly unique skills they deliver, which will offset the loss of revenue for the ADR lawyer's time in those disputes that don't settle.

When pricing is addressed, so must compensation be addressed. Returning to the "follow the money" maxim, a compensation scheme that rewards individual partners principally based on the number of hours they sell or work, or some combination of the two, does not incentivize a product that truncates hours (such as ADR). Thus, to proliferate ADR within the firm, the compensation scheme must dovetail with the pricing, product, and staffing scheme in a manner that rewards individual partners who are successful at earning cost-savings premiums generated by the ADR pricing structure. For instance, rewarding partners based in part on realization rate would accomplish this goal.

Interestingly, this model neatly addresses the training conundrum and offers an opportunity to upgrade litigation pricing as well. First, it converts the plethora of litigators into premium billers. Just as important, it isolates those with trial experience as the ultimate deliverers of value, because it is only when ADR fails that this supreme skill, so to speak, is put in play. As a result, it too should demand a higher hourly and/or result premium.

It should go without saying that if a law firm wants to proliferate a profitable ADR practice, it must create a place for it in the firm, train lawyers in the technique, and reward them for success. A law firm that has combined all these essentials, in all areas of client service, would have an extraordinary competitive advantage.

CHAPTER 11

Public Relations for Lawyers

David Graves

Overview

In any crowded marketplace, positive name recognition will give a company, an individual, or a law firm a competitive advantage. The search for this advantage can be long and frustrating. The service you supply your clients may be outstanding, yet at the same time, you may find the growth of your practice stalled while other firms seem to prosper. If there was a single action that could be taken to spur the growth of a practice, it probably would have been bottled long ago.

Many firms rely on a number of devices to tell the world that they are capable and available. "Relationship building" is usually the primary source of new business. Memberships in community and business organizations, lunches with clients and prospective clients, and networking are activities grouped under this heading.

Relationship building has a narrow focus. It allows you to reach a limited audience at a specific time. Many lawyers turn to advertising to increase name recognition and business, but not all firms can afford an advertising campaign that will make them stand out from the pack, and others simply choose not to advertise.

Seeking out a larger audience through producing and distributing brochures and newsletters, delivering speeches, conducting seminars, writing articles for publication, and seeking news media coverage of your activities usually requires additional planning, time, and, occasionally, expense. However, the returns on these "credibility-building" activities can be much larger than those realized through relationship-building activities.

This chapter will concentrate on elements of credibility building, grouped under the broad umbrella of public relations. Public relations gives you an opportunity to tell your story from your perspective. It is, in fact, another device (like the private lunch) that allows you to tell a prospective client that you can provide the service the prospective client requires. The only differences are the forums you use to tell the story, your style of presentation, and the size of the audience you address.

Unlike advertising, which can be judged on newspaper circulation or radio or television ratings, the actual value of public relations can be difficult to gauge because not all its elements are tangible, and the benefits accrued may not be felt immediately. Mounting an effective public-relations campaign is like building a wall. If you look at the project stone by stone, it appears to be going nowhere. Only after the bricks have been placed together and the wall is completed can the project be judged for what it was meant to accomplish. Similarly, the effectiveness of a public-relations campaign can be determined only when all the elements have been executed.

Though most advertising campaigns are measured in terms of weeks, or perhaps months, an effective public-relations campaign may take a year or more to accomplish its goals. Public relations is frequently used to change perceptions, whereas advertising is used to create impressions. It is much more difficult to do the former than the latter. Also, because public relations does not usually rely on the use of purchased space or time in newspapers, radio, or television, its success depends, in part, on your ability to convince others (such as the news media) to help you tell your story. This will be made easier if you have a high-quality story to tell.

The most successful public-relations campaigns are the ones grounded in a positive message. Even when the campaign is a reaction to a negative event, you can establish or reestablish a positive image through public relations if your basic message is positive and truthful. If your message lacks those two basic ingredients, then your efforts will fail.

This chapter will cover some of the very basic elements of public relations that can be practiced by an individual lawyer or by a firm. Before we get to those elements, however, there are some initial steps to take.

Sampling the Marketplace

You may think you know how others perceive you, but without data to support your beliefs, you may find that you spent time and money on an effort that was doomed from the beginning because your planning was based on erroneous assumptions. Before you begin marketing yourself through public relations, you must have a clear picture of how the marketplace sees you, what your strengths and weaknesses are perceived to be, and where prospective clients place you in comparison with your competition. Research will enable you to establish a benchmark from which to develop your public-relations campaign. It will give you the perspective you need to frame the important questions you must ask yourself as you develop your campaign.

Market research can also give you information on the legal needs of the marketplace and the developing trends that will govern supply and demand in the months and years ahead. For example, your research may show that employers see a growing trend in wrongful-termination suits being filed against them, and that they perceive they have a growing need for legal counsel in this area. You identified a significant portion of the marketplace that has a growing need. If you use your resources properly, you can reach this audience with the message that you have the skills to help solve this problem.

A carefully considered research program can provide data to establish a market profile, which can be used to develop a variety of marketing plans for different practice groups or areas of specialization. If you have faith in the data that has been collected, a carefully planned and executed market research project can give you the information you need to plan your firm's development for several years.

Sample Questions

Naturally, the specific questions included in your research will be shaped by what you hope to learn. However, there are some standard queries that will assist in setting guidelines for your future public-relations campaign. Key questions may include the following:

1. Which law firms in your area are you most familiar with?
    - In answering this question, respondents are frequently prompted with a list of firms from which they can choose. Respondents can also be asked to rank the firms by level of awareness. Answers collected on this question will tell you the level of your name recognition compared with other law firms.
2. Which law firm do you use as your primary counsel? And why?
    - Respondents would not be prompted here. The answers to this question frequently show the major difference between which law firms have the greatest name awareness and which firms are actually retained.
3. Are you satisfied with your current law firm?
    - The subheadings within this question will tell you a great deal about what potential clients want in a law firm in terms of representation, service, and billing. It also sets the stage for the next question. A high negative response will show you areas of potential success. Of course, your firm may be one of those that respondents mention when expressing lack of satisfaction.
4. What are the most important factors in retaining a law firm?

- Responses in this area may supply you with your overall marketing message. If respondents mention quick response to inquiries as the most important factor, then you should mention rapid response to client inquiries in your message. If a large number of respondents say they want a firm that can anticipate problem areas and work with the client to head off problems, this tells you to formulate a message of "looking out for the best interests of the client."

5. In which areas of your business do you expect to increase the use of outside counsel?
   - The answers to this question will provide insights about the future growth of your firm, either through new hires or positioning your firm's marketing efforts.

Other questions may deal with respondents' negative or positive impressions of advertising or news stories concerning law firms, or respondents' perceptions of your firm in terms of staff, billing, or typical clients.

Having the data will save money and aggravation. Knowing where you stand in the marketplace gives you the insights needed to determine the direction and extent of your public-relations program. If your research tells you that your target audience has never heard of you, then you obviously have a major problem. In such a case, you must start from scratch to build your name, and your campaign must be more aggressive. If, on the other hand, you learn that you are highly regarded, you should concentrate on maintaining that image. A maintenance program will require less effort but no less clear an understanding of your overall goals. Once those goals are established, you are ready to identify the tools that will help you reach them.

There are a number of nationally recognized market research companies that specialize in working with law firms, and many reputable local researchers who have the expertise to tailor field studies to the needs of a legal practice.

Searching for the Soul of Your Firm

Once you or your researcher has asked the right questions of your prospective clients and has compiled their answers in a form that provides a clear understanding of your opportunities and obstacles, then you need to ask the right questions about yourself. This self-examination should be done periodically. Changes in the marketplace and in your own personnel can result in changes in cultures within law firms or within individual practice groups. To keep pace with these changes, ask yourself some basic questions.

Who Are We?

This may sound like a preschool approach to writing a public-relations plan, but it is frightening how few law firms have a good answer to this question. Many times, public-relations campaigns are mounted without this question ever being *asked,* let alone answered. If you do not understand your practice, your efforts will be scattered and will fail to accomplish anything. Whether you are in individual practice or part of a firm, you need to have a mission statement that clearly defines your practice. This statement will be the standard against which your public-relations activities will be measured. Be certain the statement is simple, clear, and accepted by the key players in your practice.

Who Are We Trying to Reach?

Imagine the ideal client. Think about that client's business or lifestyle. What kind of work will that client bring to your practice? This prospective client is your target audience. You must know who the members of this audience are, what is important to them, what they read, how they think, and their vocabulary before you can begin to communicate with them.

The challenge is to place yourself within this audience. Every audience member asks, "What's in it for me?" Your task is to create a public-relations program that tells the audience, from their perspective, why your message is so important that they should listen to it, understand it, and retain it.

What Do We Want Them to Know About Us?

The most difficult part of communicating with an audience is deciding what *not* to say. An audience can be easily overburdened with information or distracted by too many competing messages. You may have many wonderful stories to tell about you and your firm, but if you try to tell them all at the same time two negative things can happen: The audience may remember the least important story, or it may remember nothing at all.

Also, regardless of the medium you select to communicate with the target audience, there will always be constraints on the space and time available to get your message out. Therefore, your message needs to be crafted to minimize those constraints by focusing on a single concept. For example, if your practice concentrates in corporate law, and you believe your primary audience would be those likely to retain corporate counsel, the fact that you are interested in sports law would only clutter your message and confuse your target audience.

What Is Our Budget, in Finances and Human Resources?

Your plan will fail if the resources to fund your efforts are not in place from the beginning, and if you are not committed to seeing your plan through to the end. If you want to use your own personnel to manage your campaign, you must give them the tools and time they need to be successful and make certain the person managing the program has prior public-relations or media-relations experience. If you find you cannot pull the right people from other tasks to do the job, then you should retain outside public-relations professionals.

There are various relationships and billing options that a public-relations agency or consultant will consider. These include (1) a retainer based on the number of hours your consultant expects to work on your account each month; (2) a project fee for development, coordination, and management of your program; or (3) an hourly fee for services. Together you can analyze your goals and create a budget that fits your needs.

What Are the Most Effective Ways of Reaching This Audience?

In most cases, there are a variety of avenues to follow to deliver your message. Deciding which are best should be done only after you answered all the questions preceding this one. You may decide that offering to speak before key trade or professional organizations, writing articles for release in trade publications, or volunteering as a legal resource to a news program or radio talk show are the most attractive venues for you. Be certain that the audiences to whom you will be speaking or writing are your key audiences.

Do We Have a Consensus?

The key people in your firm must support the public-relations campaign. Everyone must contribute to reaching the target groups identified by your research. Without total support, something as simple as drafting a news release on a personnel appointment can take weeks. In critical situations, when immediate action is required to take advantage of an issue or situation, recalcitrance on the part of a key individual will mean a missed opportunity for you and likely media placement for a competitor.

Who Will Call the Shots?

When events are breaking, there is little time for consensus building. This means there needs to be one individual who has the authority to make important decisions when they need to be made. This person must have a clear understanding of your public-relations goals.

Writing the Plan

Your goal in developing a public-relations plan should be to make yourself stand out from the crowd of lawyers and competing law firms. You need to be innovative, committed, and patient. You do not need to alter the culture of your firm or participate in a program that makes you uncomfortable. Public relations should be a realistic projection of you and your firm. Bringing together all the disparate parts of the data you assembled through market research and internal evaluation, and putting them into an action plan, may seem daunting. However, if you use the information in an orderly manner, you will see that the elements of the plan are really lying before you.

Situation Analysis

The situation analysis includes the conclusions drawn from your research. It should clearly define your firm's position in the marketplace, your firm's strengths and weaknesses, a profile of the competition, and your opportunities for development.

Statement of Goals and Objectives

Careful analysis of the data you assembled will give you a clear understanding of where you want your firm to head and where you expect it to be by the end of a foreseeable period of time. This is the heart of your plan and the vision that should motivate your firm. All your marketing plans should flow from this statement—it is the single most important element of the plan. As you enumerate individual action steps, they should be viewed as steps that bring you to your goal.

Program Elements

These are the bricks that will build the wall we discussed a little earlier. You may not believe the items listed here are essential to the success of your plan, and you might have ideas of your own that will work for you and your firm. There are dozens of potential action steps you can take to increase your visibility or to change perception. The important thing to remember is your target audience—that ideal client—with whom you must communicate to make your plan a success. Make sure the steps you take will bring you closer to that audience.

PUBLICITY

The easiest way to bring attention to you or your firm is to distribute news releases on key hirings, promotions, or honors. Keep them simple. Get to the point quickly and keep the release to one page whenever possible. Provide the "Who, What, When, Where, and Why," accompanied by a five-by-seven-inch, black-and-white glossy photo (taken by a professional photographer) and addressed to the appropriate person at the publication.

Conduct a media survey to determine which publications your target audience reads and which will publish your information. Your best bets will be bar association publications, business newspapers, or the business sections of daily newspapers. Weekly hometown newspapers, and alumni (both undergraduate and law school) newspapers and magazines, will almost always use publicity material.

A more newsworthy, but also more sensitive, source of publicity is information associated with participation in important court decisions. Distributing this information will require your client's prior approval. It will also require careful authorship. The general news media does not have the space, the time, or the inclination to use a heavily footnoted release that makes sense only to other lawyers. Your release will require an understanding of both the news media and the audience toward whom a release will be aimed.

Develop a list of the publications you targeted. The list should include the names of editors and key reporters, along with phone and fax numbers and e-mail addresses. Update the list at least twice a year and survey members of your firm periodically to learn which publications they believe are important for the development of their practices.

NEWS MEDIA RESOURCE

Tangential to publicizing your participation in important court decisions is the cultivation of the news media as a forum to present your expertise on legal issues. The news media frequently needs lawyers who can provide clarity and relevance in connection with court decisions or legal issues affecting readers, viewers, and listeners.

The topic may be as sensational as a murder trial, but it is usually more mundane. News items on issues such as changes in the tax codes, employee benefits, or financial planning take much more space and time than do the front-page events. If you or your firm has expertise you want to claim, and if you have a willingness to work with the news media and under constant deadlines, you will find the notoriety provided by the news media will enhance your firm's name recognition. For example, a now internationally known lawyer began his rise to prominence by calling radio stations in the Boston, Massachusetts, area and offering to interpret important local and national court decisions in terms that the stations' listeners could understand. These early proactive forays into media relations eventually allowed this lawyer to become a network television commentator, which in turn led him to become defense counsel in several highly publicized criminal cases. This course is not attractive to everybody, but modifications of the plan can help you establish yourself as a legal resource for the news media and for your targeted audience of potential clients.

One tool that will help you attract media attention is a media guide that briefly identifies your firm, your areas of expertise, and the lawyers who are willing to make themselves available for interviews. Include lawyers' phone and fax numbers and e-mail addresses, and update the guide regularly to remove names of lawyers who have left the firm and to add names of those who have joined. Call the newspapers, magazines, radio stations, and television stations within your market. Find out who is responsible for assigning reporters their stories or securing talent for on-air appearances. Talk to these people. Send them a copy of your guide and follow up with a phone call to make sure they receive it.

Working with the news media is probably very different from anything you have ever done. Whereas lawyers are trained to get to the specifics of a case, the news media is usually looking for broader interpretations that will interest as many audience members as possible. If you are not accustomed to being interviewed by reporters, you should participate in a media interview training program to learn the ground rules and how you can best perform under those rules. The program should include an overview of how a newsroom functions, how stories are assigned, what reporters look for, the need to focus on one or two messages, and how to integrate those messages into your answers.

SPEAKING ENGAGEMENTS

An enormous number of local, regional, and national trade and professional associations look for experienced speakers who can present topics of interest to their members. Generally, to be accepted as a speaker, you must be able to provide something of value to the audience without engaging in a blatant pitch for business. Speakers are expected to entertain and to educate. If you decide to undertake this activity, your presentation should be crisp, pointed, and not too long. If possible, use a computer presentation program to generate slides or overheads.

Regardless of your level of presentation skills, you can benefit from attending a presentation training program. Giving yourself an opportunity to practice, particularly if the session is videotaped and replayed for critique, can be a great eye-opener that allows you to break through to a higher performance level.

ARTICLES

Publishing an article that readers value will provide you with instant credibility. If the article is placed in a publication that is read by your target audience, the long-term benefits to your practice can be enormous. Many trade publications and weekly business publications use bylined articles with little or no editing, as long as the article meets their specifications for subject matter and length.

Many trade and professional publications will also give you a photostat or "slick" of the article under their banner for a reasonable price. These can be reprinted and used as a direct-mail piece to current or prospective clients.

If you believe you don't have the time to write articles, review the presentations you have made recently. They can usually be transformed into articles with very little effort. Also, internal communications or brief articles written for your firm's newsletter can usually be expanded for publication.

OP-ED

The op-ed (that is, opposite the editorial) pages of newspapers provide a wonderful forum for articulate people to present opinions on nearly every topic to a readership that is informed, educated, and involved in issues that concern the community. If this readership sounds like your target audience, then you should consider preparing articles for submission to the op-ed editor of your local or regional newspaper. Your article may not touch specifically on the practice of law, but it will make you more visible to the highly valued potential client who traditionally reads the op-ed page.

There is a great deal of competition for the limited space available on these pages. This means you must work for an advantage over those looking to be published. Winning a place on the op-ed page requires an awareness of important community issues, an ability to write to a nonlawyer audience, and a willingness to keep your word count within restrictions. Submitting a piece for consideration will also require some media-relations work. You should make direct contact with the person responsible for placement to learn the paper's criteria for publication. Personal contact with the editor will enhance your chances of placement. Developing positive relationships with the people who write and edit the news is essential if you want placement. (Developing these relationships will be further discussed later in this chapter.)

SEMINARS

Conducting seminars for your clients and prospective clients on topics of interest will likely bring in new clients and perhaps convince existing clients to increase their use of your firm. Some seminar topics might also be newsworthy. Seminars on energy deregulation or sexual harassment, for example, might interest a business reporter. If you believe the content of the seminar is groundbreaking or will be informative to a large audience, then a reporter or editor might consider the seminar topic or the seminar itself as a possible news story. Issue a media advisory that provides general information about the seminar and follow up with phone calls.

Your obvious goal in presenting a seminar is to get as much marketing mileage out of it as you can. Spread your net wide in issuing invitations. Be sure you fill the room. One way of doing this is to find a media partner, a business paper, or the business page of a local daily newspaper to provide advertising and editorial space for the seminar. The newspaper's payoff is in positioning itself as an educational resource for the business community. Your payoff is in enhanced name recognition and increased attendance through repetitive mention.

Finding a credible media partner as a cosponsor of events will increase familiarity between your firm and the publication. This in turn may increase the chances of the newspaper seeking your firm as a knowledgeable observer of the legal profession and a worthy commentator on legal issues.

ADVERTORIALS

The only difference between an op-ed article and an advertorial is that you pay for placement of the advertorial. Paying for the space keeps you off the op-ed page, but it allows you to select the section of the paper that fits the content of your article. You may also be able to place the advertorial on a page that carries no other advertisements. A classic location is right in the middle of the business section page carrying the stock market quotations. A boxed article designed to attract attention increases the likelihood that your article will be read.

SPONSORSHIPS

Program or organizational sponsorships are another way of raising your firm's visibility. If your research shows that prospective clients appreciate doing business with professional organizations that participate in the community, then you need to provide support for those programs. Examples include sponsoring mock trials in high schools, organizing school field trips to courts, making public-service announcements on legal matters, funding public broadcasting programs, or engaging in adopt-a-school, adopt-a-highway, adopt-a-park, and clean-up programs where your staff wears hats or T-shirts with your firm's name prominently positioned.

EMPLOYEE ACTIVITIES

Participation in employee programs not only increases your visibility with prospective clients, it increases enthusiasm among your most important public—your employees. In fact, employees can be the driving force behind some of the firm's best public-relations efforts.

In one example, a law firm employee's daughter managed a shelter for battered women and their children. The employee organized a holiday gift drive within the firm for the women and children living at the shelter. More than one hundred gifts were delivered to the home. The firm hired a professional photographer to shoot photos of employees delivering the gifts and the shelter manager accepting them. The photo, accompanied by a news release, was sent to local newspapers. One of those papers featured it in a special holiday section spotlighting companies that were doing something special for the public.

It is not unaltruistic to balance your sponsorships with the hope that your actions will result in greater name recognition for your firm. Remain focused on the group you want as clients. Seek out those events they are likely to attend or support, and make yourself a part of those events.

BOARD MEMBERSHIPS

Another example of community involvement is participation in key community organizations such as Boy and Girl Scouts, Boys and Girls Clubs, United Way, the Heart Association, or the Cancer Foundation. Your goal should be to secure board memberships that will result in high-level contacts with potential clients and prominent positioning in the community. The organizations you join will distribute news releases on the appointments, in which you and your firm will be mentioned.

Execution

Putting your public-relations plan into motion requires as much patience as planning. The natural thing to do would be to rush into production as quickly as possible. There are, however, a few things to remember as you give life to the plan.

First, when seeking publicity in the print media, recognize that you are just one of many law firms and other professional organizations looking for publicity in a limited amount of space. The competition for this space and editors' attention is intense. A blizzard of paper thrown at editors does not guarantee publication. In fact, it may result in the opposition reaction. Every editor must judge the relative value of each piece of information from the reader's perspective. Do not deluge an editor with news releases, articles, announcements, and story ideas over a short period of time. You will find that a timed release of high-quality information, delivered over a period of weeks or months, will get you more coverage than a deluge of material that holds little or no interest to the editor or readers.

There are exceptions, but normally the best way to receive coverage of your announcements is to make judicious use of your information and the contacts you have developed at your targeted publications. Success in placing one article or a release does not mean that you will have immediate success the next time. The decision to use your material is based on a number of factors, including space availability, correlation between your announcement and other available material, and the editor's level of interest.

Second, you must be reasonable about what you can generate in a given period of time and about what your target publications and other news sources can use during that time. Your public-relations plan should include a schedule of events and announcements based on those reasonable expectations. If properly coordinated, your plan will likely take at least a year to unfold. Securing name recognition and changing or enhancing perceptions cannot be accomplished with a single blow. Even basic announcements and news releases should be spaced to provide a timed-release effect. Frequent name mentions in the media over an extended period will create greater name recognition than a huge number of announcements appearing at the same time.

Third, remember that although publishing an article can mean months of rewriting and reconfiguring, you may find that the same article can be used by different publications. For example, if your firm has multiple offices, you may be able to place the same article in the weekly business publications serving those locations or in a trade publication that concentrates on a particular field.

Fourth, you will find that some of your efforts are seasonal and that your efforts need to be forward looking. Many trade and professional associations, for example, do not meet during the summer months. The chances that you will be asked to address these groups at this time of year is minimal. However, the organizations may use the summer to schedule speakers for fall and winter events. Seminars should also be scheduled to coincide with the planning of prospective clients. Do not wait until April 15th to schedule tax seminars; schedule them close to the end of the calendar year, when prospective clients are starting to think about taxes.

Finally, one of the best ways to prepare a public-relations schedule is to develop a matrix showing the months of the year at the top and a list of planned activities on the side. You will find that some of your activities (such as the development and dissemination of news releases) will be ongoing, while other activities (such as writing and placing articles) may be done only periodically. Whatever elements you include in your plan, the time line you develop for its execution needs to be sensitive to your target audience members, their business operations, and the time when they are most receptive to receiving your message.

Evaluation

The easiest way to evaluate a public-relations campaign is to see an immediate increase in the amount of business you are doing. However, the increase may be the result of other factors, such as advertising, a hot economy, increased referrals, or clients increasing their use of your firm. The impact of public relations is difficult to gauge. Its success is more often sensed in increments than realized in a sudden rush of business.

If you are looking to find a unit of measurement for your public-relations placements, use a news-clipping service or your own staff to track the publications receiving your releases or covering your activities as news stories. The number of column inches of "ink" you receive can be translated into dollar amounts by comparing the space received as a result of your public-relations efforts with what the publication would charge for an equal amount of space purchased as advertising.

High attendance at your seminars is another clear indication that you are hitting the mark in attracting attention to your firm or your practice. Provide comment cards for the attendees that ask how they heard about the program, the factors that were important in convincing them to attend, and what they felt were the most interesting or important elements of the program. This data may not be the most scientific you will gather, but it will provide information on the people you are attracting.

The best evaluation of your public-relations efforts would come from new research data assembled at the conclusion of your program. If you have been successful in changing public perception about who you are, or if you have managed to create awareness of your firm, it will be apparent in the new data.

Conclusion

Even if you plan, write, execute, and evaluate the most ingenious public-relations program ever conceived, you will fail abysmally unless you are committed to providing outstanding service to your clients. Public relations, like advertising, can take you only to within sight of success. Becoming truly successful depends on you and your firm's ability to provide what your clients need in a timely and professional way. Public relations creates an implied promise to the client or customer. In your audience members' minds, you can and will do what they need to have done. If you cannot deliver on the implied promise, you will not only lose the clients you might have gained through your public-relations efforts, you will also create your worst public-relations nightmare—dissatisfied clients who will likely tell everyone they know that you did not deliver.

Conversely, your greatest public-relations asset is the client who loves to talk about his or her relationship with your firm. Those who believe they have made good decisions want to talk about it. They want people to know that they are intelligent and astute, and that they have good business sense. The ripple effect these satisfied clients create is the ideal vehicle to carry your message to the public.

CHAPTER 12

Successful Marketing for the Solo Practitioner and Small-Firm Lawyer

Murray Singerman

Introduction: Choosing Solo or Small-Firm Practice

As a law student I aspired to the same type of job that my school buddies did—the large-firm associate. Just like the other three hundred future lawyers in my graduating class, I envisioned success as the seven-year partner track.

But when I obtained the coveted position and started working in a large firm, I began to have a recurring, insistent dream. I dreamed of being my own boss, of deciding my own destiny, of running my own practice. After a year of planning, I resigned my position and struck out on my own. I soon discovered that *most* American lawyers choose to practice alone or in small firms.

I believe that many lawyers opt for running their own offices because it provides personal and financial satisfaction. As a solo practitioner or small-firm lawyer, you control your own destiny. You decide what type of practice you want, rather than being assigned an area of law by a managing partner. You determine your standard of living, rather than placing your financial fate into the hands of a management committee. You decide how hard you want to work and how you want to spend your time, rather than meeting a 2,000 billable-hour requirement. You avoid the seven- to ten-year-long worry of not knowing whether the firm will make you a partner. You answer only to yourself and your clients, rather than constantly worrying about what your superiors think of you. You reap the benefits of your hard work, rather than sharing your profits with tens or even hundreds of other lawyers. When you combine these attractions with the ability to make a good living, solo and small-firm practice become extremely attractive to many lawyers.

Solo and small-firm practice also may be the only option for lawyers who cannot secure positions with larger firms. In a tight job market, this is nothing to be ashamed of. By graduating from law school and passing the bar, these lawyers fulfilled the prerequisites to practice law. In another place and time, when there weren't so many lawyers, they probably would have had job offers. If you are one of those lawyers, don't sell yourself short. View your situation as an opportunity to create your own rewarding practice.

Success in solo and small-firm practice is readily attainable within two years of opening a practice, even when starting is difficult. When you begin with no clients and without seven or eight years' work at a well-known firm, you probably have limited resources and can't invest huge sums in advertising or other marketing. Moreover, there are no shortcuts to success, nor are there any guarantees. But with dedication and hard work, you can attain your goals. By knowing how to market a practice effectively, by understanding the process, and by having control of it, a solo or small-firm lawyer can ensure a steady stream of clients.

Diagnostic Quiz: Personality Traits Needed for Success in Solo and Small-Firm Practice

Success in any enterprise, including solo or small-firm practice, requires positive thinking, self-confidence, and absolute commitment. By taking the following quiz, you will most likely discover that you already possess the personality traits necessary to market a solo or small-firm practice successfully.

Question 1

Did you apply to law school despite unencouraging or bleak job prospects, or after the late 1980s? If you did, you are willing to take calculated risks. Even though you knew finding a job wouldn't be easy, you took the risk that you'd be fortunate enough to be hired.

Question 2

Did you choose to go to law school because you might be able to help people and make a good living doing it? If you did, you have personal integrity, you are caring, and you want to enjoy a comfortable lifestyle.

Question 3

Did you really read every single class assignment in law school, or do you fall into the category of students who failed to read many, if not the majority, of class assignments? And when you were less than 100 percent prepared, did you find a way to cram in the ten minutes before class so that if you were called upon, you could salvage some of your dignity? If this sounds like you, you're creative and efficient.

Question 4

Did you graduate from law school and pass the bar exam? If you did, you know what commitment means. You have the ability to make a commitment, and meet it. You're determined. You have drive. You can motivate yourself. You're self-reliant.

Question 5

When you sat for the bar exam, were you convinced that you failed and were you surprised and relieved when you received your positive results? If you did, you know what it means to triumph and overcome a challenge. You've gained confidence in yourself.

The characteristics necessary to make it as a solo or small-firm lawyer include these: willingness to take risks, empathy and caring, integrity, desire for a comfortable lifestyle, creativity, efficiency, commitment, willingness to carry things through to completion, determination, self-motivation, self-reliance, knowing what it means to triumph and overcome a challenge, and self-confidence.

Of course, having these traits isn't enough. You also need to master the formula and techniques necessary to get and keep a steady stream of clients.

Formula for Success

The purpose of this chapter is to present a formula for success, give an overview of the process, and convince you of the steps you need to take to succeed. Before learning to master the details of each separate area of marketing, you must fully understand how the component parts mesh together. I often argue from analogy and personal experience. My goal is to excite your imagination—to motivate you and help inspire belief in your untapped capabilities.

Marketing is not a science, but an art. Like any art form, it ceases being creative when it becomes imitation. Many lawyers believe they can effectively market a practice by imitating the marketing strategies of medium and large firms, or other solo practices and small firms. Though all effective marketing relies upon some common and proven principals, individual successes are built on the subtleties of a lawyer's practice, personality, and market. As a solo lawyer, I cannot compete with medium and large firms. I don't have the financial resources to experiment with or sustain a marketing strategy that isn't assured of immediate success. I lack the resources to meet all the needs of corporate clients traditionally served by medium and large firms. Assuming that medium and large firms design marketing strategies to meet *their* budgets and to target *their* clients, it would be foolish of me to adopt their practices.

It would also be shortsighted to imitate the marketing strategies of other solo and small-firm lawyers. Although we may have similar resources and pursue clients who share similar economic situations, our differing personalities and practices necessitate marketing approaches that fit our individual needs. In short, don't imitate! Create!

Case Study

To introduce you to the process of successfully marketing a solo or small-firm practice, I'm returning to your days of law school and the problem method of teaching. I'm sure you remember those lengthy narratives and the painstaking (and sometimes painful) analysis you were required to undertake if you were on the hot seat. The story I'm about to share and analyze won't be as painstaking—and certainly not as painful—but it still has great instructive value for depicting the marketing process at work.

My office is located in Columbia, Maryland, a beautiful planned city equidistant between Washington, D.C., and Baltimore, Maryland. On Wednesday, January 10, 1996, John called to schedule an appointment. John received my direct-mail brochure, which included copies of articles I've written and testimonial letters. We arranged to meet the next day at 11:30 a.m. John needed the two hours to drive to Columbia. He lives in western Maryland, a mountainous, coal-mining area.

John was devastated. The Internal Revenue Service (IRS) had scheduled an auction of his property for Wednesday, January 17, only six days away and the day after Martin Luther King's birthday, a federal holiday when the IRS is closed. The revenue officer handling John's case planned to auction his car wash facility and eight rental properties.

The first question I had for John was why he waited until the eleventh hour to seek help. He explained that where he lived, there were no tax lawyers. Two years earlier, when his problems first came to light, he responded to a direct-mail flyer from a Baltimore bankruptcy lawyer, whose name he could not recall, and paid him $600 to solve his problems. The lawyer did little more than take John's $600 and make one call to the IRS, and, to John's frustration, he never followed up or solved John's problems. (Incidentally, I later discovered the name of the lawyer in John's paperwork. The lawyer attended one of my seminars to learn how to improve his marketing skills. Obviously there are other skills he needs to address.) When John received my direct-mail brochure, he was encouraged by the testimonials but nevertheless was wary. He called several other tax lawyers listed in the Yellow Pages, but decided to make an appointment with me.

I reviewed the history of the tax liability with John. My initial reaction was that John was not the person liable for the taxes. The revenue officer had not sufficiently investigated to determine who should be responsible for the taxes. After reviewing the information, I believed the revenue officer was pursuing the wrong person. I sat with John for nearly two hours. I described the process we needed to take to challenge the IRS, the risks involved, and our chances of prevailing. John signed a power of attorney, which would enable me to represent him before the IRS. He returned the next day with a $5,000 retainer and more information.

Because the auction was scheduled to take place in four days, I knew I had my work cut out for me that weekend. To make matters worse, the IRS was closed on Monday because of the holiday. With the auction scheduled for Wednesday at 10:00 a.m., I had one day to convince the IRS to call it off. This last-minute auction was the first I ever faced. I turned to a treatise I had been using for nearly a year, relying upon its advice. On Tuesday, I filed a Form 911, Taxpayer Assistance Order, with a ten-page legal memorandum, explaining why John wasn't liable and that the IRS should call off the auction. I sent it to every office and official I could think of: the District Director, the Chief of Collection, the Chief of Special Procedures, the Branch Chief, the revenue officer, and his group manager.

The revenue officer's reaction was predictable. In his dialect, he declared, "Meester Seengerman, we are gonna have ourselves an auction." As I recall, he shouted "Yeehaw" as he hung up the phone. (Although, truth be told, he probably just hung up.) Special Procedures reviewed the file and politely declined to get involved. The other offices referred me to Special Procedures. I hit a dead end. I returned to my treatise, which advised this: If all else fails, attend the auction, point out the procedural errors committed by the revenue officer, let the potential buyers know you believe the IRS violated your client's Fourth Amendment rights, and state that you intend to file a quiet title suit in state court to determine who owns the property. Tell the potential buyers that if they get the property, it won't be without a fight and extensive litigation.

On Wednesday, the day of the auction, I left my house at 7:00 a.m. to make the two-hour drive to western Maryland. The auction of the car wash was scheduled for 10:00 a.m. I made my speech to the buyers and the shocked revenue officer. When I finished, none of the buyers offered a bid. I was elated, to say the least, and impressed with my lawyering skills. At 2:00 p.m. we arrived at the auction of the rental properties. As I began my speech, the revenue officer interrupted me. From his pocket he drew out his IRS identification badge and announced, "I am an officer of the United States of America. It is a felony to impede a revenue officer of the Internal Revenue Service from carrying out his duties under the Internal Revenue Code. Meester Seengerman, unless you desist immediately and move to the other side of the street, I will cite you for criminal behavior with a punishment of three years in prison and a fine of $5,000."

What would you have done? At that point, my heart dropped into my stomach. Like a dog who puts his tail between his legs, I moved to the other side of the street. All I could envision was sitting behind bars while my wife and four kids went hungry. The revenue officer auctioned the rental properties, receiving close to $50,000.

The drive back to my office seemed interminable. When I finally arrived, I made a beeline for the treatise and took it from my desk. For the first time, I read the author's name, looked him up in *Martindale-Hubble,* and dialed. "Hello, this is Murray Singerman. I bought your book and followed your advice. I have just been threatened with going to jail because of what you advised." As my voice grew louder and louder, there was dead silence on the other end of the phone. When I finished, a warm deep voice asked me to describe what happened. I detailed the events—how John first came to me five days earlier; how I researched, wrote, and filed my Form 911; how I challenged the revenue officer at the auction; and how I was threatened. I heard a gentle chuckle. "Welcome to the club, my friend. Among practitioners, the IRS is notorious for threatening and using scare tactics to make lawyers back down. And by the way, you did a fabulous job."

After I calmed down, I was delighted to accept Tom's offer to act as co-counsel. Together, over the next two weeks, we forced the IRS to return the car wash, void the sale at the auction, and return the rental properties. The voiding of the sale took two months. The IRS unit handling the process told me it had never voided a sale in Baltimore and didn't know how to do it. Upon the return of the car wash, I filed a bankruptcy for John to ensure that he would receive a fair hearing before a judge. Throughout the eight-month case that followed, I kept John informed of how we were progressing. Because John's case was a huge success, I shared it with clients and referral sources, making sure I did not disclose John's identity.

The Marketing Process

An exciting story—hardly what you'd expect from a tax lawyer. I believe that analyzing this story will help you understand and remember the marketing process, which has four major steps: (1) marketing groundwork, (2) self-promotion, (3) interpersonal skills, and (4) client service.

MARKETING GROUNDWORK

OVERCOME YOUR FEARS

Long before John picked up the phone and called, I had already come to believe in my capabilities as a lawyer. I made it through law school with a respectable grade average, passed the bar exam with proud scores, and worked as a clerk in a firm and for a judge. I had the self-confidence to realize that what I didn't know I could learn from a book. And what I couldn't find in a book, I'd learn from someone who would teach me. By focusing on what I could *learn,* rather than on what I did *not* know, I overcame my number-one fear: not being able to practice law proficiently on my own.

I then overcame my number-two fear: not being able to attract clients. I accomplished that by teaching myself everything I could about marketing, by setting goals, and by taking steps to achieve them. Once I had my marketing plan in place, my fear of starving faded and I began building my practice.

You must take this first step—overcome this first hurdle—to master the marketing process: Identify and overcome your fears, whatever they may be.

Otherwise, a sense of paralysis sets in, leaving you frozen in a state of inactivity, and worrying about what may happen.

COMMIT TO MARKETING

Second, to lay marketing groundwork properly, you must commit to the practice of marketing. Embrace the idea that you must market your practice just as enthusiastically as you have embraced the idea of practicing law. Without consistent marketing you won't be able to practice law, because you won't have the clients you need to achieve your personal and financial goals. To be good at something, a person must like doing it. So you must learn to appreciate marketing.

Most people are not born to market. Although you may be a terrific legal technician, you probably were never taught how to market. Consequently, you may be uncomfortable with the idea of actively pursuing clients and referral sources. At best, you may view marketing as a necessary evil. But worse than that, you may think marketing is not what professionals should do. You may equate marketing with being a huckster, or America's gadfly—the used-car salesperson.

The key to making marketing a best friend is to adopt an understanding of it that creates no discomfort—one that meshes with your personality. Marketing is not advertising, not promotion (offering a 20-percent discount to get someone in the door), and not selling, although it embraces some or all of these concepts. For now, accept this definition: Marketing is what a lawyer does to get and keep clients. You are probably asking, "Well, what is that?"

Marketing is everything a lawyer does: choosing an area in which to concentrate, deciding where to locate an office, learning how to establish authority and credibility, and understanding how to tell people you can help them, convince them to become your clients, and serve them. The marketing plan you choose will consist of techniques and decisions that best fit your personality, and that emanate from your strengths. (This definition presupposes enough introspection to determine your strengths and weaknesses.) Don't believe that only one mold of a successful rainmaker exists. You can become a rainmaker in your own right, finding your own path to success.

John came to me because I have always been comfortable marketing my practice. I market consistently, using a wide range of techniques that mesh with my strengths. I look at marketing as an enjoyable challenge, one that enables me to meet many incredibly interesting people. And although my wife must drag me to parties (where I will not market because I separate my business and personal lives), I look forward to business/social gatherings with gusto. They give me opportunities to market.

DEFINE YOUR "PROFESSIONAL IDENTITY"

The next step in laying marketing groundwork requires you to define your "Professional Identity," which answers the question, "So what do you do?" I'll tell you mine: I protect people from the IRS, work out their tax problems, make sure they keep their assets, and keep them out of jail. If you base your marketing on your Professional Identity, you will learn how to gain a steady stream of clients without hard selling and without discomfort. When you formulate your practice in terms of how you help people, you can share that information without pressure or being uncomfortable.

Before you formulate your Professional Identity, you must choose your area of concentration and decide how you will present that to the public. In a sense, marketing a law practice is similar to marketing a retail product. A lawyer must deal with issues of supply and demand, perceived and actual need, determination of those who require the services the lawyer offers, and the extent of competition. One of the reasons I chose tax law, apart from the consistent excitement and pathos (yes, I am serious!), is because there aren't many tax lawyers in my geographical location. At the same time, there are many people with tax problems. I know of equestrian lawyers, adoption lawyers, and computer lawyers. By exploring the marketplace, you can discover an area that attracts you and that will offer you the chance to carve out a profitable niche. Even general practitioners should find a niche that they can use as a springboard for other services.

John responded to my marketing efforts, because he clearly understood my Professional Identity. Without confusion or guessing, he knew that I dedicated my practice to solving tax problems and protecting property. John responded to what he read and came to me to save his property.

TARGET YOUR CLIENTS

Once you have defined your Professional Identity, you need to find and target your prospective clients. I send direct mail to taxpayers against whom the IRS has filed tax liens. The county clerk makes these liens available to the public. The local business newspaper publishes them. John's name appeared on one of those lists. My direct-mail brochure was aimed at John, much like an arrow flies toward its target. I hit the bull's-eye for many different reasons, but primarily because my marketing was directed at the right person.

By zeroing in on your best prospects, you can maximize your marketing dollars. A correct determination of your target market can save you thousands of dollars. If you mail to the general population, you will waste money on people who have no interest in your services. The more you refine your list, and the more you focus your message on the group most interested in your services, the higher your return on your marketing investment.

STAND OUT AND BE CHOSEN

Marketing groundwork also requires you to distinguish yourself from the crowd. You must make your practice stand out from everyone else's practice, and ensure clients choose you over the competition. You must establish yourself as an authority by writing articles, giving seminars, or hosting radio programs, for example. Find topics that showcase your expertise and interest your audience.

From my experience with John, I learned that you do not have to establish credibility and authority by yourself. By bringing Tom into the case, I not only solved John's immediate problems, I also used John's case and what I learned from Tom as a basis for articles and seminars enabling other lawyers and professionals to see me as an authority. In addition, I established myself as an authority in the eyes of the IRS. They have come to treat me with a wary respect. You must distinguish yourself by obtaining superior legal results. No one says you have to do it alone. Build mentor relationships as soon as you can.

LEARN ABOUT YOUR TARGET MARKET

The last step in marketing groundwork is learning all you can about your potential clients—your target market. Discover what they expect from a lawyer, what they think about legal services, what is important to them, what they need immediately, and what they need in the long run. Based on this treasure of information, let them know you can meet their immediate needs, even exceed their expectations, with superior service and for a fair fee.

REAP THE RESULTS OF LAYING YOUR MARKETING GROUNDWORK

I attribute a degree of my rapid success to laying the proper groundwork for my marketing. I am comfortable with my Professional Identity—the knight in shining armor who slays the IRS dragon and saves helpless taxpayers. I have found and targeted my prospects—middle-class people and small businesses with tax problems. I have positioned my practice carefully and caused it to stand out—many people now refer others to me, and many clients choose me.

I'll tell you how I knew I was on the right track. The first time I visited a potential referral source, my first "cold call," I was extremely nervous. I made an appointment with an accountant who knew a friend of mine. I was worried about stupid things: Did I have stains on my tie? Did my socks match? But the minute I opened my mouth and began describing my practice and capabilities, I became assured and confident, even though I didn't have a single client. Because of my past experience, the articles I'd published, and my continuing legal education, I felt I could speak with confidence. What was scheduled as a fifteen-minute meeting lasted an hour. To date, this accountant is my strongest referral source. My marketing groundwork paid off. And as with most referral sources, I left the meeting with the promise of future business.

Contrast that with Jane Doe Lawyer who rented an office where I first started out. Without ever mastering the basics, she threw large sums of money into advertising—television commercials, full-page ads in the Yellow Pages, and large display ads in advertising mailers. Sadly, she received very little response from her investment. Eventually she couldn't afford the rent and moved her office to her home. I knew she was destined to fail. Jane Doe had not properly laid the groundwork for marketing. She lacked an understanding of her Professional Identity, her marketplace, her competition, the services she should offer, and her target group of potential clients. She was not able to communicate her expertise or how she would meet the expectations and needs of potential clients. She was wasting her money. To avoid such a disaster, you must establish the basics of marketing before venturing out into the marketplace.

SELF-PROMOTION

Once you have properly laid your marketing groundwork, you can effectively profit from self-promotion. Self-promotion includes any method of letting people know about your Professional Identity: announcements, advertising, brochures, direct mail, newsletters, networking, public relations, radio and television ads, seminars, and speeches, among dozens of other methods. Self-promotion can be the savior or the slayer of a solo practice. The wise use of self-promotion can produce impressive returns, but haphazard use can bankrupt you.

Let me share a success story and a failure story—both my own. First, the success: For four months, I worked on one of my main marketing tools—a client-focused brochure (the one to which John responded). I drafted the brochure, hired an editor and a graphic designer, and used a top-notch printer. The total investment in the brochure was about $4,000, which included postage. The return on my investment in my first year was approximately $25,000. I kept working on it, trying different techniques, inserts, and accompanying material. In my second year, this brochure brought me $50,000 in business.

Now, the failure: Before I developed my brochure, I followed the lead of most new solos and took out an ad in the Yellow Pages. This was a beautiful, color ad that contained my logo and captured all I felt I needed to say. I designed it with the salesperson for the Yellow Pages. (A big mistake.) My investment was close to $1,000. My return on the investment was $0. For one year, I waited for the phone to ring because of that ad. No calls came. I stopped running the ad when it came up for renewal.

Now why did my brochure work, but my Yellow Page ad fail? The answer is simple. Without a solid theory of self-promotion that's proven to work, you could spend your life's savings without getting a single response. Self-promotion material must accomplish many tasks. First and foremost, it must communicate your Professional Identity and how you distinguish yourself, your expertise, and your superior services. The material must overcome the hesitations and concerns of potential clients. But that's not enough. It's incredibly important that potential clients make use of the self-promotion material.

My Yellow Pages ad failed because I never asked a crucial question—one that the salesperson had no interest in answering. Do my potential clients scan display ads to find a lawyer? I later discovered that people who have tax problems do not scan display advertisements looking for a tax lawyer. They turn to the directory of specialties and look under the "Tax Law" heading. A specialty listing costs about one-tenth of what a display advertisement costs. I have resumed using the Yellow Pages, but in a way that works for me. Instead of spending $2,000 for a display, I now spend $200 for a specialty listing. And even though I spend far less than I did on Yellow Page advertising, I have increased my return by a much larger amount.

One of the most important means of self-promotion is networking. Many lawyers associate networking with brash backslapping, giving business cards to everyone, and joining service organizations solely to get clients. But networking can be enjoyable and stress-free. Like other types of self-promotion, networking is a way of letting referral sources and potential clients know you can help them, or their friends or clients. You can alleviate much of the stress associated with networking by viewing it as an opportunity to give other people information, or to get information from them. I enjoy sharing an article I wrote with referral sources and clients, making invitations to a seminar, and involving other professionals in my intellectual pursuits by discussing interesting cases. To me, networking is how I build professional relationships. I don't feel the need to act as though I like someone to get his or her business. When I network, my professional friends and colleagues understand that I'm calling or writing about business. And if my relationship with one of those people develops into a friendship beyond business, we both know it's based on genuine respect, not flattery for the sake of business.

INTERPERSONAL SKILLS

It's not enough to be skilled at marketing and self-promotion. You must do much more than simply get a potential client into the office; you must also know how to create a relationship using interpersonal skills. In most law schools, interpersonal skills are not part of the curriculum. We are not taught how to listen to our clients, or how to manage our client encounters.

LISTENING SKILLS

Many lawyers find it hard to master good listening skills. After all, most of us have been trained to talk, not listen. But listening skills are imperative. They allow you to learn what really motivates your prospective clients. They help you meet their needs, not yours. Ultimately, we want satisfied clients who will bring us other clients.

The harshest lesson I learned practicing law relates to listening skills. It involves the only instance in which I was fired by a client. Dr. B and his wife called me after receiving my opening announcement and general brochure. The doctor and his wife were casual friends of mine. They had some tax problems and wanted to see me. Well, it took a long time for the truth to come out, but the doctor owed over $85,000 in taxes, was carrying $65,000 in credit card debt, and had an annual deficit of $36,000 in his household income. The IRS and the state taxing authorities were applying heavy pressure, threatening to shut him down. After analyzing the situation, I made a reasonable recommendation: File bankruptcy to discharge the credit card debt and to handle the tax liabilities. I also suggested that his wife get a job as soon as possible, and I sent him to an accountant who specializes in medical practices, with the hope of increasing his income. The next day I received a call telling me, "You're fired." "Why?" I asked. "Because we aren't the kind of people who file bankruptcy." What I missed, and never really listened for or heard, was what mattered most to my clients. It wasn't the stress of dealing with the taxes, or the credit card debts, or the annual deficit. It was their dignity. They live in a small community that has a lot of doctors. They give to charity, live in a nice house, and drive nice cars. Filing bankruptcy was the ultimate embarrassment. I never caught it, and I should have. Today, if presented with the same situation, I would not make a specific recommendation. Instead, I would present them with various options, addressing the consequences of each. I would discuss in detail the impact of the different options on their lifestyle, the medical practice, and finances. Because I wasn't keyed into listening, I wasn't as sensitive as I should have been.

By the time I met with John, I had learned my lesson. I listened carefully to what he wanted. Although he was deeply concerned with keeping his property, he wanted someone to stand up to the IRS for him even more. The revenue officer handling John's case treated him like a criminal. John wanted to get a fair shake from the IRS. By attending the auction and stating his case to the bidders, some of whom were his neighbors, I helped John stand up to the IRS.

NONPRESSURE SALES

Another interpersonal skill I learned by the time John came to see me is nonpressure selling. When you meet with a client, you need to know how to ask for the client's business and get the retainer check. You can make this job many times easier if you know how to *make your intangible work tangible.* I take a great deal of time in an initial meeting to show a potential client what must be done on the case. I go through a sample case file to illustrate the necessary work. For tax clients, I have created a fictional file containing IRS forms, a protest appeal, a tax court petition, and court motions, to help give a sense of how much work must be done. I make my intangible work—the work I have not done for the client—more tangible. This helps the client understand what the retainer check covers. A client who appreciates the enormity of his or her problem, and the work needed to solve it, usually rushes to write a retainer check.

John was pleased to give me a hefty retainer; not because I forced him with threats that he would lose everything he had, but because I made him appreciate the problems ahead and the amount of work needed to address them.

OFFICE DESIGN

An area of interpersonal skills often overlooked is your office design, which should support and mesh with your marketing strategy. Where you locate your practice, how you operate your office, what it looks like, and how you dress—among other design decisions—should reflect the marketing and self-promotion decisions you have made.

For example, if you want to establish a tax practice that targets professionals and small businesses, you need to choose an office in an area that's convenient to them and looks like an office they'd expect. You need to dress the part as well. Were you to set up an office in a red-light district, buy secondhand furniture, and dress in blue jeans every day, you'd probably have difficulty attracting clients, even if you were technically adept. Admittedly, this example is extreme. But one lawyer with whom I consulted was having difficulty getting midsized companies to hire him, even though he was technically proficient and had a solid marketing campaign. Although he wore attractive suits and chose a desirable location, he regularly wore a small, gold-ball earring. We decided that for business, he would remove it because it might put off conservative business executives who make the decisions to hire legal counsel. Your design decisions should likewise support your marketing and help your practice grow, not work against it.

CLIENT SERVICE

Client service is another area in which most lawyers need improvement. I view client service as a form of marketing, where clients become your best referral sources.

Let me illustrate the importance of relationship management and client service. For months, I tried to convince an accountant to send most of her tax-problem cases to me. Before I met her, she sent most of them to a lawyer five minutes away from where I am located. On one of the first cases she sent me, I negotiated a settlement with the IRS for less than ten cents on the dollar. And as with all my clients, I tried hard to give superior client service. After I solved this client's tax problems, the accountant said she would start sending me referrals but still needed to spread her referrals around, to ensure that she would receive work from many lawyers.

Several months later, a new client called—this time referred by the taxpayer whose case I settled with the IRS. This new client did business with the other client, who told him I did a good job and was accessible. It turns out that the accountant had previously referred the new client to one of my competitors. But that lawyer didn't return calls, didn't get the work done when promised, and wasn't enthusiastic. The new client became dissatisfied and started looking for another lawyer when he happened to run into the original client who sung my praises. I got the new client's business because I *do* return calls, I *do* get the work done when promised, and I *am* enthusiastic. So, in the end, both clients came to me, even without a direct referral from the accountant. And now, because I satisfy her clients (which, in turn, is a good reflection on her), she refers me 90 percent of her clients with tax problems. Client service pays off. Go the extra mile.

John responded to my direct-mail piece partly because it contained testimonial letters from clients and referral sources attesting to my ability to solve their problems. Why speak for yourself, when a more convincing source will do it for you?

Conclusion

Make sure you master the four mileposts a lawyer needs to succeed in solo and small-firm practice: marketing groundwork, self-promotion, interpersonal skills, and client service. If you are committed to investing what it takes, motivated to meet a challenge, and want to experience the pride of accomplishment, then try solo or small-firm practice. It's probably the job you've always been looking for.

SECTION 4

Maintaining Your Program

CHAPTER 13

Marketing Training

James A. Durham
(William J. Flannery Jr. also contributed to this chapter)

Introduction: Setting the Stage

Most lawyers are ill-equipped to meet the challenge of being required to develop new business. This is true not only because they have not been taught the requisite skills, but also because of deep-seated resistance to the very notion of business development.

Historically, ethical restrictions have precluded aggressive marketing, and there has been a pride in the legal profession that said, "I'm a licensed lawyer and I didn't go to law school to be a salesperson." The fact that most firms were sufficiently profitable in the past with just a few major rainmakers also contributed to the lack of marketing by most lawyers.

Further, the resistance most lawyers have to "management" (or, more accurately, "being managed") limits their interest and involvement in business development initiatives. The reason many lawyers joined larger law firms, rather than becoming solo practitioners, was to leave administrative headaches to someone else; they also wanted the steady flow of work that comes from the so-called "rainmakers." They do not, however, like being told what to do.

To be sure, there have always been lawyers who could get new business just by sharing a cab to the airport with somebody. The reality is that great lawyers *can* be great salespeople. The unsettling point, however, is that many rainmakers are tired—tired of bearing such a significant responsibility, and tired of the increasing effort required to face the incredible competition that has emerged. Simply stated, lawyers who work in law firms founded or grown by such titans had better find ways to replenish the supply of clients before the Great Ones fade off into the sunset. (Marketing is, in many respects, a matter of succession planning!) It is in this new competitive environment that firms have begun to offer a variety of marketing training programs.

The Advent of Training

It is certainly a watershed that training exists on a fairly widespread basis, often involving significant investments of lawyer time and money. Sometimes lawyers need to be dragged into training programs kicking and screaming—usually after some enlightened managing partner or management committee insists on their participation. In recent years, however, it is clear that the resistance has ebbed dramatically. What makes the very existence of marketing training so remarkable is that it suggests the transformation of professional attitudes and the professional culture of most law firms. Lawyers are learning that they cannot simply "market" in the traditional sense, by writing and speaking to their peers ("reputation building"); they are learning that they must change the way they approach and manage entire practices. The good news is that they are coming to realize that marketing is best done by delivering extraordinary service to existing clients and by building meaningful relationships within their networks, not by pushy sales pitches and discounting. As lawyers learn this, they become even more receptive to training.

Implicit in their willingness to be trained is the lawyers' realization that they do not need to have a certain type of personality to succeed at building a practice. In every endeavor, there are "naturals," and there are those who have to learn the skills of the trade painstakingly. In music, the person with perfect pitch isn't necessarily as successful as the journeyman with modest natural gifts who practices constantly. And sports offers obvious examples. In golf, there are those who, like Tiger Woods or Bobby Jones, are innately gifted, and those who, like Ben Hogan or Nancy Lopez, have worked notoriously hard to compete. In the fullness of time, all these athletes have commanded equal respect from the historians of the game.

This same pattern can be seen in the legal profession. Countless numbers of lawyers who believed they could never bring in business because they were not natural rainmakers now have solid six- and seven-figure "books of business" as a result of learning and practicing the fundamentals of service, communication, "value-added" concepts, and relationship building. The transformation in lawyer attitudes once marketing is redefined in these terms is palpable.

Today, it is actually possible at some law firms to use a word like "selling" as part of a skills training program, in part because of competition fears and in part because lawyers now understand it to mean "relational sales." Even five years ago, you would not have dared mention the "s" word to most lawyers.

The Nature and Extent of Training

Regardless of who does marketing training, it will not be effective if it is an isolated event. It must be a component part of an integrated business development and overall strategic plan. Training should blend with, support, or modify the strategic plan.

Many law firms have gone as far as they can go in developing conventional marketing tools (such as brochures, newsletters, seminars, published articles, and media relations). These are essential to a successful overall marketing program, but the benefits of these tools cannot easily be quantified. On the other hand, training lawyers to expand relationships with current clients and to win work from new clients *can* result in specific, measurable increases in revenue. Moreover, a firm can improve client satisfaction and client retention dramatically by offering business development and client service training to nonlawyer staff persons. By showing these individuals what a critical role they play in the firm's success, they get energized to deliver incredible service to everyone who deals with the firm.

If you ask lawyers what they want to learn during training, their answers typically include these: how to develop a strategic business development plan, how to leverage present work to gain new work, how to find the time to market, how to target appropriate clients for additional work, how to discover the client's perspective, how to talk to strangers, and how to network more effectively. If lawyers are asked what they see as the greatest obstacles to business development, they typically mention these: fear of looking like a pushy salesperson, not enough time, not enough reward for marketing *efforts* (only for results), lack of information about the firm's existing clients and contacts, insufficient understanding of other practice areas, and a general lack of teamwork in the firm. These answers illustrate that training cannot be done in a vacuum, and that firms need to address serious management and cultural issues if they want newly trained lawyers to be successful business producers.

The Training Process

Training can be broken into a number of distinct stages. It makes good sense to start with individual training that addresses the expressed desires and concerns of the lawyers. This can be followed by—or supplemented with—relational sales training and programs designed to improve communication skills (particularly "active" listening and presentation skills). Next, you can teach the lawyers how to form client-focused teams, and to tailor targeted strategies to capture new business. All this can be supplemented with individual coaching. I must reiterate, however, that training, like any successful marketing effort, must have the strong ongoing support of firm leadership. The level of management support is directly proportional to the level of measurable success and the depth of cultural change that flows from the training. (More about this later in this chapter.)

Making the Case for Training

What should happen when there is *no expressed demand* for training in your firm? Typically, it is left up to management (or the person in charge of marketing) to identify the firm's needs and "make the case" for training to the lawyers. If successful at selling the training concept, then typically the marketing director or marketing partner must manage the entire process. In essence, the law firm marketer needs to do his or her homework, identify the options, develop a plan, and make something happen. When proposing a training program, he or she should anticipate a lot of questions (and objections), such as these: "Do we really need this?" "What is the measurable benefit?" "Can this stuff really be learned?" (Many lawyers think one either knows it or doesn't know it from birth.) "Consultants don't understand our business." "It costs too much."

Studies show that the most common complaint about lawyers is that they are not good listeners. (This helps perpetuate the image of arrogance that haunts lawyers.) So, maybe it makes sense to start by proposing a training program for "active listening." Regardless of how rational it may be, however, this type of "soft skills" training is particularly hard to sell to lawyers.

It also may make sense to start by offering training on a "pilot" basis. Training has a better chance of getting off the ground if people are assured that those responsible for training will elicit feedback from the participants, and assess the "value" of the training before committing to a major program.

Selecting a Trainer

The marketing director or marketing partner (the person typically responsible for developing or arranging training programs) can have a real impact on the firm by managing the training process effectively. This important role is not without risk, however, because the law firm marketer will also be held responsible for the results of training. Accordingly, it is important to get as many members of the firm as possible involved in the selection of the trainers. Although most trainers have a good understanding of the *substantive material* that should be covered in a training program, a trainer must offer a lot more than basic knowledge and checklists for a training program to succeed.

Assuming the firm cannot do the training itself, for most types of training (there are exceptions) you will be best served by a trainer who has considerable experience working with lawyers and law firms. Law firm experience should not, however, be the sole criterion; it is helpful but not dispositive. Getting a trainer with a personality that is a "good fit" can also be critical.

Whether you plan to offer presentation skills, "working a room," developing case budgets, or sales training, the person in charge of training should use his or her network of contacts and as many resources as possible to find the person best suited for *each* undertaking. (Seldom will "one size fit all.") The effort should include asking for referrals, reviewing information on the Web, conducting personal interviews, and checking multiple references. The person responsible for training should also present the firm with options for trainers and programs, and make recommendations based on his or her sense of which programs will fit in the firm's culture.

A so-called "name brand" training organization can have credibility with the lawyers, but you must be careful to avoid "canned" or "cookie-cutter" programs. You should not hesitate to ask a trainer about specific changes he or she plans to make in a "typical" program to address issues that are unique to your firm. Do not rely solely on friendships or personal loyalty to select a trainer, either. Choosing the wrong trainer can be a setback to the firm's efforts (and even one's career).

Ultimately, I would suggest looking for a trainer with excellent knowledge of the legal industry, a *practical* understanding of lawyers' specific challenges, a flexible approach, an ability to withstand the most intense lawyer scrutiny, and a proven track record. You should get marketplace feedback from a variety of prior clients (not just those of the consultant's choosing) on the value of the proposed program.

Management's Role

Keep in mind that there is no perfect program or ideal person for the challenging job of lawyer training. What has worked famously at one firm may not have any measurable impact somewhere else. Much of the success of a training program is dependent on the firm's willingness to support, reward, and even enforce the application of the skills and processes taught in the training.

In other words, if the lawyers do what they are taught (such as rehearsing before beauty contests, spending time "off the clock" advancing client relationships, organizing into client teams, supervising junior lawyers, and managing matters better), their efforts must be recognized and appreciated, even if the payoff is not immediate. Instead, many firm structures create roadblocks and penalize lawyers for these activities because they result in less billable time, too much independent authority, increased infrastructure requirements, and other expenses. The mixed messages that management can send will frustrate even the most enthusiastic trainees. Also, if no systems of accountability or measurement are put in place, results will be minimal.

The success of the training also depends on the attitudes of the participants. Were they willing volunteers or were they forced by management to attend the training? Were they the "best and the brightest," or were they part of the remedial group? The best results tend to occur when those in attendance are volunteers, but you should always try to mix some stars or skeptics into the program. Obviously, if the skeptics see value in the program, more volunteers will appear for future programs.

Other Variables

The success of a training program can also be tied to two other key points. One is the willingness of the trainer to be flexible, and the other is the law firm marketer's ability to manage expectations.

Flexibility

Because the impact of law firm training can vary considerably, depending on the firm's culture and the makeup of the attendees, it is essential that the trainer have the capability (and willingness) to adapt the program to the specific needs and constraints of the firm and the group members. Make sure the trainer creates a program to achieve *your* specific goals, not the trainer's.

Training programs can be packaged in a series of sixty- to ninety-minute workshops, or a single program can extend over several full days; now training can even be technology based, using interactive multimedia approaches. The best programs will have the participants role play, strategize, and do exercises to practice new skills.

Managing Expectations

Speaking of goals, even the best training programs can have only a limited impact in the first instance. If the program goals are not clearly defined and limited, the attendees will be disappointed. And even when you have established realistic expectations, it is important to have a well-defined plan to follow up, monitor, and support the initial training program, because it is from the ongoing reinforcement, encouragement, and accountability that you will see results.

Conclusion

We certainly have come a long way from the days when marketing was seen as a diminution of professional practice, and the idea of marketing training was almost insulting to most lawyers. In fact, for all that remains to be done, marketing training has accomplished more than many might have expected.

Law firm marketing is no longer just about helping law firms generate more revenue. Good training actually contributes to the profession by reaffirming the primacy of the client. This moves the profession closer to its roots, and can help enhance the perceived value of legal work. Marketing, rightly understood, plays a key role in this reaffirmation because it is ultimately about getting lawyers to be helpful and to communicate more effectively.

Following is a list of some possible training programs. Although the list is not exhaustive, it will offer plenty of options from which to choose the training program that is right for your firm.

Some Marketing-Related Training Program Options

- Listening Training
- Client Service Training (for lawyers and staff)
- Client Satisfaction Interview Training

- Presentation Skills Training (for lawyers who run meetings, give speeches, and participate in beauty contests)
- Cross-Selling Training
- Networking Skills Training
- Relational Sales Training
- Case Management and Budgeting Training
- Responding to Requests for Proposals (winning beauty contests)
- Marketing Time Management
- Media Training
- Key Client Retention and Growth
- Leadership, Management, and Delegation Training
- Communication Styles
- Personal Business Planning
- Alternative Fees
- Talking with Clients about Fees
- Effective Billing Strategies

ABOUT THE EDITORS

Hollis Hatfield Weishar

Hollis Hatfield Weishar is president of Hollis Weishar Marketing, in East Greenwich, RI, a practice devoted to working with professionals, primarily lawyers, accountants, and architects. Ms. Weishar is a frequent speaker and is the author of *Marketing Success Stories . . . Personal Interviews with 66 Rainmakers,* published by the ABA Law Practice Management Section in 1997. She has worked as a marketing consultant to professional service firms throughout the United States and Canada since 1986. She assists her clients with the creation, development, and implementation of marketing, client relations, and business development programs. Services include strategic planning for firms, practice groups, and individuals; individual coaching of professionals; marketing training for professionals and support staff; client relations programs and client interviews; market research and focus groups; business development and targeted marketing programs; proposal writing; advertising; brochures, newsletters, and collateral materials; and public relations.

Ms. Weishar has a bachelor's degree in marketing and has been actively involved for a number of years with the Legal Marketing Association (LMA), the Society for Marketing Professional Services (SMPS), and the Association for Accounting Marketing. She currently serves on the ABA Publishing Board as well as serving as President for the LMA's New England Chapter.

James A. Durham

Jim Durham is president of The Law Firm Development Group, Inc., a firm dedicated to changing the way lawyers and clients work together. Mr. Durham has practiced business law for over 15 years, during which time he also worked with Mintz, Levin, Cohn, Ferris, Glovsky and Popeo, P.C., one of New England's largest law firms. As Mintz Levin's Director of Client Development, he developed uniquely successful client service and client satisfaction programs, in addition to having senior responsibility for marketing strategies, practice development, and marketing training.

A master in the art of client relationship strategies and business development, Mr. Durham has led firms worldwide in seminars, trainings, and retreats designed to attract new clients, increase referrals, maintain a first-class image and reputation, develop alternative fee structures and partnering relationships, win "beauty contests," develop strategic plans, and create effective branding and positioning strategies. Using his expertise in client relations and business development, Mr. Durham has developed an interactive, CD-ROM training program called "Just Think . . . about Clients™," a revolutionary training tool that teaches lawyers—individually at their own speed—the importance of client service, as well as how to develop better relationships and time management. Mr. Durham currently spends considerable time in a management consulting role, assisting law firm management in the implementation of innovative changes.

Mr. Durham is a graduate of Emory University School of Law and Harvard University. He is also a founder of the highly successful Law Firm Marketing Directors Institute, which is co-sponsored annually by the Legal Marketing Association.

ABOUT THE CONTRIBUTORS

Stephen Barrett

Presently director of practice development at Paul, Hastings, Janofsky & Walker LLP, in Los Angeles, California, Steve Barrett has been active in large law firm marketing for more than 10 years. He is a seasoned business marketing, communications, and public-affairs professional, with nearly 25 years of experience in creative problem solving, marketing, and communications. Mr. Barrett has been director of practice development with the 630-lawyer firm of Paul, Hastings, Janofsky & Walker LLP for five years, joining it from Choate, Hall & Stewart LLP, in Boston, Massachusetts, where he had been that firm's director of marketing.

Mr. Barrett previously headed corporate communications for the Aetna Life & Casualty Companies, Hartford, Connecticut, and founded and headed LMS/Barrett Public Relations, in Providence, Rhode Island, which was the largest New England public-relations firm outside Boston. Clients of LMS/Barrett included law firms and many other consumer-product, high-tech, financial-services, and business-to-business organizations. Mr. Barrett also held marketing and corporate communications positions with the public-relations firm Creamer Dickson Basford, and managed public relations for the Power Systems Group of Combustion Engineering, Inc.

Mr. Barrett received a dual degree in political science and journalism from Syracuse University.

Burkey Belser

Designer and illustrator Burkey Belser has won over 150 awards in every major field of graphic design: publication, illustration, trademark, and collateral. His work has been honored by every major national and international design competition, and every major legal competition, including over 20 NALFMA Your

Honor Awards, 16 LAMMIES (Law Firm Advertising and Marketing Awards), and 7 ABA Dignity in Advertising Awards.

An accomplished writer and public speaker, Mr. Belser has written for the *Washington Post,* the *Los Angeles Times,* the *American Lawyer,* the *National Law Journal,* and many other industry magazines. He regularly speaks about marketing communications to professional audiences, such as the ABA, the Association of Legal Administrators, the Legal Marketing Association, the American Institute of Graphic Arts, and the American Trial Lawyers Association. He served for two years (1988–1990) as the president of the Art Directors Club of Metropolitan Washington, a 750-member, 45-year-old organization.

Mr. Belser has been listed in *Who's Who in the East* since 1989. Recently, he was awarded a Presidential Design Award by President Bill Clinton for his design of Nutrition Facts, the food-labeling initiative that now appears on all consumer food packages.

As president and creative director of Greenfield/Belser, Mr. Belser oversees all its marketing communications strategy and creative development. Formed to meet the marketing communication needs of professional service firms, Fortune 500 corporations, and publishers, Greenfield/Belser offers a full range of services from strategic communications planning through creative implementation. Mr. Belser has been the driving force behind the firm's outstanding business success and creative acclaim. Over the last decade, Greenfield/Belser has grown substantially in size and reputation. Today the firm works with clients all over the United States, and over 80 percent of its work is with law firms.

Stephen Brewer

Stephen Brewer is president of Brewer Business Development LLC. He has been in the advertising, marketing, and market research business for more than 30 years. His firm produces proprietary and franchised research surveys for law firms throughout the country. He has conducted management retreats and consulted with more than 100 major law firms in the areas of strategic planning, firm mergers and acquisitions, business development, sales training, and market research.

William J. Flannery Jr.

William J. Flannery is founder and president of The WJF Institute, located in Austin, Texas. The Institute's primary focus is client development and client relationship management, law firm marketing, and marketing support programs. The WJF Institute also trains lawyers and provides related consulting services in substantive legal skills, law firm management, and leadership. Over the past 10 years, The WJF Institute has conducted intensive, small-group training sessions for over 4,500 attendees.

Mr. Flannery graduated from the University of Maryland and started his career at the Department of Justice as an instructor. He later joined the Johns-Manville Corporation in its Washington, D.C., office, then joined the IBM Corporation in Washington, D.C. While at IBM, he attended the University of Baltimore Law School, graduating in 1973. Mr. Flannery also attended the IBM/Harvard Advanced Business Executive Education Institute Program. His IBM career included assignments in marketing training, product marketing, large-account marketing, corporate marketing planning, large-system management, IBM corporate executive briefing program, corporate strategic planning, finance, litigation management, personal computer product development, and technology for the legal profession. He was instrumental in creating the IBM Legal Profession Marketing Group, established in 1980 in response to the growing technology systems needs of private-practice lawyers, courts, governments, and in-house counsel in the United States and overseas.

Mr. Flannery is a frequent speaker at various legal conferences and meetings. He has been a special advisor to the ABA and the Association of Legal Administrators (ALA) on technology and marketing. He has served as a member of the ALA's Long-Range Planning Committee. He has been a member of the ABA's Law School Curriculum Committee, and has lectured in law schools, graduate schools, and undergraduate schools in the United States and overseas on strategic planning, technology, and marketing. Mr. Flannery has published numerous articles on marketing, technology, and law firm management in law journals and legal publications.

David Graves

David Graves is vice president of the RDW Group, Inc., in Providence, Rhode Island. He has designed and implemented successful public and media relations programs for major clients in the fields of legal services, public utilities, conventions and tourism, cable television, and construction. He has more than a dozen years' experience in issues management and crisis communications and has trained hundreds of executives in media interview and presentation skills. Mr. Graves began his career in communications as a broadcast journalist in Boston in the 1970s. He worked as a reporter, anchor, and news director at radio stations in New Hampshire and Rhode Island before becoming assignment editor and later news manager at the ABC television network affiliate in Providence. He is a graduate of Holy Cross College and a recent recipient of the Publicity Club of New England's Bell Ringer Award.

Lawrence M. Kohn and Robert N. Kohn

Lawrence M. Kohn and Robert N. Kohn are brothers and principals of Kohn Communications in West Los Angeles, California. The firm specializes in helping lawyers bring in new clients by focusing on interpersonal interaction. Both speak regularly across the country to law firms and bar associations helping lawyers—especially those who are uncomfortable with the marketing process—learn how to build a book of business.

Susan Raridon Lambreth

Susan Raridon Lambreth is a Director with Hildebrandt International, the largest international management consulting firm for the legal profession. She has her J.D. and M.B.A. Ms. Lambreth has also authored over 50 articles and has given over 300 presentations on law firm strategic planning, practice management, and marketing issues. She currently serves as a member of the seven-person ABA committee on the Research on the Future of the Legal Profession, as well as the ABA House of Delegates.

Kelly Kiernan Largey

Kelly Kiernan Largey is the Director of Client Services of Fish & Richardson P.C., a national intellectual property and technology law firm with 150 lawyers. She served as President of the Legal Marketing Association (formerly NALFMA) in 1993. A member of the American Bar Association, she served as a judge for the ABA's Dignity in Advertising Awards in 1993 and served on the ABA's Commission on Advertising from 1997 to 1999.

Ms. Largey graduated from Wellesley College, where she was elected to Phi Beta Kappa, and earned a law degree from Notre Dame Law School. During law school, she clerked for the United States District Court for the Northern District of Indiana. She practiced law for two years following law school and is admitted to the bar in Massachusetts, New Jersey, and Illinois. She serves on the Prostate Cancer Core Group for the Massachusetts Chapter of the American Cancer Society and has been active as a prostate cancer patient advocate.

Roberta Montafia

Roberta Montafia is director of marketing for Appleby Spurling & Kempe, in Hamilton, Bermuda. She was previously the marketing director for a major Boston law firm as well as a member of the Boston Bar Association's Volunteer Lawyer's Family Practice Group. She has both domestic and international experience in law firm marketing and administration, having worked in London and Brussels. Ms. Montafia is a member of the Bars of the Commonwealth of Massachusetts and the State of Florida, the American Bar Association, the Bermuda International Business Association's Marketing Committee, and Women in Trade. A past board member of the Legal Marketing Association's

New England Chapter, she is currently a board member of the Bermuda Marketing Association. Ms. Montafia is a graduate of the University of Massachusetts and Suffolk University School of Law.

Murray Singerman

Murray Singerman holds a B.A. from Yeshiva University. He earned his J.D. and L.L.M. in taxation from the University of Baltimore. Mr. Singerman concentrates in tax controversy.

Gregory H. Siskind

Gregory H. Siskind is the author of the ABA's best-selling book, *The Lawyer's Guide to Marketing on the Internet,* and he is the founding partner of Siskind, Susser, Haas & Devine, one of the nation's largest immigration law firms. Mr. Siskind was one of the first lawyers in the country to establish a World Wide Web site for his law firm, and the firm's site has now received more than 13 million hits. Additionally, his immigration law newsletter is now delivered to more than 21,000 e-mail subscribers in all 50 states and in 125 countries. Mr. Siskind's Internet experiences have been profiled in a number of publications, including the *New York Times,* the *Wall Street Journal,* the *Washington Post, USA Today, American Lawyer,* and the *National Law Journal.* He has lectured on the subject of law firm Internet marketing to thousands of lawyers in the United States, Canada, and the United Kingdom.

Peter D. Zeughauser

Peter D. Zeughauser is a legal industry consultant with ClientFocus in Corona del Mar, California. He consults to law firms, corporate clients, and vendors to the legal profession in the areas of strategic planning, strategic client relationship planning, marketing, running and winning RFPS for legal services, compensation structures, and the win-win pricing of legal services. He is a management columnist and contributing editor of *The American Lawyer* magazine, a member of the College of Law Practice Management and a former Chairman of the American Corporate Counsel Association. Portions of his chapter first appeared in his "Inside Track" law firm management column in *The American Lawyer* magazine.

INDEX

Law Firm Partnership Guide: Strengthening Your Firm. Addresses what to do after your firm is up and running, including how to handle: change, financial problems, governance issues, compensating firm owners, and leadership.

Law Law Law on the Internet. Presents the most influential law-related Web sites. Features Web site reviews of the *National Law Journal's 250*, so you can save time surfing the Net and quickly find the information you need.

Law Office Policy and Procedures Manual, 3rd Ed. A model for law office policies and procedures (includes diskette). Covers law office organization, management, personnel policies, financial management, technology, and communications systems.

Law Office Staff Manual for Solos and Small Firms. Use this manual as is or customize it using the book's diskette. Includes general office policies on confidentiality, employee compensation, sick leave, sexual harassment, billing, and more.

The Lawyer's Guide to Creating Web Pages. A practical guide that clearly explains HTML, covers how to design a Web site, and introduces Web-authoring tools.

The Lawyer's Guide to the Internet. A guide to what the Internet is (and isn't), how it applies to the legal profession, and the different ways it can—and should—be used.

The Lawyer's Guide to Marketing on the Internet. This book talks about the pluses and minuses of marketing on the Internet, as well as how to develop an Internet marketing plan.

The Lawyer's Quick Guide to E-Mail. Covers basic and intermediate topics, including setting up an e-mail program, sending messages, managing received messages, using mailing lists, security, and more.

The Lawyer's Quick Guide to Microsoft® Internet Explorer; The Lawyer's Quick Guide to Netscape® Navigator. These two guides de-mystify the most popular Internet browsers. Four quick and easy lessons include: Basic Navigation, Setting a Bookmark, Browsing with a Purpose, and Keeping What You Find.

The Lawyer's Quick Guide to Timeslips®. Filled with practical examples, this guide uses three short, interactive lessons to show to efficiently use Timeslips.

The Lawyer's Quick Guide to WordPerfect® 7.0/8.0 for Windows®. Covers multitasking, entering and editing text, formatting letters, creating briefs, and more. Includes a diskette with practice exercises and word templates.

Leaders' Digest: A Review of the Best Books on Leadership. This book will help you find the best books on leadership to help you achieve extraordinary and exceptional leadership skills.

Living with the Law: Strategies to Avoid Burnout and Create Balance. Examines ways to manage stress, make the practice of law more satisfying, and improve client service.

Marketing Success Stories. This collection of anecdotes provides an inside look at how successful lawyers market themselves, their practice specialties, their firms, and their profession.

Microsoft® Word for Windows® in One Hour for Lawyers. Uses four easy lessons to help you prepare, save, and edit a basic document in Word.

Practicing Law Without Clients: Making a Living as a Freelance Lawyer. Describes freelance legal researching, writing, and consulting opportunities that are available to lawyers.

Quicken® in One Hour for Lawyers. With quick, concise instructions, this book explains the basics of Quicken and how to use the program to detect and analyze financial problems.

Risk Management. Presents practical ways to asses your level of risk, improve client services, and avoid mistakes that can lead to costly malpractice claims, civil liability, or discipline. Includes Law Firm Quality/In Control (QUIC) Surveys on diskette and other tools to help you perform a self-audit.

Running a Law Practice on a Shoestring. Offers a crash course in successful entrepreneurship. Features money-saving tips on office space, computer equipment, travel, furniture, staffing, and more.

Successful Client Newsletters. Written for lawyers, editors, writers, and marketers, this book can help you to start a newsletter from scratch, redesign an existing one, or improve your current practices in design, production, and marketing.

Survival Guide for Road Warriors. A guide to using a notebook computer (laptop) and other technology to improve your productivity in your office, on the road, in the courtroom, or at home.

Telecommuting for Lawyers. Discover methods for implementing a successful telecommuting program that can lead to increased productivity, improved work product, higher revenues, lower overhead costs, and better communications. Addressing both law firms and telecommuters, this guide covers start-up, budgeting, setting policies, selecting participants, training, and technology.

Through the Client's Eyes. Includes an overview of client relations and sample letters, surveys, and self-assessment questions to gauge your client relations acumen.

Time Matters® in One Hour for Lawyers. Employs quick, easy lessons to show you how to: add contacts, cases, and notes to Time Matters; work with events and the calendar; and integrate your data into a case management system that suits your needs.

Wills, Trusts, and Technology. Reveals why you should automate your estates practice; identifies what should be automated; explains how to select the right software; and helps you get up and running with the software you select.

Win-Win Billing Strategies. Prepared by a blue-ribbon ABA task force of practicing lawyers, corporate counsel, and management consultants, this book explores what constitutes "value" and how to bill for it. You'll understand how to get fair compensation for your work and communicate and justify fees to cost-conscious clients.

Women Rainmakers' 101+ Best Marketing Tips. A collection of over 130 marketing from women rainmakers throughout the country. Features tips on image, networking, public relations, and advertising.

Year 2000 Problem and the Legal Profession. In clear, nontechnical terms, this book will help you identify, address, and meet the challenges that Y2K poses to the legal industry.

TO ORDER CALL TOLL-FREE:
1-800-285-2221

Qty	Title	LPM Price	Regular Price	Total
______	ABA Guide to International Business Negotiations (5110331)	$ 74.95	$ 84.95	$________
______	ABA Guide to Lawyer Trust Accounts (5110374)	69.95	79.95	$________
______	ABA Guide to Legal Marketing (5110341)	69.95	79.95	$________
______	ABA Guide to Prof. Managers in the Law Office (5110373)	69.95	79.95	$________
______	Anatomy of a Law Firm Merger (5110310)	24.95	29.95	$________
______	Billing Innovations (5110366)	124.95	144.95	$________
______	Changing Jobs, 3rd Ed.	*please call for information*		$________
______	Compensation Plans for Lawyers, 2nd Ed. (5110353)	69.95	79.95	$________
______	Complete Internet Handbook for Lawyers (5110413)	39.95	49.95	$________
______	Computer-Assisted Legal Research (5110388)	69.95	79.95	$________
______	Computerized Case Management Systems (5110409)	39.95	49.95	$________
______	Connecting with Your Client (5110378)	54.95	64.95	$________
______	Do-It-Yourself Public Relations (5110352)	69.95	79.95	$________
______	Easy Self Audits for the Busy Law Firm	*please call for information*		$________
______	Finding the Right Lawyer (5110339)	14.95	14.95	$________
______	Flying Solo, 2nd Ed. (5110328)	29.95	34.95	$________
______	Handling Personnel Issues in the Law Office (5110381	59.95	69.95	$________
______	HotDocs® in One Hour for Lawyers (5110403)	29.95	34.95	$________
______	How to Build and Manage an Employment Law Practice (5110389)	44.95	54.95	$________
______	How to Build and Manage an Estates Law Practice	*please call for information*		$________
______	How to Build and Manage a Personal Injury Practice (5110386)	44.95	54.95	$________
______	How to Draft Bills Clients Rush to Pay (5110344)	39.95	49.95	$________
______	How to Start & Build a Law Practice, Millennium Fourth Edition (5110415)	47.95	54.95	$________
______	Internet Fact Finder for Lawyers (5110399)	34.95	39.95	$________
______	Law Firm Partnership Guide: Getting Started (5110363)	64.95	74.95	$________
______	Law Firm Partnership Guide: Strengthening Your Firm (5110391)	64.95	74.95	$________
______	Law Law Law on the Internet (5110400)	34.95	39.95	$________
______	Law Office Policy & Procedures Manual (5110375)	99.95	109.95	$________
______	Law Office Staff Manual for Solos & Small Firms (5110361)	49.95	59.95	$________
______	Lawyer's Guide to Creating Web Pages (5110383)	54.95	64.95	$________
______	Lawyer's Guide to the Internet (5110343)	24.95	29.95	$________
______	Lawyer's Guide to Marketing on the Internet (5110371)	54.95	64.95	$________
______	Lawyer's Quick Guide to E-Mail (5110406)	34.95	39.95	$________
______	Lawyer's Quick Guide to Microsoft Internet® Explorer (5110392)	24.95	29.95	$________
______	Lawyer's Quick Guide to Netscape® Navigator (5110384)	24.95	29.95	$________
______	Lawyer's Quick Guide to Timeslips® (5110405)	34.95	39.95	$________
______	Lawyer's Quick Guide to WordPerfect® 7.0/8.0 (5110395)	34.95	39.95	$________
______	Leaders' Digest (5110356)	49.95	59.95	$________
______	Living with the Law (5110379)	59.95	69.95	$________
______	Marketing Success Stories (5110382)	79.95	89.95	$________
______	Microsoft® Word for Windows® in One Hour for Lawyers (5110358)	19.95	29.95	$________
______	Practicing Law Without Clients (5110376)	49.95	59.95	$________
______	Quicken® in One Hour for Lawyers (5110380)	19.95	29.95	$________
______	Risk Management (5610123)	69.95	79.95	$________
______	Running a Law Practice on a Shoestring (5110387)	39.95	49.95	$________
______	Successful Client Newsletters (5110396)	39.95	44.95	$________
______	Survival Guide for Road Warriors (5110362)	24.95	29.95	$________
______	Telecommuting for Lawyers (5110401)	39.95	49.95	$________
______	Through the Client's Eyes (5110337)	69.95	79.95	$________
______	Time Matters® in One Hour for Lawyers (5110402)	29.95	34.95	$________
______	Wills, Trusts, and Technology (5430377)	74.95	84.95	$________
______	Win-Win Billing Strategies (5110304)	89.95	99.95	$________
______	Women Rainmakers' 101+ Best Marketing Tips (5110336)	14.95	19.95	$________
______	Year 2000 Problem and the Legal Profession (5110410)	24.95	29.95	$________

***Handling**
$10.00-$24.99....................$3.95
$25.00-$49.99....................$4.95
$50.00+ $5.95

****Tax**
DC residents add 5.75%
IL residents add 8.75%
MD residents add 5%

Subtotal	$________
***Handling**	$________
****Tax**	$________
TOTAL	$________

PAYMENT

☐ Check enclosed (to the ABA) ☐ Bill Me
☐ Visa ☐ MasterCard ☐ American Express

Account Number Exp. Date Signature

Name Firm
Address
City State Zip
Phone Number E-Mail Address

Mail: ABA Publication Orders, P.O. Box 10892, Chicago, Illinois 60610-0892 ♦ Phone: (800) 285-2221 ♦ FAX: (312) 988-5568

E-Mail: abasvcctr@abanet.org ♦ Internet: http://www.abanet.org/lpm/catalog

Source Code: 22AEND499

CUSTOMER COMMENT FORM

Title of Book: ______________________________

We've tried to make this publication as useful, accurate, and readable as possible. Please take 5 minutes to tell us if we succeeded. Your comments and suggestions will help us improve our publications. Thank you!

1. How did you acquire this publication:

☐ by mail order ☐ at a meeting/convention ☐ as a gift

☐ by phone order ☐ at a bookstore ☐ don't know

☐ other: (describe) ______________________________

Please rate this publication as follows:

	Excellent	Good	Fair	Poor	Not Applicable
Readability: Was the book easy to read and understand?	☐	☐	☐	☐	☐
Examples/Cases: Were they helpful, practical? Were there enough?	☐	☐	☐	☐	☐
Content: Did the book meet your expectations? Did it cover the subject adequately?	☐	☐	☐	☐	☐
Organization and clarity: Was the sequence of text logical? Was it easy to find what you wanted to know?	☐	☐	☐	☐	☐
Illustrations/forms/checklists: Were they clear and useful? Were there enough?	☐	☐	☐	☐	☐
Physical attractiveness: What did you think of the appearance of the publication (typesetting, printing, etc.)?	☐	☐	☐	☐	☐

Would you recommend this book to another attorney/administrator? ☐ Yes ☐ No

How could this publication be improved? What else would you like to see in it?

____

Do you have other comments or suggestions? ______________________________

Name ______________________________

Firm/Company ______________________________

Address ______________________________

City/State/Zip ______________________________

Phone ______________________________

Firm Size: ______________ Area of specialization: ______________

We appreciate your time and help.

Fold

POSTAGE WILL BE PAID BY ADDRESSEE

AMERICAN BAR ASSOCIATION
PPM, 8th FLOOR
750 N. LAKE SHORE DRIVE
CHICAGO, ILLINOIS 60611-9851

Fold